In the steps of John Wesley

The Church of the Nazarene in Britian

by

Jack Ford, B.D., Ph.D.

First Fruits Press
Wilmore, Kentucky
c2017

In the steps of John Wesley: the Church of the Nazarene in Britain.
By Jack Ford.

First Fruits Press, © 2017

ISBN: 9781621717027 (print), 9781621717034 (digital), 9781621717041 (kindle)

Digital version at place.asburyseminary.edu/academicbooks/22/

First Fruits Press is a digital imprint of the Asbury Theological Seminary, B.L. Fisher Library. Asbury Theological Seminary is the legal owner of the material previously published by the Pentecostal Publishing Co. and reserves the right to release new editions of this material as well as new material produced by Asbury Theological Seminary. Its publications are available for noncommercial and educational uses, such as research, teaching and private study. First Fruits Press has licensed the digital version of this work under the Creative Commons Attribution Noncommercial 3.0 United States License. To view a copy of this license, visit http://creativecommons.org/licenses/by-nc/3.0/us/.

For all other uses, contact:

First Fruits Press
B.L. Fisher Library
Asbury Theological Seminary
204 N. Lexington Ave.
Wilmore, KY 40390
http://place.asburyseminary.edu/firstfruits

Ford, Jack, 1908-
   In the steps of John Wesley: the Church of the Nazarene in Britain / Jack Ford. – Wilmore, KY: First Fruits Press, ©2017.
   351 pages; cm.
   Includes bibliographical references.
   Originally presented as the author's thesis (doctoral)--University of London.
   Reprint. Previously published: Kansas City, Mo. : Nazarene Publishing House, ©1968.
   ISBN: 9781621717027 (pbk.)
   1. Church of the Nazarene--Great Britain--History. 2. Holiness churches--Great Britain--History. 3. Great Britain--Church history. I. Title.
BX8699.N335 G74 2017   289.9

Cover design by Jon Ramsay

asburyseminary.edu
800.2ASBURY
204 North Lexington Avenue
Wilmore, Kentucky 40390

First Fruits Press
The Academic Open Press of Asbury Theological Seminary
204 N. Lexington Ave., Wilmore, KY 40390
859-858-2236
first.fruits@asburyseminary.edu
asbury.to/firstfruits

In the Steps of
John Wesley

The Church of the Nazarene in Britain

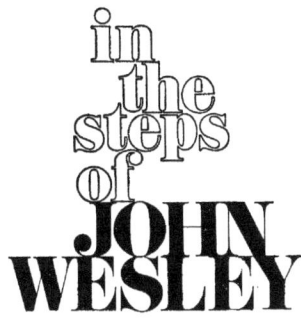
In the Steps of JOHN WESLEY

The Church of the Nazarene in Britain

by

JACK FORD, B.D., Ph.D.

A thesis accepted for the degree of Doctor of Philosophy in Theology in the University of London

Printed by
NAZARENE PUBLISHING HOUSE
Kansas City, Missouri, U.S.A.

Dedication

To my wife Muriel,

and the

Holiness People

Preface

Not only for the sociologist but also for the church historian the microcosm of the sect has special value. Factors and trends too complicated to be easily discerned in the great and ancient communions stand out sharply in the select society. In the study of the three movements which are the subject of this thesis, the Church of the Nazarene in Britain, the International Holiness Mission and the Calvary Holiness Church, causes of division can be learned afresh, familiar patterns of faith and order emerge, the evolution of the sect into a denomination and towards a church takes place, but with particular modifications which warn us not to make our categories nor our rules of development too rigid, and the desire for unity, given momentum by the pressure of internal and environmental forces, bears fruit in their uniting in a larger denomination.

The history of these three movements is drawn from primary sources and fully annotated. Their origin is traced back to the British Holiness Movement of the latter part of the nineteenth century, which is shown to owe a real debt to the American Holiness Movement. Their faith and church order is analysed, their attitude to the world indicated and explained and the doctrine of Holiness to which they give special emphasis is defined and discussed, with special reference to John Wesley's teaching of entire sanctification. An attempt is made to compare their belief in Holiness and its expression in church life and towards the world with movements and individuals in Christian history holding a similar belief. A short summary of conclusions is given concerning factors in their origin and features in their development. Criticisms of their doctrine are considered and its value is indicated, and suggestions are made concerning their contribution to society and to the Church.

—J. FORD

Abbreviations

SPECIAL

BIDF	British Isles District (of Church of the Nazarene) Files.
CHCDCM	Calvary Holiness Church Delegates Conference Minutes
CHCECM	Calvary Holiness Church Executive Council Minutes.
HMJ	Holiness Mission Journal.
IHMECM	International Holiness Mission Executive Council Minutes.
MBDMPPC	Minute Book of Deacons Meetings of Parkhead Pentecostal Church.
MBIDCN	Minutes of British Isles District of Church of the Nazarene.
MBIDPCN	Minutes of British Isles District of Pentecostal Church of the Nazarene.
MBPCS	Minute Book of Pentecostal Church of Scotland.
PBIDCN	Proceedings of British Isles District of Church of the Nazarene.
PCS	Pentecostal Church of Scotland.

GENERAL

ERE	*Encyclopaedia of Religion and Ethics,* ed. James Hastings.
Wesley	Where "Wesley" appears alone, the reference is to John Wesley.

Contents

PART I: HISTORICAL

CHAPTER 1.	Introduction	11
CHAPTER 2.	The Church of the Nazarene in Britain	35
CHAPTER 3.	The International Holiness Mission	90
CHAPTER 4.	The Calvary Holiness Church	139

PART II: ANALYTICAL AND COMPARATIVE

CHAPTER 5.	Their Faith and Church Order	185
CHAPTER 6.	Their Attitude to the World	205
CHAPTER 7.	Their Special Emphasis: Holiness	222
CHAPTER 8.	Their Relationship to Holiness Movements in Christian History	243
CHAPTER 9.	Conclusion	270

PART I
HISTORICAL

CHAPTER 1

Introduction

THE ORIGIN OF THE CHURCH OF THE NAZARENE

The American Holiness Movement

To understand the British branch of the Church of the Nazarene, which is the subject of this thesis, it is necessary to consider in some detail the rise of the Church of the Nazarene in America. This had its origins in the American Holiness Movement[1] as the British part of it owes its rise to the British counterpart.

Warfield traces the beginnings of mystical perfectionism in America to the Quakers. They preceded the Methodists by almost a century and becoming respected members of the community in some measure prepared the minds of the people for the Wesleyan message.[2] But beyond doubt it is Methodism which has made the main contribution to the doctrine of perfection in America, and all its outstanding exponents have either been Methodists or in a greater or lesser degree been indebted to Methodism. The leaders of the Oberlin School, C. G. Finney and Asa Mahan, were influenced by Wesley's *Plain Account of Christian Perfection,* although in some respects they deviated from it.[3] Thomas Upham, to use his wife's expression "was begotten in the Gospel" by Mrs. Phoebe Palmer, and Mrs. Upham herself was brought into the experience of entire sanctification by the testimony of a Methodist.[4] Rev. and Mrs. W. E. Boardman[5] and Mr. and Mrs. Pearsall Smith,[6] who exercised such an influence in America and Europe through their writings and preaching, had fertile contacts with Methodism. And in the words of W. E. Sangster all the Holiness denominations stem-down from the founder of Methodism.[7]

What is usually regarded as the American Holiness Movement began in the period following the Civil War. Prior to the war Finney and Mahan and other members of the Oberlin School had preached Holiness all over the country, and for twenty years Phoebe Palmer's "Tuesday Meeting for the Promotion of Holiness" had been a means of leading hundreds of Methodist ministers, including two bishops and three prospective ones, to claim the experience of entire sanctification. Boardman had published his *Higher Christian Life* in 1858, the year of the mid-century revival which reaped a harvest of between 500,000 and a million converts.[8] Then came four years of fratricide. The Holiness Movement was both a reaction against the bloodshed and a participation in the mood of post-war reconstruction.

The first general Holiness camp meeting held at Vineland, New Jersey, in 1867, from which came the National Association for the Promotion of Holiness,[9] was predominantly Methodist though professedly interdenominational in character.[10] Others came into being as a result of its success and in the early days received the support of the Methodists. Prominent Methodists like Dr. and Mrs. (Phoebe) Palmer, John S. Inskip, James Caughey, J. A. Wood, Daniel Steele and Bishops Hamline, Matthew Simpson, Thomas A. Morris, and Jesse T. Peck played an important part in the promotion of the movement. In 1886 Bishop Mallalieu wrote that more than at any time in the history of Methodism, God's people were seeking the blessing.[11] But so far from being confined to one denomination the movement overflowed to the other churches where a way had been prepared for it by the Oberlin School and the writings of Boardman. Congregationalists like Finney, Mahan and A. M. Hills; Presbyterians like Boardman and Pearsall Smith; Quakers like David B. Updegraf and Professor Dougan Clark; Baptists like A. B. Earle, A. P. Graves, George Morse and E. M. Levy; and the Episcopalian layman, Dr. Charles C. Cullis, gave breadth to the movement. Lewis R. Dunn declared in the *Methodist Quarterly Review* in 1873 that Episcopalians, Quakers, Presbyterians and Baptists were forsaking sectarian controversy to proclaim with their Methodist brethren the purifying grace.[12] A spate of literature bore forward the Holiness message. In 1888 at least four publishing houses were engaged exclusively in the publishing of Holiness journals, and twenty-seven Holiness periodicals were circulating. By 1892 the periodicals had increased to forty-one.[13]

Yet it would be false to suggest that there was unanimous support for this proclamation of Holiness. In the Methodist Church itself there was always a hard core of resistance to it, which increased as the century moved to its close. The fact that the ministers were divided in their attitude meant that members who were led to claim entire sanctification by one minister could encounter opposition from his successor, as was the case with F. A. Hillery and his associates in St. Paul's Methodist Episcopal Church in Providence.[14] Then there was the fear on the part of the officials that the association of their members in Holiness bands and camp meetings might lead to the creation of cliques and issue in schism.[15] Between 1792 and 1881 there were at least thirteen schisms from the Methodist Church. Two were on the issue of language, like that of the Evangelical Association; five were racial, resulting in the creation of coloured Methodist groups; and of the other six two were related to Holiness: the Wesleyan Methodist (1843), obliquely, and the Free Methodist (1860), directly. But almost all of them gave a new prominence to Holiness when they were separated from the parent body.[16] In such circumstances the official caution was understandable. Moreover, while many leading advocates of Holiness were loyal and responsible churchmen, some of the Holiness evangelists were irresponsible extremists who sought to precipitate Holiness sects without cause or even taught that no church order was necessary at all.[17] Some of the bands lapsed into fanaticism and repelled sensible and spiritual observers.[18] On the other hand, adherents of the Holiness

14 • *In the Steps of John Wesley*

movement saw much in the churches which disturbed them: worldliness, formality and, towards the close of the century, a denial by denominational scholars of what they regarded as Christian fundamentals and by some Methodist professors a repudiation of the Holiness doctrine which they treasured as the founder's grand depositum.[19]

The last ten years of the nineteenth century witnessed the rise of about the same number of separate Holiness groups. At least half of them united in the Pentecostal Church of the Nazarene.[20]

The Rise of the Church of the Nazarene in America[21]

The Church of the Nazarene dates its origin as a denomination from the union of the Pentecostal Church of the Nazarene with the Holiness Church of Christ at Pilot Point on October 8th, 1908.[22] Previously the Association of Pentecostal Churches of America, an Eastern Holiness denomination, had united with the Church of the Nazarene, which originated in California, to form the Pentecostal Church of the Nazarene. To understand the genesis of the church which came into being in 1908 it is necessary to trace the origins of the three denominations which gave it content and shape.

The Association of Pentecostal Churches of America

On July 21st, 1887, the People's Evangelical Church was organized in Providence, R.I., with F. A. Hillery as the pastor and fifty-one members. They had previously been members of St. Paul's Methodist Episcopal Church where under the ministry of Rev. T. J. Everett in the early eighties many had been led to claim entire sanctification. Everett's successors, however, did not share his emphasis and as a result of a dispute between successive pastors and the official board originating in the prospect of the church being used for money-raising suppers and entertainments and involving the cancelling of the church's Holiness meeting, a small group formed the South Providence Holiness Association on May 12th, 1886, with Hillery as president.[23] A weekly meeting was commenced at 163 Oxford Street and sixty members of the church gave their support. When the pastor, E. D. Hall, removed from office all the Sunday School teachers

Introduction • 15

belonging to the association a Sunday School[24] and other church services were commenced, resulting in Hillery being expelled from the Methodist Church. The outcome was the People's Evangelical Church.[25]

The newly formed church entered into fellowship with likeminded groups of Christians in the area such as the independent church at Rock, Massachusetts (1882),[26] the Mission Church at Lynn (1889), a similar church at Attleboro, and the Bethany Mission in Keene, New Hampshire (1889), and delegates from local Holiness associations in the suburbs of Boston. The fellowship of these Holiness groups was furthered, and incidentally the influence of the People's Evangelical Church extended, by the publishing by Hillery from September, 1888, of a small monthly journal entitled "Beulah Items".

The informal fellowship existing between the aforementioned groups took a more concrete form in the inauguration of the Central Evangelical Holiness Association at Rock on March 13th and 14th, 1890. Membership was confined to representatives of "holiness churches, associations or bands" and such ministers or evangelists whose application should be approved by the executive committee. W. C. Ryder, pastor at Rock, was elected president and Hillery vice-president. It consisted in its first year of about ten churches.[27]

The churches which entered into the association were Congregational in church government. Though all were united in the Methodist doctrine of perfection, they had no sympathy with the Methodist practice of episcopacy.

Although reports of spiritual blessing and numbers of seekers were given at the annual meetings of the association, the number of churches affiliated to it remained about ten. There were two main reasons for this. Firstly, a group of ministers who believed in the Holiness message in New England sought to retain likeminded members in their churches by forming the General Holiness League in 1891. For a time it arrested the drift away from the churches, but tension soon developed, particularly in the Methodist churches. To the north, in Vermont, a similar organisation was formed by Methodists about the same time called the Vermont

16 • *In the Steps of John Wesley*

Holiness Association, which in 1892 appointed H. F. Reynolds, a promising young Methodist minister, to conduct Holiness conventions and revivals. Secondly, another alternative to the Central Evangelical Holiness Association presented itself to Methodist ministers adhering to the Holiness message. Early in 1892 extensive Holiness revivals took place in the Evangelical Association in eastern Pennsylvania. Some Methodist ministers and groups of believers in the Holiness message in and around Boston seized the opportunity of identifying themselves with an existing denomination with Methodist origins and church order which stood for the faith which they loved.

Thus there were at least three courses open to those in New England who had embraced the Holiness message: they could find fellowship with those likeminded in such organisations as the General Holiness League; they could join the Evangelical Association; or they could form an independent church and find a wider fellowship in the Central Evangelical Holiness Association. And whatever course they chose they were welcomed at united Holiness rallies.[28]

About the same time as the formation of the Central Evangelical Holiness Association in Massachusetts a Congregationalist, William H. Hoople, the son of a millionaire leather merchant, came into contact with Charles BeVier, a Methodist, who was instrumental in his claiming the experience of entire sanctification.

On January 4th, 1894, they began a mission among the poor in an old saloon at 123 Schenectady Avenue, which developed into the Utica Avenue Tabernacle. Here was formed at the close of the year the interdenominational New York State Holiness Association, with BeVier as president and Hoople as one of the vice-presidents. Two more churches were organised the following year, all three being Congregational in government.

In October, 1895, H. F. Reynolds, whose friend O. J. Copeland had preceded him in Brooklyn to open a granite business, joined forces with Hoople. He had left the Methodists that year, disturbed by the increasing opposition his converts were experiencing from pastors who opposed his teaching concerning Holiness. In December, 1895, the three churches previously mentioned formed themselves into the Association of Pentecostal Churches of America.

It was not long before Reynolds and Hoople entered into negotiations with the churches of the Central Evangelical Holiness Association and at a meeting in Hoople's home in November, 1896, members of the two associations voted to recommend the union. The name and constitution of the Association of Pentecostal Churches of America were adopted. In April, 1897, seven of the churches of the Central Evangelical Holiness Association joined the denomination, which had accessions also from newly organised churches around New York City. In addition, some who had remained in the Methodist Church were drawn into the growing denomination with its distinctive witness to Holiness. Further accessions came from the Evangelical Association. Some ministers who had entered it to raise up Holiness churches found it difficult to accept the direction of German-speaking bishops, who lived five hundred miles away, in a work raised up by others. Tension issued in division in most of the congregations of the New England Evangelical Association Conference, and most of those who left joined the Association of Pentecostal Churches of America.[29]

The Church of the Nazarene

While the Association of Pentecostal Churches of America was taking shape and extending on the eastern seaboard, Bresee's Church of the Nazarene was developing in the West.

Phineas F. Bresee has a unique place in the history and the hearts of Nazarenes. The church in the East began and developed through the labours and association of a number of men with gifts of leadership. Bresee was the founder of the western church. The delegates of both the eastern and southern churches recognised his leadership in union negotiations and the Church of the Nazarene today shows historical insight in naming him as its founder.

It would be difficult to exaggerate the debt which Bresee owed to the Methodist Episcopal Church. He was born on December 31st, 1838, on his father's farm in Franklin, Delaware County, Western New York. His parents were earnest

18 • *In the Steps of John Wesley*

Christians, members of the Methodist Church, in which Phineas was converted and later ordained an elder in 1861. In 1860, he married Marie E. Hibbard of Davenport, daughter of a well-known Methodist family. In 1872, he was elected a delegate to the General Conference in New York.[30]

In 1883, Bresee moved with his family to California and was called to the pastorate of the Los Angeles First Methodist Church. Previously, while at Chariton (1867 to 1868) he had claimed the baptism with the Holy Spirit but he arrived in Los Angeles "not in the clear enjoyment of the blessing". Largely through the influence of some of the members at First Church he found a new enduement of the Spirit. Within three years the membership was doubled and he experienced similar success as pastor of the First Methodist Church in Pasadena from 1886 to 1890. After a year's pastorate in Asbury Church, Los Angeles, Bishop Mallalieu appointed him presiding elder for the Los Angeles district and encouraged him in his plan to organise Holiness revivals during the coming year. But in 1892, Bishop Vincent, who had little sympathy with Bresee's emphasis, appointed him as pastor of the Simpson Church, the one church which had refused to co-operate with his Holiness crusade. After serving a year there and the following year at Boyle Heights Church, he accepted an invitation to be one of the superintendents of the Peniel Mission, an undenominational mission for the poor. Contrary to his hope and expectation, this involved his leaving with profound regret the ministry of the church which had given him his opportunity to serve and honoured him with many privileges.[31]

The Peniel engagement lasted less than a year. In spite of the prosperity of the work in attendance and seekers for blessing, Bresee was asked to withdraw.[32] The notice came so unexpectedly that Bresee was compelled to make a swift decision. Encouraged by supporters, he commenced services in Main Street near Peniel Hall on October 6th, 1895, and announced that a new denomination was being inaugurated to provide a full salvation church for the poor. J. P. Widney, a close friend, president of the University of Southern California and a fellow Methodist, who had supported him at Peniel Hall, became co-founder of the new denomination and gave it the name of the "Church of the Nazarene" as bringing out the lowliness of Jesus and His association with the "toiling . . . sorrowing heart of the world". By this step Bresee and Widney severed their connection with the Methodist Church. It deemed their action unwise but recognised their motives as sincere: "our people will not oppose this new organization in honest efforts to save men".[33]

The new church, which brought together influential Christians and recent converts from among the poor, combined the marks of a church in preaching and sacraments with the enthusiasm of the early Salvation Army. Its membership grew from 82 to 350 in the first year and the building had to be enlarged. By the end of 1897 other churches had been organised in Berkley, Pasadena and Elysian Heights, Los Angeles. In January, 1898, the *Nazarene* was published as the official organ of the denomination.

The church was organised on democratic principles. Bresee and Widney were made general superintendents, but a church board made up of trustees and stewards shared full responsibility for the temporal side of the work. As other churches were added, ministers were ordained by the vote of the congregation, but the general superintendents' approval was required before ordination became final.

The first *Manual* was drawn up in October, 1898, at a delegated meeting of the four churches of the denomination, held in the mother church. It was based on the Discipline of the Methodist Church, with a simplified version of its General Rules (1896 ed., pp. 30-31). In his aim to recover the simplicity and power of primitive Christianity,[34] Bresee sought to reduce articles of doctrine and conduct to their minimum. It was expected that members would not be members of secret orders and would not use tobacco but such items were included in the category of "Special Advice".

Originally it had been stipulated that the office of General Superintendent should be for life, but there was a growing feeling among the members that this should be an annual office. Accordingly both Bresee and Widney resigned. For some time Widney, a quiet-mannered man, had felt out of place in the highly emotional services which Bresee conducted. He took the opportunity of the change not to stand for re-election and returned to the Methodist Episcopal

Church. He left, however, on the friendliest terms with Bresee.[35]

Up to 1902 the Church of the Nazarene spread slowly in the direction of raising up new churches, and those which were organised were located in California. But by the turn of the century Bresee became convinced that a national Holiness church was needed to conserve the gains of the Holiness revival, and he devoted all his energies to this end.

The first six years of the twentieth century witnessed a nationwide extension of the Church of the Nazarene, in which C. W. Ruth, Bresee's assistant at the Los Angeles First Church, took the initiative. Churches were organised in Washington, Utah, Illinois, Nebraska, Idaho, Montana, Texas, Minnesota, Indiana and Kansas. In 1906, there were 45 local churches and 3,385 members. Missionary work begun in 1897 among the Spanish people in Los Angeles extended until by 1907 it included other areas in southern California and in Texas, and two missionaries and a national worker in India. In 1902, the Pacific Bible College was opened in Los Angeles to train those offering for Christian service. Four years later its location was removed to a site near Los Angeles donated by Mr. and Mrs. Deets and its name was changed to Deets Pacific Bible College. From the printing of the *Nazarene Messenger*[36] a publishing house developed to such an extent that by 1905 Rev. C. J. Kinne was engaged as business manager.[37]

Meanwhile the Association of Pentecostal Churches of America had been developing in the East. By 1907 it consisted of 48 churches, extending from Maine to Iowa, with a membership of 2,313. A college, commenced at Saratoga Springs, New York, in 1900, as the Pentecostal Collegiate and Bible Training School,[38] had an enrolment by 1907 of eighty-four students. The *Beulah Items* magazine, renamed the *Beulah Christian* in 1892, was serving the denomination with a considerably increased circulation. Moreover four mission stations had been opened, three in India and one in Cape Verde Islands, with a missionary personnel in the region of a dozen. H. F. Reynolds had come into increasing prominence as the secretary of the missionary work, the only full-time connexional officer in the denomination.[39]

Introduction • 21

The Union of the Church of the Nazarene and the Association of Pentecostal Churches of America

From the time that Ruth met Hoople and Reynolds at the Allentown Camp Meeting in 1903, the two movements which they represented gravitated towards union. A decisive step was taken when J. N. Short, H. N. Brown and A. B. Riggs[40] accepted the invitation to attend the Nazarene Assembly in 1906 as representatives of the Pentecostal Churches. Here a plan of union, formulated by Bresee, was adopted by the Assembly, and Bresee, Ruth, H. D. Brown and Girvin were appointed as fraternal delegates to the Pentecostal Annual Meeting in Brooklyn the following April. In the interval the proposed union was discussed in the *Nazarene Messenger* and the *Beulah Christian* and the Pentecostal Churches were asked to send representatives to the Annual Meeting with instructions on how to vote concerning it.[41]

At Brooklyn what was substantially the Nazarene plan of union was adopted. A compromise was reached between superintendency and Independency with the agreement that the authority of the superintendents should "not interfere with the independent action of the fully organized church".[42] The resolutions for union were adopted with great enthusiasm. The name of the "Pentecostal Church of the Nazarene" was taken and the Nazarene *Manual* was adopted as a "working basis", with an invitation to the Pentecostal Churches to suggest any modifications they thought desirable.

The first General Assembly of the new denomination at Chicago from October 10th to 16th was mainly a time of strengthening the spiritual bonds. Present in response to an open invitation to all Holiness bodies and participating in the legislative committee were representatives from the Holiness Church of Christ, which united with the new denomination the following year.

The Holiness Church of Christ

The Holiness Church of Christ was the result of the union of the New Testament Church of Christ and the Independent Holiness Church.

The New Testament Church of Christ was founded in Milan, Tennessee, in 1894, by Robert Lee Harris, a west

Texan known as the "Cowboy Evangelist". He had served as a missionary in Monrovia, French West Africa, and had had connections with the Free Methodist Church and the Methodist Episcopal Church, South. He left the latter because of its "worldliness" and the decision of the West Tennessee Conference to exclude "unauthorised, self-styled evangelists" from its churches.[43]

In the spring of 1894, he and his wife moved to Milan, Tennessee, with Mr. and Mrs. E. H. Sheeks, with thom they had spent the winter in Memphis, and took up residence with Mr. and Mrs. R. B. Mitchum, who like the Sheeks had been deeply influenced by Harris's ministry. Shortly after his arrival there he published a pamphlet on "The Government and Doctrine of the New Testament Church" in which he declared that the New Testament taught that each congregation should be strictly autonomous, ordaining its elders (or bishops), electing its deacons to care for the secular needs of the church and, when necessary, administering the sacrament, normally the duty of the elders.[44] Pouring was the correct mode of Baptism. Holiness as a second work of grace was the privilege and obligation of believers, and separation from worldliness in dress and amusements, from the use of tobacco and alcohol and from membership in secret societies was the New Testament standard of conduct.

Harris was already known in Milan as the result of a Holiness tent meeting which he had conducted the previous year. At the close of the second campaign on July 9th, 1894, in the last stages of tuberculosis, he "set in order" the first congregation of the "New Testament Church of Christ" with thirteen members.[45] When the tent was taken down in the autumn the little flock was given shelter for a time in a Cumberland Presbyterian meeting house, and when Harris died, on November 26th, his funeral was conducted by a minister of that denomination before a large congregation in the local Opera House, to which the new group had moved.[46]

The founder gone, the future lay in the balance. Appropriately, it was women who succoured the infant denomination, foremost among them being Mrs. Harris, Mrs. Sheeks and Mrs. Mitchum. Scorning survival, they turned to a strategy of attack and by the turn of the century churches,

Introduction • 23

mostly small, had been established in west Tennessee, Arkansas, northern Alabama and Texas.

Gradually, as the church extended and the need of guidance and of the supply of pastors was felt, the rigid Congregational pattern was modified. It began with the annual meeting of the mother church at Milan in December, 1899, being attended by representatives from nearby churches. Two years later an annual meeting was arranged at Jonesboro and each congregation was expected to send a representative. The annual meeting became the Annual Council with power to settle vexed questions, pronounce on issues not expressly dealt with in Scripture and ordain elders. Two important decisions of the first annual meeting at Milan were that the local church had the right to accept as members those who believed in baptism by immersion rather than by pouring and that women as well as men were eligible for ordination, on the strength of which Mrs. Harris and Mrs. Sheeks applied for ordination and were ordained. At the Fourth Annual Council at Hillville, Tennessee, in September, 1902, it was decided to have copies of the *Government and Doctrine of the New Testament Church* printed with the statement on baptism modified to suit the decision of the Council. Thus important modifications of its original pattern of baptism and Congregationalism were introduced without which the later union with the Pentecostal Church of the Nazarene would probably have been impossible.[47]

Meanwhile the church had developed in Texas to such an extent that in response to numerous suggestions Mrs. Harris, now Mrs. Cagle, sent out a call to the churches in Texas to send representatives to a general meeting at Buffalo Gap in December, 1902. Eleven churches sent sixteen ministers and eight laymen. By this time in the east able men were assisting and gradually preceding women in the extension and government of the church. In the west, apart from the pioneer labours of Mrs. Cagle and her assistant, the church had grown by the addition of capable men such as W. E. Fisher, and there was no shortage of ministers. The general meeting, renamed the Western Council, affirmed the Congregational form of government but had no scruples about publishing its minutes and a statement of doctrine and form of government in a yearbook entitled *Council and Guide*

24 • In the Steps of John Wesley

of the *New Testament Church of Christ*. Similarly, in the east, R. B. Mitchum, the chairman of the Eastern Council, repeatedly stressed the advisory as opposed to the mandatory nature of the Council's decisions. Nevertheless, the evolution of the Councils meant that the church had representative and authoritative bodies to negotiate a union with other Holiness groups in 1904.[48]

Foremost among those seeking union with the New Testament Church of Christ was the *Independent Holiness Church*. It was a descendant of the Texas Holiness movement.

The first phase of the Holiness movement in Texas was the Holiness revivals conducted by Hardin Wallace, a Methodist preacher, in 1877. Besides independent bands, these resulted in the formation of the interdenominational Texas Holiness Association in 1878, and the Northwest Texas Holiness Association, formed by Methodists in 1883. The Free Methodists soon established a foothold, and in northern Texas Dennis Rogers raised up a group of small congregations which he organised as the Holiness Church Association of Texas about 1886. From about 1890, the Methodist Episcopal Church, North, established a membership among leading exponents of Holiness dismissed by the southern branch. But in spite of all these Holiness organisations, there were some believers in the Holiness message who were without a church home until the formation of the Independent Holiness Church.

The first step in its formation was the initiation of the Holiness Association of Texas in 1899 at an informal meeting in the home of C. B. Jernigan, a former Methodist, at which were present Dennis Rogers, of the Holiness Church Association, C. A. McConnell, representing a group of Holiness bands recently organised by a Cumberland Presbyterian pastor, and C. M. Keith, editor of the *Texas Holiness Advocate*. The new association was midway between an interdenominational association and a church. It met a real need and increased rapidly.

But in Jernigan's opinion many of the Holiness people were still without a church home. When, therefore, in 1901 he received the call to pastor a congregation at Van Alstyne, created as a result of a revival campaign in which he shared, he took the plunge and named it the "Independent Holiness

Introduction • 25

Church".⁴⁹ Other congregations were added, in spite of opposition from many in the Holiness Association of Texas who feared that such a step would divorce the support of the older denominations for the association and who perhaps doubted the ability of Jernigan, described by H. C. Morrison as "an unknown wood chopper", to lead an adequate denomination. Nevertheless by 1904, with Jernigan as president and J. B. Chapman, later to become one of the ablest general superintendents of the Church of the Nazarene, as secretary, the new denomination had grown to twenty-seven churches.⁵⁰

As the result of a meeting with W. E. Fisher in 1903, and his friendship with J. D. Scott, whom he met in 1901, Jernigan became convinced of the advisability of the union of the Independent Holiness Church with the New Testament Church of Christ. So it came about, after preliminary negotiations, that delegations from the two churches met at Rising Star, Texas, where the Third Annual Council of the New Testament Church of Christ was held on November 22nd, 1904. It was hoped that a larger union comprehending the Pentecostal Mission, of Nashville, the Pentecostal Union, the Union Mission Association, the Holiness Baptist Church and any other Holiness organisation interested in the project would come into being, but for one reason or another none of these entered into it.

The New Testament Church of Christ and the Independent Holiness Church found a basis of union in the following terms: the right of the local congregation to call and ordain ministers and to conduct its business affairs; the right of women to be ordained; subscription to a doctrinal statement based largely on that of the New Testament Church of Christ; belief in entire sanctification and separation from secret societies, intoxicants, drugs, etc.; baptism as a condition of membership, but the mode was left to the conscience of the candidate. It was recommended that the name of the united church should be the "Holiness Church of Christ".

The union was consummated at Pilot Point, Texas, November 7th to 12th, 1905, and the following were elected to office: Rev. R. M. Guy, president; Rev. C. B. Jernigan, first vice-president; R. B. Mitchum, second vice-president; Rev. Mrs. E. H. Sheeks, recording secretary, and Rev. J. D. Scott, corresponding secretary. (All were from the New Testament Church of Christ except Jernigan.) By the union seventy-five[51] churches were brought into the same denomination which were divided into three annual councils: Western Texas, Eastern Texas and Arkansas Councils.[52]

The chief need of the united denomination was an adequately trained ministry. By 1906, Bible schools were being supported at Buffalo Gap and Pilot Point, Texas, and at Vilonia, Arkansas, to supply this need. In that year the *Holiness Evangel* was inaugurated as the church's official journal, with Jernigan as the editor. An ambitious programme of rescue and home mission work was vigorously prosecuted. Rest Cottage, at Pilot Point, was sponsored and support was given to three other homes for unmarried mothers. Further afield, by 1908, missionaries were labouring in India (four), Japan (two) and Mexico (two).

The concentration on home and foreign missions diverted the emphasis of the church from the establishing of Holiness churches in America with the result that from 1905 and the union with the Nazarenes in 1908 only fifteen new congregations were added. But, more important to the union, these very activities gave rise to the appointment by the Arkansas Council of a council evangelist, a rescue home agent and a missionary-cum-treasurer, connexional offices which foreshadowed a district superintendency. Thus a further step was taken in the direction of Nazarene church government.

The Union of the Pentecostal Church of the Nazarene and the Holiness Church of Christ

At the first General Council after union, November 20th to 25th, 1906, the Holiness Church of Christ was invited by the Nazarenes and the Association of Pentecostal Churches to send delegates to the union meeting in Brooklyn the following April. Shortage of funds prevented the delegation from attending, but delegates were present and participating in the legislative committee at the Chicago meeting in October, 1907. In an editorial in the *Holiness Evangel* Jernigan declared, "They gave us all we asked for", and quoted the articles on the second coming of Christ and divine healing which had been added, and the section on abstentions which had been stiffened to suit the Southerners. It was

Introduction • 27

agreed that the next General Assembly of the Pentecostal Church of the Nazarene should meet jointly with the General Council of the Holiness Church of Christ at Pilot Point, on October 8th, 1908.

Discussion of the prospective union in the journals of the respective denominations helped to prepare the minds of the delegates, but union was not achieved without thorough discussion, some heated debate and the statesmanlike forbearance of the chairman, Phineas Bresee. The Southerners wanted rules to legislate such matters as dress and the use of tobacco, whereas the Nazarenes preferred "advices". Concessions were made on both sides, more, perhaps, by the latter than the former, and union was achieved amid scenes of great enthusiasm.[53]

Other Unions

At Pilot Point the history of the Church of the Nazarene as it exists today begins. Each of the three denominations involved in the union there, eastern, western and southern, made its contribution to the constitution which denominations joining the church later were expected to accept. Since that time the church has grown by the multiplication of churches and the increase in their membership and, to a much smaller degree, by the accession of other Holiness denominations.

In September, 1908, on the eve of Pilot Point, the fifteen churches of the Pennsylvania Conference of the Holiness Christian Church joined the Pentecostal Church of the Nazarene.[54] In 1911, a small addition came from the union of churches of the Holiness branch of the Louisiana Conference of the Methodist Protestant Church.[55] In 1915, the Pentecostal Mission, founded by J. O. McClurkan, a Cumberland Presbyterian minister, with headquarters at Nashville, after hesitating for over ten years, united with the church. With it came "a missionary force of considerable strength, doing work in India, Cuba, and Central America"[56] and the Trevecca College.[57] In 1922, the Laymen's Holiness Association, based in North Dakota, officially united with the Church of the Nazarene.[58] Originally it had been a Methodist organisation which grew out of the Jamestown Camp Meeting but was reconstituted as an interdenominational association in

28 • *In the Steps of John Wesley*

1919. Most of the leaders and about a thousand of its members eventually became Nazarenes.⁵⁹

THE ORIGINS AND MILIEU OF THE
CHURCH OF THE NAZARENE IN BRITAIN

This then was the church with which the three British Holiness denominations which are the subject of this thesis united: the Pentecostal Church of Scotland in 1915; the International Holiness Mission in 1952; and the Calvary Holiness Church in 1955.

All of them were indigenous churches in the sense that they were founded by Britons and composed of Britons. They had their origins in the British Holiness Movement. The High Church phase of it, the Oxford Movement, with its thirst for personal holiness and devotional worship, preceded its evangelical counterpart by several decades.⁶⁰ The trend of the former was to Rome; the inspiration of the latter was from America. It was an outcome of the '59 Revival, which began in a noonday prayer meeting in New York and brought new life to the churches in Britain.⁶¹ Among those who participated in the revival were the Americans, Charles G. Finney,⁶² an outstanding revivalist and a teacher of Holiness of the Oberlin School, James Caughey,⁶³ a Methodist preacher of full salvation who made an indelible impression on William Booth,⁶⁴ and Dr. and Mrs. W. C. Palmer,⁶⁵ leading exponents of the Wesleyan doctrine of entire sanctification. Even more influential in the propagation and exposition of the Holiness message were the American Presbyterians, Rev. and Mrs. W. E. Boardman⁶⁶ and the American Quakers, Mr. and Mrs. R. Pearsall Smith.⁶⁷ The leader of the second phase of the revival was D. L. Moody, who attributed his success as an evangelist to an experience of the Spirit's fulness⁶⁸ which he sought under the influence of two zealous members of the American Holiness Movement, Mrs. Sarah A. Cooke and Mrs. Hawxhurst.⁶⁹ He gave his prayerful support to the Brighton Convention in 1875⁷⁰ out of which the Keswick Convention developed. Thus by sharpening the spiritual appetite of Christians and bringing them into contact with those who taught a deeper Christian experience the '59 Revival gave birth to the evangelical phase of the British Holiness Movement.

Introduction • 29

This phase of the movement found expression in three main directions: denominationally, interdenominationally and extradenominationally. The writings of Boardman and the Pearsall Smiths had a wide circulation in England. Mrs. Boardman quotes an account by Dr. Cullis of breakfasts at which her husband and Pearsall Smith spoke to the Free Church ministers of London, each denomination separately, in 1873.[71] Other breakfast meetings followed. A. T. Pierson estimates that about two thousand four hundred preachers attended these meetings between 1874 and 1875. Conferences at Broadlands, Oxford and Brighton brought thousands of clergy, ministers and laity under the challenge of the "Higher Life".[72] Even after Pearsall Smith's tragic collapse[73] the quest for the highest in the Christian experience continued. In Methodism, Cliff College and the Southport Convention with their emphasis on the Wesleyan presentation of Holiness had their origin in the milieu of this period.[74] Interdenominationally, the movement gave birth to the Keswick Convention (1875),[75] the Faith Mission (1886),[76] the Star Hall, Manchester (1889),[77] the Pentecostal League (1891)[78] and kindred organisations. Thirdly, as a result of it such denominations arose as the Salvation Army (1878),[79] the Holiness Church,[80] the Independent Holiness Movement (1907),[81] the three denominations with which we are dealing and numerous undenominational missions with entire sanctification as a basic doctrine.[82] Besides these were two branches of the American Holiness Movement, the Pentecostal Union (from 1917 renamed the Pillar of Fire) and the Metropolitan Association, which were established in Britain in 1909[83] and 1904[84] respectively, and continue to the present time.

Four missionary societies belonging to this century have operated on full salvation lines, publishing literature with the Holiness testimony and offering an opening to members of the Holiness Movement who have felt the call to missionary service. They are the Japan Evangelistic Band (1903),[85] the Japan Rescue Mission (c. 1922),[86] the India North West Mission (c. 1922), and the Oriental Missionary Society, of which the American founders, Mr. and Mrs. Charles E. Cowman, visited Britain in 1905, met Holiness leaders such as Reader Harris, David Thomas and George Wooster and had appointed representatives by 1909.[87] More

30 • *In the Steps of John Wesley*

recently, in 1936, the Irish Evangelistic Band was formed on the pattern of the Faith Mission to work mainly in Eire. The Emmanuel Holiness Church began in 1916 as an independent church, branched out into the Emmanuel Bible School in 1921, commenced a missionary work on 1924, added several churches in England and became a denomination in 1947.[88]

After an initial period of indecision during which speakers who taught complete cleansing from sin and those who taught the counteraction of sin by the Spirit were both invited to speak on its platform, Keswick, under the influence of Evans J. Hopkins, H. W. Webb-Peploe and Handley C. G. Moule adopted the latter interpretation.[89] The other movements mentioned above held to the Wesleyan interpretation of cleansing from inward sin, and at times the distinction between them and Keswick has been sharply drawn. This will be referred to later. Since the movements to which this thesis refers all adhered to the Wesleyan interpretation, it is this interpretation which will figure mainly in our study.

NOTES ON CHAPTER 1

[1] Elmer T. Clark, *The Small Sects in America* (New York: Abingdon Press, rev. ed.), p. 74.

[2] B. B. Warfield, *Perfectionism* (New York: Oxford University Press, 1931), II, 338.

[3] *Ibid.*, p. 54.

[4] *Ibid.*, pp. 358-59.

[5] Mrs. Boardman, *Life and Labours of Rev. W. E. Boardman* (London: Bemrose and Sons, 1886), chap. iii.

[6] Warfield, *op. cit.*, pp. 502-3.

[7] W. E. Sangster, *The Path to Perfection* (London: Hodder & Stoughton, 1943), p. 6.

[8] J. Edwin Orr, *The Second Evangelical Awakening in Britain* (London: Marshall, Morgan and Scott, 1953), pp. 35-37.

[9] John L. Peters, *Christian Perfection and American Methodism* New York: Abingdon Press, 1956), p. 134.

[10] *Ibid.*, pp. 134 ff; Clark, *op. cit.*, p. 73.

[11] Timothy L. Smith, *Called unto Holiness: the Story of the Nazarenes* (Kansas City: Nazarene Publishing House, 1962), p. 20.

Introduction • 31

¹²*Ibid.*, pp. 22-23.
¹³Peters, *op. cit.*, p. 139.
¹⁴See pp. 14-15 below.
¹⁵Peters, *op. cit.*, pp. 140-41.
¹⁶Clark, *op. cit.*, pp. 60-69.
¹⁷Peters, *op. cit.*, p. 140; Smith, *op. cit.*, p. 28.
¹⁸Smith, *op. cit.*, p. 27; Peters, *op. cit.*, p. 146.
¹⁹William W. Sweet, *The Story of Religions in America* (New York: Harper and Brothers, 1930), pp. 499-501; Peters, *op. cit.*, pp. 150-80.
²⁰Peters, *op. cit.*, pp. 148-49.
²¹In giving this brief survey of the origin of the Church of the Nazarene in America I have chosen to follow mainly the official history, Timothy L. Smith, *op. cit.*, supplemented by M. E. Redford, *The Rise of the Church of the Nazarene* (Kansas City: Nazarene Publishing House, 1951). These books, besides being written by specialists in the subject, are readily accessible. However, these histories have been used against the background of my research in original sources during visits to North America in 1957 (four months), 1960 (four months) and 1964 (three months).
²²The date was fixed by the General Assembly, 1923. See *Manual of the Church of the Nazarene* (Kansas City: Nazarene Publishing House, 1923), par. 467, and J. B. Chapman, *A History of the Church of the Nazarene* (Kansas City: Nazarene Publishing House, 1926), p. 33.
²³The Secretary's Records of the South Providence Association for the Promotion of Holiness, May 12th, 1886 (in the files of the First Church of the Nazarene, Providence).
²⁴Commenced January 16th, 1887. *Ibid.*, 12-1-87.
²⁵The main sources for the preceding paragraphs, besides those indicated, are the Records of the People's Evangelical Church of Providence, R.I., and *The People's Evangelical Church*, organized July 21st, 1887. *Revised Manual.* Both in the files of the First Church of the Nazarene, Providence. Also Smith, *op. cit.*, pp. 54-57 and Redford, *op. cit.*, pp. 82-85.
²⁶Year in brackets is year of origin.
²⁷Smith, *op. cit.*, pp. 57-58, and Redford, *op. cit.*, pp. 87-92.
²⁸Smith, *op. cit.*, pp. 58-64.
²⁹Smith, *op. cit.*, pp. 63-64 and 66-71, and Redford, *op. cit.*, pp. 98-106.
³⁰Smith, *op. cit.*, pp. 91-93; J. B. Chapman, *A History of the Church of the Nazarene* (Kansas City: Nazarene Publishing House, 1926), pp. 120-21; E. A. Girvin, *Phineas F. Bresee: A Prince in Israel* (Kansas City: Pentecostal Nazarene Publishing House, 1916), pp. 23-71.
³¹Girvin, *op. cit.*, pp. 51-52, 72-102, and Smith, *op. cit.*, pp. 94-106.
³²The reasons are nowhere stated. Bresee preferred "to draw a veil" over "the treatment accorded to me", Girvin, *op. cit.*, p. 103. The Fergusons left it to the judgment day, *Peniel Herald*, Vol. I, No. 13 (Oct., 1895), p. 2. *The Los Angeles Times* (Oct. 7, 1895), p. 6, declared he was "frozen out". Cited by Brickley, see below. Smith suggests a difference with the Fergusons concerning methods, *op. cit.*, p. 109. Don-

32 • *In the Steps of John Wesley*

ald P. Brickley in *Man of the Morning* (Kansas City: Nazarene Publishing House, 1960) hints that the Fergusons disliked Bresee's emotionalism. See pp. 127-31.

³³*Californian Christian Advocate*, October 9th, 16th, 23rd, and 30th, 1895, cited by Smith, *op. cit.*, p. 112.

³⁴"Primitive Christianity" is mentioned each time in two of the early interviews which Girvin had with Bresee in 1896, *op. cit.*, pp. 121-23.

³⁵Smith, *op. cit.*, pp. 109-21; Girvin, *op. cit.*, pp. 99-153; Redford, *op. cit.*, pp. 47-62; Brickley, *op. cit.*, pp. 139-45.

³⁶Commenced as the *Nazarene* in 1898. The name was changed in 1900.

³⁷Smith, *op. cit.*, pp. 122-50; Redford, *op. cit.*, pp. 60-81; Girvin, *op. cit.*, pp. 152-306.

³⁸Transferred to North Scituate in 1902 and renamed the Pentecostal Collegiate Institute.

³⁹Smith, *op. cit.*, pp. 74-90; Redford, *op. cit.*, pp. 106-13.

⁴⁰All former Methodist preachers.

⁴¹The investigating committee of the Providence church, while favouring unity among "all distinctly holiness churches", looked with a Congregationalist disfavour on the Nazarene *Manual* and sharply questioned the authority of the Missionary Committee to enter into union discussions with the Church of the Nazarene. It nevertheless recommended that the church's representatives at the Annual Meeting be instructed to vote in favour of union! (Records of the People's Evangelical Church, Providence, R.I. Annual Meeting, January 3, 1907.)

⁴²*Manual* of Pentecostal Church of the Nazarene, 1907 (Los Angeles: Nazarene Publishing Co.), pp. 16-17.

⁴³R. L. Harris, *Why We Left the Methodist Church* (Memphis, 1893).

⁴⁴In no other group which joined the Church of the Nazarene did church order figure so prominently as in this. In the Association of Pentecostal Churches of America the Congregational form of government was regarded as the *bene esse* of the church. In the New Testament Church of Christ it seems to have been regarded by Harris and his followers, in the early days at least, as part of the *esse* of the church.

⁴⁵Original Minutes of Church of Christ, organised by Rev. R. L. Harris at Milan, Tennessee, July 9th, 1894 (in the files of M. E. Redford, Trevecca Nazarene College, Nashville), p. 1.

⁴⁶Redford, *op. cit.*, pp. 114-18; Smith, *op. cit.*, pp. 153-54; C. B. Jernigan, *Pioneer Days of the Holiness Movement in the Southwest* (Kansas City: Pentecostal Nazarene Publishing House, 1919), p. 116; and the writer's research in Rev. M. E. Redford's collection of early documents of the New Testament Church of Christ.

⁴⁷M. E. Redford, *op. cit.*, pp. 118-26; Smith, *op. cit.*, pp. 154-58; Jernigan, *op. cit.*, pp. 117-19.

⁴⁸Redford, *op. cit.*, pp. 126-29; Smith, *op. cit.*, pp. 155-59; Jernigan, *op. cit.*, pp. 119-21.

⁴⁹"So as to distinguish it from the Holiness church that came from California some years before, that had about become extinct." Jernigan, *op. cit.*, p. 111.

⁵⁰Smith, op. cit., pp. 161-68; Jernigan, op. cit., pp. 97-115; Redford, op. cit., pp. 130-35.

⁵¹Per Smith, op. cit., p. 175. Jernigan gives "about one hundred", op. cit., p. 123.

⁵²Smith, op. cit., pp. 168-71; Jernigan, op. cit., pp. 122-23; Redford, op. cit., pp. 135-37.

⁵³Smith, op. cit., pp. 171-77, 214-23; Redford, op. cit., pp. 137-42, 147-49; Jernigan, op. cit., pp. 123-27.

⁵⁴Smith, op. cit., pp. 229-30.

⁵⁵Ibid., pp. 233-34; Jernigan, op. cit., pp. 31-32.

⁵⁶Proceedings of the Fourth General Assembly of the Pentecostal Church of the Nazarene, Kansas City, Sept. 30 to Oct. 11, 1915, p. 50.

⁵⁷Smith, op. cit., pp. 180-99; Redford, op. cit., pp. 154-58.

⁵⁸"The General Assembly of 1919, in response to memorials from thirty-five District Assemblies, changed the name of the organization to 'Church of the Nazarene'." (Manual, 1923, par. 14). At the close of the nineteenth century "Pentecostal" conveyed the idea of "second blessing Holiness." By 1919 it had come to be associated with the *glossolalia*.

⁵⁹Smith, op. cit., 298-315; Redford, op. cit., pp. 164-69.

⁶⁰For an interesting comparison between the holiness emphasis in Methodism and the Oxford Movement see E. E. Jorden, "The Ideal of Sanctity in Methodism and Tractarianism" (unpublished Ph.D. thesis, University of London, 1958), esp. pp. 386-87.

⁶¹J. Edwin Orr, *The Second Evangelical Awakening in Britain* (London: Marshall, Morgan & Scott, 1953), passim. Although, as Dr. Orr indicates, revival broke out in Canada about the same time as the Fulton Street prayer meeting began, it was the American revival with its origin in the prayer meeting which so deeply influenced Britain.

⁶²Charles G. Finney, *An Autobiography* (London: Salvationist Publishing and Supplies), chaps, xxviii, xxix, xxxiv & xxxv.

⁶³Orr, op. cit., pp. 126, 127, 143, 157, 231.

⁶⁴Harold Begbie, *Life of William Booth* (London: Macmillan and Co.), I, 9 et passim.

⁶⁵Orr, op. cit., passim.

⁶⁶Steven Barabas, *So Great Salvation* (London: Marshall, Morgan and Scott, 1957), p. 16.

⁶⁷Ibid., pp. 17-24. Dr. Barabas states that Pearsall Smith, though a Quaker by upbringing, spent most of his active life as a member of the Presbyterian Church.

⁶⁸J. C. Pollock, *The Keswick Story* (London: Hodder & Stoughton, 1964), p. 18.

⁶⁹Sarah A. Cooke, *Wayside Sketches* (Grand Rapids, Mich.: Shaw Publishing Co., rev. ed., n.d.), pp. 49-50.

⁷⁰Barabas, op. cit., pp. 23-24.

⁷¹Mrs. Boardman, *Life and Labours of Rev. W. E. Boardman* (London: Bemrose & Sons, 1886), pp. 156 ff.

⁷²Arthur T. Pierson, *Forward Movements of the Last Half Century* (New York: Funk & Wagnalls Co., 1905), pp. 18-19.

⁷³Pollock, op. cit., pp. 34-36.

[74] For the origins of Cliff College in 1884 see J. I. Brice, *The Crowd for Christ* (London: Hodder & Stoughton, 1934), pp. 34 ff. For the origins of the Southport Convention see *To the Uttermost* (London: Epworth Press, 1945), pp. 12-15. It began in 1885.

[75] Pollock, *op. cit.*, p. 38.

[76] I. R. Govan, *Spirit of Revival* (Edinburgh: Faith Mission, 1938), p. 37.

[77] E. K. Crossley, *He Heard from God* (London: Salvationist Publishing & Supplies, 1959), p. 65.

[78] Mary R. Hooker, *Adventures of an Agnostic* (London: Marshall, Morgan & Scott, 1959), p. 111.

[79] Begbie, *op. cit.*, p. 386.

[80] Began about 1880. In 1884 there were thirteen churches. See *Holiness Advocate*, ed. Mrs. S. Chambers, January, 1884, back cover. (British Museum).

[81] G. W., *The Work of the Holy Ghost in Modern Times* (Leicester: J. W. Hemmings & Capey, 1919), p. 21.

[82] In his report as district superintendent at the District Assembly of the Church of the Nazarene in 1917, after referring to the Faith Mission, the Pentecostal League, Star Hall, etc., George Sharpe declared, "There are other independent missions and churches all over the land. ... We accept them as sharers with us in the war against sin ..."

[83] *Discipline of Pillar of Fire* (Zarephath, N. J.: Pillar of Fire, 1926), p. 23.

[84] Letter from Pastor Thomas W. Gilling of the Metropolitan Association to the writer, 6-4-65.

[85] Mary W. Dunn Pattison, *Ablaze for God: Life Story of Paget Wilkes* (London: Oliphants, 3rd ed., 1938), p. 81.

[86] Geo. Dempsey, the founder, visited Japan in 1918, *HMJ*, Oct., 1918, p. 76. The Japan Rescue Mission ceased to operate in Japan about 1940 or 1941. Letter from Rev. J. H. Liversidge to the writer, 31-3-65.

[87] *HMJ*, Oct., 1909, p. 111.

[88] See Reviews issued by J. & L. Drysdale, *Emmanuel. "Fourteen Years After"* (Birkenhead: 1931), and J. D. & L. M. Drysdale, *"Emmanuel". 25 Years After* (1941), and letter from Rev. Stanley Banks to writer, 25-3-65.

[89] Pollock, *op. cit.*, chap. viii.

CHAPTER 2

The Church of the Nazarene in Britain

THE PENTECOSTAL CHURCH OF SCOTLAND

EVENTS LEADING UP TO IT

Sharpe's Early Days in Scotland and U.S.A.

The Pentecostal Church of Scotland was the outgrowth of the religious experience and the ministry of George Sharpe. The son of a Scottish miner, he was born on April 17th, 1865, at the Rotten Tree, near Craigneuk, in the Parish of Dalziel, Lanarkshire. He describes his father as "a good man with a beautiful disposition", who was active in church work, bearing office and teaching in the Sabbath School. In later years, he was promoted to be under manager in the colliery. His mother, a native of Camlachie, Glasgow, whose parents were weavers, was fully occupied with the care of a large family of thirteen children, five of whom died in childhood. It was not until later life that she came into a conscious experience of God, and her son, George Sharpe, baptised her.

Young George Sharpe attended school in Craigneuk. At the age of twelve he became a message boy in a hardware shop. Leaving two years later, he subsequently entered the

36 • *In the Steps of John Wesley*

office of Colville's iron and steel works near his home. Here, to use his own words, "he sowed his wild oats". Nevertheless, he continued to attend church, where he alternatively trembled at the thought of judgment and was attracted by the preaching of the Cross.

In the spring of 1882, during a religious revival in his neighbourhood, he was drawn almost against his will into an evangelistic meeting in a dance hall. In this dingy conventicle, under the preaching of Malcolm Ferguson, unordained and without college training, the young member of the parish church knelt at the penitent form and prayed God to forgive his sins and make him His child. The following day, confronted by one of his workmates, he boldly testified to the decision he had made and there came an assurance into his heart that he was accepted of God. The young clerk became a changed man. The Bible, the church and the company of Christians took the place in his life previously filled with pastime and pleasures.[1]

Some two or three years after his conversion, Sharpe "was brought face to face with the call to preach". His eldest sister promised to meet all expenses if he would go through Edinburgh University and enter the ministry of the Church of Scotland, but a sense of inferiority prevailed and he declined the offer.[2] After months of indecision, he made a full surrender to God for service at a meeting in the Motherwell old town hall at which Rev. Nelson Countee, a former slave was the preacher.[3]

Shortly after, in the summer of 1885, Sharpe was made a tempting offer by Mr. Rose, president of an industrial concern in Cortland, New York State, U.S.A., to represent his firm in France, where they intended opening a new factory. He accepted the offer, resolving as a salve to his conscience to be a lay preacher in America and France. But while en route the project of the new factory in France was abandoned, and the young clerk-cum-preacher arrived in New York on Feb. 26th, 1886, to find that he had left an office in Scotland to work in a factory in America. He joined the Methodist Episcopal Church in Cortland. Within a few weeks he accepted an invitation to be the pastor of a small country church at Elmstump, and for some nine or ten months he ministered to the farmers and their families who

The Church of the Nazarene in Britain • 37

made up the congregation of his first pastorate. A yet more remarkable seal on his call to the ministry followed. Dr. C. C. Wilbor, the pastor of the Cortland Church, where he was still a member, told him that the official board of the church were prepared to assist him to enter training for the ministry. Sharpe accepted the offer, and within a few weeks he entered college.[4] He left at the completion of his course full of zeal and high purpose.[5]

During his college days, he was student supply at Oran in 1887. The following year, he became assistant pastor at Gouveneur in the Watertown District of the Northern New York Conference of the Methodist Episcopal Church,[6] and he remained there until 1890, when he was appointed as pastor at Depeyster, in the same district. In April, 1893, he was ordained an elder, and in April 1894, he was put in charge of the church at Hamilton in the Utica District. Four years later, Sharpe was sent in 1898 to Chateaugay, in the St. Lawrence District. All his appointments were in the Northern New York Conference.[7] In each case Sharpe claims that the church was established and extended under his ministry, the level of giving was raised and considerable improvements were made to the property at Depeyster and Hamilton.[8]

The effectiveness of his ministry was enhanced by the whole-hearted co-operation of his wife. On Nov. 17th, 1887, during his first year in college, he had married Jane Brayton Rose. Born about the same time and in the same district,[9] they had already entered into courtship when Jane's father, a master builder, took his family to America in 1884. It was Jane's uncle who made the offer to Sharpe which brought him across the Atlantic.[10]

While Sharpe was at Chateaugay, Major L. Milton Williams, of the Salvation Army, was invited by the church to conduct special services. He was the first Holiness preacher to conduct a revival campaign in one of Sharpe's churches.[11]

Sharpe describes the services as follows:

"In a short ministry of less than two weeks the country for twenty miles around was under deep conviction. In every afternoon meeting the subject was holiness. Every evening there was more on the subject. . . . There were preachers seeking the experience. My own loved wife prostrated herself before God until she rejoiced in the fulness of the blessing. But what of the preacher himself?"¹²

Sharpe was a Methodist preacher and was not only well acquainted with the Methodist doctrine of Holiness but was also mentally convinced that it was correct.

Now he was convinced that the Scriptures taught such an experience was possible and obligatory on all who would walk in God's perfect will. The finest Christians in his church, loving, prayerful and co-operative, testified that they had received it, and were praying that their pastor might enjoy it too. He felt that "the pressure of truth and the Holy Ghost" were upon him.

At the close of an afternoon service, alone in his church he faced the issue. Dropping on his knees at the organ bench, he consecrated himself unreservedly to God. In spite of the fact that he experienced "no ecstatic joy", he believed that the work was done. Then, when he testified in the evening service to God's sanctifying work in him, he states: "suddenly the Holy Ghost came and filled the cleansed temple. Praise God. He witnessed that the work was done."¹³

From this moment, George Sharpe became a Holiness preacher. The results of the revival campaign conducted by Major Williams were conserved by a visit from Rev. E. F. Walker (who re-appears later in the story), a Presbyterian minister and an able Holiness teacher. Holiness conventions were held at intervals. The services of the church were well attended and the worshippers rejoiced in a sense of the Divine Presence. Sharpe claims that "in the records of the General Church at that time, Chateaugay exceeded all other churches in per capita giving for benevolences". He and his church were an influence for temperance reform in the town. He writes, "Here I had my ideal church and a satisfied ministry."¹⁴

In the summer of 1901, Sharpe and his family spent a holiday in Scotland. For some time he had felt a concern for his native land.¹⁵

No opportunity to preach among "his ain folk" was missed, and while visiting his brother in Ardrossan he was invited to preach in the Congregational church¹⁶ there. He was asked if he would accept the pastorate, subject to a call. The Scottish-born minister of the American Methodist Episcopal Church was faced with a heart-searching decision. Calvinistic Scotland was likely to be a hard field for a preacher of the Wesleyan doctrine of entire sanctification. But Scotland was his native land, and it seemed to Sharpe that God was saying, "Now is the opportunity for you to return to the land of your birth and preach the preaching which I bid Thee."[17] The church officers were assured that should their call be forthcoming it would be accepted. Within a few short weeks of his return to Chateaugay, the call came and was accepted.[18]

The Parkhead Pentecostal Church

Sharpe's ability in promoting both the spiritual and material interests of his pastorates was demonstrated in Ardrossan as clearly as in the States. From the time of his induction on Nov. 24th, 1901, Sharpe carried the work vigorously forward, his evangelistic methods with their American flavour stirring the members and creating interest in the district. It was soon felt that the original scheme to erect a church costing £2,000 was inadequate for the growing congregation, and plans were drawn up for a building costing £4,500. The new church was dedicated on 16th October, 1903, large enough to accommodate over 600 people. During this period the church membership rose from 127 to 200. But at this point Sharpe became conscious "of an undercurrent being fostered by officials against the doctrine of holiness",[19] and shortly afterward he had a distinct impression that he ought to resign. He felt it again when the church opposed his intention to assist at the Mooers Holiness Camp Meeting in New York in the summer of 1905, because they thought his absence would disappoint summer visitors to Ardrossan. It was the beginning of the end. He resigned from the pastorate of the church at Ardrossan, and on the second Sunday of September, 1905, he became the pastor of the Parkhead Congregational Church.[20]

From the outset of his ministry in Parkhead, Sharpe felt a twofold conviction: first, that he should preach what he found in the Bible, and, secondly, that he should preach his experience and his convictions. His dynamic preaching and his evangelistic method proved as effective in Parkhead as they had in Ardrossan. Sharpe claims that "every department in the church was ablaze with new interest, the membership grew every month while the growth of the Sabbath School was phenomenal."[21]

Yet, in spite of the remarkable increase in numbers, some were dissatisfied, and in little over a year from the time of his induction, Sharpe was evicted from the pastorate. In Sharpe's opinion

> possibly three things led up to this. First, the Holiness services conducted by the pastor which did not find favour with two classes, those who never attended them and those who attended them irregularly. Second, a letter sent by the pastor while in the United States where he was a worker in a camp-meeting. In this he described a scene there and expressed the wish that something of the same nature might happen at home.[22] Third, a sermon preached on 'Worship the Lord in the beauty of holiness.' It was claimed that the sermon was provocative of strife because the preacher had said that while he was pastor of the church he could do no other than preach the glorious doctrine of holiness.[23]

From all accounts, it is clear that Sharpe's preaching of instantaneous entire sanctification was the real point at issue. Inevitably there were contributory causes. Sharpe states that at a meeting between him and the officials "many things were said against him of a most trivial nature",[24] but the call, prepared by the officials, and read out by the pastor, on Sunday, September 23rd, 1906, puts the real issue beyond dispute:

"A special church business meeting will be held (D.V.), Saturday first, at 5 p.m.

"All church members are requested to be present at this meeting at which our Pastor's attitude on the question of Holiness will be discussed."[25]

Feeling ran high in the meeting which ensued. Eventually, after regrettable scenes, a motion was carried that the members should dispense with the services of Mr. Sharpe as from that date and give him two months' salary.

The next step was taken by one of the deacons. As the meeting broke up in disorder, Robert Bolton called together under the gallery all who still wanted Sharpe to be their preacher. About 80 responded. They prayed and sang, and, in the words of Robert Bolton Junior, "it was there they founded the Pentecostal Church."[26] The Great Eastern Road

Halls were secured for services the following day and filled for the evening service. It was evident that the preacher without a church did not lack a congregation! The church without a preacher was also well attended that evening. As he gave the announcements, an old deacon read I John 2:19: "They went out from us, but they were not of us; for if they had been of us, they would no doubt have continued with us."[27] The two parties within the same church had now become two churches.

Sharpe now set about the task of organising into a church the people who gathered round him. A business meeting was called for the 6th October in the Great Eastern Road Halls. It was attended by about 60 "demitted" members of the Parkhead Congregational Church, who declared their intention to form a new church in which to worship God and to carry on agressive Christian work.[28] Sharpe was "heartily and unanimously" accepted as pastor. In his response to their action, he made clear from the outset that "the doctrine of Entire Sanctification" should "be declared as taught in the Word of God."[29]

This emphasis was necessary. Some had left their former church out of loyalty to a faithful pastor and in protest against a church which they believed had acted unjustly. By no means all had claimed the experience of Holiness which he preached.[30] Four former deacons of the Parkhead Congregational Church, Robert Bolton, a lithographer, Andrew Robertson, who worked in the cogging mill of the Parkhead Forge, Thomas Gray, an engine driver, and William Barrie, a bricklayer, were elected deacons of the new church, with Robert Bolton as senior deacon and secretary and Andrew Robertson as treasurer.[31] It was agreed that a Sabbath School should be started with Robert Bolton as the superintendent.[32] At the next members' meeting on October 17th it was unanimously decided that the name of the new church should be "The Parkhead Pentecostal Church." Sharpe had said at the time of his eviction, "If we organize a new church, the word 'pentecostal' will be in it."[33]

On October 18th the deacons met with Sharpe at the manse. At this meeting it was decided to increase the diaconate to eight, and to appoint eight managers to work in conjunction with the deacons. This was according to the Congregational pattern, the managers being entrusted with the care of the material affairs of the church, leaving the pastor and the deacons free to concentrate on the spiritual needs of the congregation.

A basis of fellowship was drawn up:

1st. We accept the Holy Bible as the Word of the living God.

2nd. Personal saving faith in Jesus Christ, the Son of God and the sacrifice for sin, is essential and necessary to fellowship in our communion.

3rd. That all applicants for membership must be at least 3 months converted before being addmitted to fellowship, and that the deacons visit such and report to their fellow deacons.

4th. We believe that with the baptism of the Holy Ghost our hearts are purified from sin and that this experience is subsequent to regeneration.[34]

But Sharpe knew that church organisation and doctrinal definition were not enough. At this first deacons' meeting, he suggested the advisability of having a fortnight's mission towards the end of the year, and characteristically, he recommended evangelists from *America,* Rev. and Mrs. Charles Stalker.

The regular services were continued in the Great Eastern Road Halls on Sundays at 11 a.m. and 7 p.m., and on Wednesday and on Saturday evenings at 8. The communion was observed at the close of the morning service on the first Sunday of each month. The Sabbath School met on Sunday at 5 p.m. From April 7th, a service was commenced on Sunday afternoon, and after May 4th it appears that the Saturday evening service was dropped, probably in favour of an open air meeting.[35]

The initial enthusiasm was maintained through the first year of the new church's history. All the services were well attended and on the Sunday evenings the hall was full. On the first Sunday no one came to "the altar"[36] to seek justification or entire sanctification, but Sharpe records that

the following week the altar was filled with seekers, and for many, many months, weeknights and Sabbath nights, and at times on Sabbath mornings, seekers were at the altar, six, seven, eight, nine, ten, eleven, twelve and thirteen at a time.[37]

The Church of the Nazarene in Britain • 43

The Parkhead Pentecostal Church combined the regular ministry and sacraments of the large denominations with the fervour of the early Salvation Army.

The evicted minister remained a topic of local interest. The people outside the churches were inclined to be sympathetic to his bold stand, but there were some in the churches who thought that he was preaching error. One thing was certain, the eyes of the community were on "Sharpe's Kirk" to see whether it would stand the test of time or fall a victim to its scythe.

Within the first few months of its existence, the newly formed church endeavoured to supply the answer. They decided to build. The second Deacons' Meeting on Feb. 9th, 1907, devoted almost its entire attention to the best methods of raising money for the project. All the resources of the church and Sunday School were marshalled, and friends and acquaintances were invited to help. Again Sharpe looked to America for assistance, and during the summer he crossed the Atlantic to raise money towards the project. On the first weekend in December, 1907, the new church in Burgher Street at Parkhead Cross was officially opened and dedicated in the presence of a large congregation. The preacher was Rev. George J. Kunz, an old friend and colleague of the pastor from America.[38]

The printed report of the church for 1907 has a triumphant ring about it. The members on the roll are given as 225. A full programme of services is announced. The pastor's letter closes with an exhortation "to love one another, the world that lies in sin, and those who may be against us".

On September 22nd, 1908, Sharpe inaugurated the Parkhead Holiness Bible School, declaring that such a school had been laid on his heart ever since the opening of the church. He defined its purposes as twofold: firstly, the training of young men and women "in all the fulness of the Gospel" in order that they might preach "an uttermost salvation for all in this and in other lands"; and, secondly, as a help to those who, "though not specially called to preach", desired to know more of "the wonderful truth of Entire Sanctification".[39] The course included Theology, Holiness, New Testament Doctrines, Exposition of Isaiah, Homiletics, Work and Methods, Grammar and English Composition.[40] This venture was taken up with enthusiasm. In the region of forty or fifty students enrolled, and between twenty and thirty completed the first year's course.[41] The teachers were Mr. and Mrs. Sharpe, their eldest daughter Katherina Elizabeth, and Mr. Joseph Robertson, the secretary of the Pentecostal League of Prayer centre at Motherwell.

Sharpe entertained high hopes. All his hopes were not to be realised, but from among the students in these early classes arose some of the first ministers of the Pentecostal Church of Scotland: notably, Andrew Robertson, the secretary and treasurer of the school, John E. Watson, Peter Clark and Robert Purvis.

ITS FORMATION AND DEVELOPMENT

Its Origin and First Assembly

When George Sharpe found himself at the head of a new church, there was no thought in his mind of it extending into a denomination.[42] But the force of circumstances which pressed him to the forefront of a new congregation made him the rallying point of a new denomination. The novelty of his eviction and of the doctrine which led to it attracted many from the surrounding district to hear him for themselves. Others were drawn, not by the novelty, but by the familiarity of Sharpe's teaching. The Pentecostal League of Prayer had eleven centres in Scotland at this time in which was propagated the identical message and Sharpe himself was a member of the League. Thus from the beginning there was nothing parochial about the Parkhead Pentecostal Church. Its influence was further extended by lay preachers and witness teams who went out from its congregation to proclaim its message of full salvation wherever openings occurred.[43]

Toward the end of 1908, Charles Rose, Sharpe's brother-in-law, arranged for a deputation[44] from the Parkhead Pentecostal Church to visit the church of which he was the choirmaster, the United Free Church, George Street, Paisley. Some of the members of the choir[45] decided to commence a similar church in Paisley. Meetings were arranged in a small room in the Good Templars' Hall in co-operation with Sharpe, who arranged to supply speakers, mainly from his Bible School. In Febrary, 1909, Dr. A. M. Hills, a prominent

American Holiness teacher, conducted special services in the Y.M.C.A., in which many people sought and claimed the experience of entire sanctification. Shortly after, on March 4th, the Paisley Pentecostal Church was organised with a membership of 40 and a Sabbath School with 50 scholars and 10 teachers in the Good Templars' Hall, moving after June 1st to the Bethany Hall[46] in New Street. Sharpe appointed John E. Watson, a manager in the Parkhead Pentecostal Church and a student in the Holiness Bible School, as the pastor.[47]

A similar movement was taking place in Uddingston. In 1907,[48] W. P. Nicholson, an evangelist of the Lanarkshire Christian Union, conducted a mission there in which many professed conversion. A young barber, John D. Drysdale, a worker in the Nicholson mission, who had claimed the experience of entire sanctification under the ministry of George Sharpe early in 1907,[49] was asked to form a Bible Class for some of the young converts. As many as forty met on a Sunday afternoon, and meetings were also held during the week for prayer, Bible study and open air witnessing. Uddingston is only six miles from Parkhead, and it became a practice for him and some of his class to attend services in the Parkhead Pentecostal Church. Eventually, on March 15th, 1909, a Pentecostal church was organised by Sharpe with a membership of 14 in the Lesser Public Hall, moving by the end of the month into Belmont Hall, Main St., a former dance hall and training hall for boxers, which was set aside for worship. At first the pulpit was supplied by different preachers, mainly from the Holiness Bible School; but the following year, Andrew Robertson, the secretary and treasurer of the Bible School and its most diligent student, became pastor of the little flock, on September 11th.[50]

About this time, another small congregation was formed at Blantyre, near Uddingston. Drysdale felt a burden for this little town, where he carried on his hairdresser's business, and toward the end of March, 1908, assisted by his sister, Mary, and Mr. Nicholson, he commenced meetings for miners' children on a Sunday evening in the Caldwell Institute which increased from 40 to nearly 180. Shortly afterwards, Sunday evening services were begun for the parents, and week-night meetings were held for them in different homes. Thus the

Blantyre Holiness Mission was formed. Drysdale left the district to take the pastorate of a Holiness congregation in Ardrossan on May 28th, 1909. The following March, at a meeting presided over by Sharpe, the Blantyre Holiness Mission elected to join the Pentecostal Church of Scotland and took the name of the Blantyre Pentecostal Church. George Dempsie, a local man, was appointed pastor on September 11th, 1910. On Nov. 19th, 1910, the congregation moved into a building of its own in Jackson St., Stonefield.[51]

The rise of these three congregations, small in themselves, faced Sharpe with important questions of policy. Paisley and Uddingston had already recognised his leadership and entered into fellowship with his congregation. They could have been given the status of branch churches with representation in the business meetings of the Parkhead church. But such an arrangement was contrary to Sharpe's conception of church polity.

"Even when other churches came into our fellowship I never could accept the idea that a 'mother Church' should lord it over another church. The same Manual, the same everything was and is the true concept of the Church of God. It was this idea that started out the union of the churches into the Pentecostal Church of Scotland."[52]

Moreover, Sharpe had become convinced that if the testimony to Holiness was to be effective and permanent, it was essential for the various congregations which held it to be brought together into a strong union with an ordered church life.

Accordingly, a call was sent out to "the Churches and Missions existing to propagate Holiness", stating Sharpe's conviction of the need of a church being organised to unite and preserve the work of Holiness and inviting them to send representatives to an Assembly in Parkhead Pentecostal Church on May 7th and 8th, 1909, to accomplish this purpose.[53] Data is lacking concerning the extent of this call, but four churches responded to it. According to the list of delegates in the minute book, the three Pentecostal churches were represented as follows: Parkhead, 17; Paisley, 14; Uddingston, 3. Two were present from the Blantyre Holiness Mission and were given recognition as corresponding members.[54]

The Church of the Nazarene in Britain • 47

The first session, on Friday evening, was inaugurated with religious exercises, after which Sharpe preached on I Corinthians 3:11, and dispensed the sacrament.[55] Then came the crucial moment. After Sharpe had read the wording of the call,

> it was moved by Messrs. R. Bolton, Watt and Turnbull representing the Pentecostal Churches in Parkhead, Paisley and Uddingston that the meeting now assembled be constituted the first Assembly of the Pentecostal Church of Scotland.[56]

Thus a denomination came into being. Sharpe was appointed chairman and John E. Watson was appointed secretary, both "pro tem".[57]

The Assembly lost no time in organising its affairs. Committees on Nominations, Organisation, Licentiates, Doctrines and Discipline, Church Extension and Evangelism, Education and Publications, Foreign Missions and Deaconesses were appointed without delay. Sharpe was the moving spirit behind this division of the Assembly into committees, which reflects his experience in American Methodism, and, probably, his contact with the Pentecostal Church of the Nazarene. Miss M. A. Hatch of Star Hall addressed the Assembly asking for co-operation in the sale of the new paper she was editing with Miss Crossley, entitled the *Way of Holiness*. It was already recognised as the official organ of the Pentecostal Church, space being allotted to the new denomination.[58]

The Assembly was addressed again in its second session by Miss Hatch, who took as her text Daniel 11:32. In the business session which followed, the first four committees reported.[59] The Committee on Nominations announced that the Executive Committee would be composed of thirteen members, of which the president, secretary, minute secretary and treasurer would be ex officio. Sharpe, Watson, John Robb and Robert Latta were respectively elected to these offices. The Committee on Organisation, besides confirming the name of the denomination, defined its membership as being

> composed of Churches and Missions which are propagating Holiness and which are in accord with and have submitted to the Declaration of Faith,

48 • *In the Steps of John Wesley*

and its object as being

> a) To encourage and create a bond of unity amongst all of like faith. b) To co-operate in founding Holiness Churches and Missions, and helping to maintain all agencies common to church work. c) To maintain the standards of Scripture, and defend and propagate the truth that pertains to sanctification as a doctrine and experience.

In its report, the Committee on Doctrines and Discipline recommended "that the printed Declaration of Faith be the standard of our church". This Declaration of Faith had been adopted and printed by the Parkhead church some months previously.[60] In its minutes of the Deacons, Managers and Trustees on 13-2-09, is the following statement:

> Mr. Sharpe in making reference to the different places and parties seeking to further holiness, Motherwell,[61] Paisley, Uddingston, Bellshill[61] etc. . . . he thought it most advisable for us to adopt a standard confession of faith . . . he mentioned having had a small book or manual sent him from America in connection with the Pentecostal Church of the Nazarines (sic), and in reading it was of the opinion that we should adopt a part refaring (sic) to the doctrine of holiness, church membership and general rules as we presently recognise and believe . . . it was unanimously agreed that we get 500 copies printed for distribution in our church and that of any body of people who may think of beginning a new church and affiliating themselves with us.

Thus, at its inception, the Pentecostal Church of Scotland based its doctrine and discipline on the *Manual* of the Pentecostal Church of the Nazarene. The section of the 1908 *Manual* to which the excerpt from the minutes refers contains a Wesleyan definition of entire sanctification and a strict standard of conduct, forbidding profanity, sabbath desecration, the use or countenancing of intoxicating liquors, uncharitable conduct, dishonesty, pride in dress, and worldly entertainment and pastimes; and enjoining courtesy, support of the church, helpfulness, love, public and private devotion, good works, seeking the salvation of the unsaved and loyalty to the church's doctrines and practices. The section in this *Manual* under the title "Special Advices" advocating support for the ministry, temperance and prohibition, and abstinence from tobacco was embodied in the discipline of the denomination, along with the *Manual's* rules of procedure in the case of immoral or imprudent conduct.[62] The report of the Committee on Licentiates and Ordination also borrowed

The Church of the Nazarene in Britain • 49

freely from the *Manual's* section on the Ministry as far as it was applicable to the new church's organisation. Provision was made for licences to preach to be given by the pastors to those who were recommended by the officials of their churches and took the prescribed course of study. Ordination was offered to those in pastorates who had passed the course of study and whose characters were approved. The same opportunity was given to women as to men, and provision was made for the recognition of the orders of ministers from other denominations.[63]

In the final session, after hearing reports from the remaining three committees[64] and the drawing up and adopting of a letter of protest directed to the Railway and Steamboat Companies concerning their disposition to run Sabbath excursions on the Clyde, the Assembly created an eighth committee, for the examination of licentiates and deaconesses. It was decided that one hundred licentiate certificates should be ordered. Prayer was then offered; the Assembly joined in the singing of the Doxology and "Leaving all to follow Jesus"; a vote of thanks was accorded the chairman and the first General Assembly of the Pentecostal Church of Scotland came to an end.[65]

In this Assembly, the lines on which the denomination was to develop can be traced. First, there is Sharpe's dominant personality. His occupancy of the chair was inevitable, where he presided, according to the rules of procedure, but with the authority of a father. Next, there is the sense of standing for fundamentals: Sharpe's sermon on Christ as the foundation, and Miss Hatch's on a vital knowledge of God. The shocked reaction of the Assembly to the idea of Sabbath excursions on the Clyde is typical of the Holiness Movement but not distinctive. It is part of a Puritan heritage shared by Calvinists and Wesleyans alike. But it indicates the reverence of the new movement for the Decalogue, and its sense of responsibility to enforce it, as far as its influence permitted, on the community as a whole. Then there is the spirit of optimism. The eyes of the Assembly were on future possibilities of extension rather than on present facts. With only one ordained minister and the immediate prospect of no more than a dozen[66] licentiates, fifty ordination and one hundred licentiate certificates were to be procured. But then one of the first committees was for Extension and Evangelism. This anticipation of growth, this belief in a coming "revival" is in evidence in all the following Assemblies. It was partly responsible for another feature of the church, its emphasis on organisation. As Sharpe reminded the delegates at the Fourth Assembly,[67] they were laying the foundations of future work.

Three other tendencies appear. The way to ordination was carefully guarded.[68] Sharpe was adamant on candidates for the ministry completing their course of study.[69] Nor would he hear of anyone without ordination celebrating the sacrament of the Lord's Supper.[70] This emphasis on a regular ministry was maintained. We have noted the debt of the Assembly via Sharpe to American ecclesiastical faith and order. This element was to find its culmination in 1915 in the integration of the new movement into the American Pentecostal Church of the Nazarene. Finally, there was the missionary trend. This is manifest in the appointment of committees for Foreign Missions and Publication. They represent a sense of responsibility to the "unenlightened" and a desire to propagate.

Its Churches

By the next Assembly, held on May 6th and 7th, 1910, in the Parkhead church, the venue of all the Assemblies, Blantyre Holiness Mission had been organised as a Pentecostal church, and its leader, George Dempsie, was given the right hand of fellowship.[71] It was anticipated that Buccleuch Holiness Church, Edinburgh, would join at the same time,[72] but a year elapsed before it was admitted at the Third Assembly, 11th to 13th May, 1911.[73] At the same time, a church at Morley, near Leeds, which had been organised in the latter part of 1910, was received into fellowship. Also at this Assembly reports were given of missions under the jurisdiction of the Home Mission Committee at the corner of Wellshot Rd. and James St., Shettleston, and Paisley Road, Glasgow.[74] In the Fourth Assembly, held 9th to 13th May, 1912, the Perth Holiness Mission, which had been constituted a Pentecostal church was formally received into fellowship. Only two other churches were added up to the time of the union with the Pentecostal Church of the Nazarene: The

The Church of the Nazarene in Britain • 51

Gildersome Pentecostal Church and the Whifflet Mission, both given recognition in the Sixth Assembly.

Before reviewing their corporate life in the various Assemblies, it would be well to take cognizance of the origin and progress of these individual churches.

Edinburgh. It appears from what records are available that the Buccleuch Holiness Church was the result of the ministerial labours of Rev. George J. Kunz,[75] a former colleague of Sharpe's in the Methodist Episcopal Church, and the financial support of Mr. and Mrs. McDougall, who provided and owned the church building.[76] Kunz returned to America after the Fourth Assembly. It seems that another congregation was formed about this time, probably as a result of a division in the Buccleuch Street church, and met for worship in a hall in Marshall Street.[77] James Jack, of Perth, was called to the pastorate of this congregation in the month of October.[78] In his report at the Fifth Assembly, he speaks of 30 members in the Marshall Street[79] church, two other branch missions in Leith and a weekly Holiness meeting in Ritchie Hall. By the following Assembly, a new place of worship had been secured in Leith Walk "through the practical help of Sister Black". In the printed Minutes of the Seventh Assembly, the membership is given as 36.

Morley. The originator of the Pentecostal Church in Morley was George Pawson, a partner in Pawson Brothers, quarry owners. As a young man, a Primitive Methodist, he had entered into the experience of entire sanctification under the ministry of James Caughey, the American Methodist evangelist. As a result of coming into contact with Sharpe at a convention at Star Hall, Manchester, he decided to sponsor a Pentecostal church in Morley, and Sharpe persuaded John E. Watson to leave Paisley to open up the new work. Watson commenced services on August 14th, 1910,[80] in premises in Albion Street belonging to Pawson Brothers and previously used as offices.[81] Organised as a church on December 12th, 1910 with a membership of 62,[82] it soon became necessary for the office buildings to be extended and on February 15th, 1913,[83] the present church building seating 600 was completed and dedicated, through the financial assistance of Pawson.[84] By the time of the Seventh As-

52 • *In the Steps of John Wesley*

sembly, the membership figure had risen to 190 and the number of children attending Sunday School was in the region of 200.[85]

Gildersome. As a result of special services conducted by Watson, regular meetings were arranged from July 16th, 1911, in a former Wesleyan chapel in "the Bottoms", Gildersome, a village about two miles from Morley. Edmund Roach, who went to Morley about the end of 1911 to assist Watson, became responsible for the Gildersome meetings,[86] and when a Pentecostal church was organised there on January 12, 1914,[87] he became the first pastor. He reported 34[88] members at the Sixth Assembly and declared that "souls were being saved and sanctified", but "he had not much progress to report". He gave a similar report in the final Assembly of 1915.[89]

Perth. On May 2nd, 1909, six members of the Pentecostal League of Prayer, who found themselves out of sympathy with their churches, inaugurated the Perth Holiness Mission, with James Jack as the leader, determining, if it was successful, to constitute it a church. Three years later, on March 21st, 1912, it was organised into a Pentecostal church with 30 members. William Stewart was elected the senior deacon, and in the Fourth Assembly he was given the right hand of fellowship. On June 8th, Rev. W. E. Smith, a Canadian, who was a minister of the Methodist Episcopal Church of America, and was present at the Fifth Assembly, was inducted into the pastorate. Under his energetic ministry a church building was secured in Alexandra Street and dedicated on Jan. 10th, 1914. The membership increased from 32 in 1912 to 40 in 1915.[90]

Whifflet. The Whifflet Mission was the outcome of kitchen meetings,[91] commencing about 1911. In August, 1912, a children's work was commenced, rising from 11 to as high as 80. In the Sixth Assembly, Mr. Nicholson, the leader, one of the students at the Pentecostal Bible College, was given the right hand of fellowship. Before the next Assembly the work had returned to a week-night meeting under the care of Mrs. Sharpe, as Nicholson had left to join the army.[92]

Home Missions at Shettleston and Paisley Road. These two missions were virtually branch missions of the Parkhead

The Church of the Nazarene in Britain • 53

Pentecostal Church and were staffed by its members. Those connected with the Shettleston Mission were expected to attend certain meetings at Parkhead.[93]

Parkhead. The formation of the Pentecostal Church of Scotland enhanced the prestige of the Parkhead church as the mother church of a denomination, but deprived it of much of its pastor's concentration. His responsibilities as president of the denomination, principal of the Pentecostal Bible College (1913) and editor of the *Holiness Herald* (1913) made increasing encroachments on his time and attention. There was a growing concern among the officials of the church which found expression in several of the deacons' business meetings.[94] Various solutions were discussed. Edmund Roach,[95] Rev. James Young [96] of Star Hall and Rev. W. E. Smith[97] of New York were all considered as assistant pastors, but of these only the first actually served in this capacity.

Sharpe continued his periodical visits to America. All these visits brought their compensation in financial assistance and closer fellowship with those like-minded on the other side of the Atlantic, but they could only aggravate the problem of Sharpe's distraction from his pastorate. However, the visits were reciprocated in full measure by American preachers visiting Scotland.

Emigration from Scotland to America made inroads into the membership.[98] Later the war added its complications.[99] Some lost heart and some fell out of sympathy. During 1911 to 1915, three deacons and seven managers resigned for various reasons, four because of removal from the district.[100] But amid all the difficulties and discouragements, the work was maintained. After rising to 275 in 1908, the church membership found its level at 250 in 1912, and fell no lower than 240 during 1915-16.[101] Throughout this period, there were those who professed conversion and sought the experience of entire sanctification.[102] As may be expected, the church finance fluctuated.[103] The Sabbath School, under the able superintendency of Robert Bolton, was an outstanding feature of the church.

Paisley. The church at Paisley prospered under the ministry of John E. Watson reaching a membership of 120 in its first year.[104] When he left to inaugurate the church in

Morley, his place was taken on October 29th, 1910, by J. H. Farmer from Star Hall, Manchester.[105] Sickness hindered his progress in study, which in turn held up his ordination, and interfered with his ministry.[106] He resigned[107] before the Fifth Assembly, at which a drop in membership from 81 the previous year to 36 was shown. By the Sixth Assembly, W. L. Telford had been installed in the pastorate. Membership declined to 30, but rose to 56[108] by the Seventh Assembly. In the report at this Assembly, Telford expressed the hope that by the next Assembly they would have a building of their own;[109] a hope which was soon realised. The Paisley Church was characterized by a zealous ministry in the open air.

Uddingston. Andrew Robertson Junior was the pastor of the church at Uddingston for almost the entire period under review, resigning in 1915. His reports at the Assemblies indicate the difficulties he experienced through the unattractive building in which the congregation worshipped, the distance of his residence from his flock and the limitations which his studies at the Glasgow University imposed upon his time and energies.

In spite of these and other hindrances, some progress was made. The membership was never large,[110] but the secretary[111] and the treasurer[112] of the Assembly were at one time both members of this church. It was during Dr. Walker's visit to Uddingston that the subject of union with the Pentecostal Church of the Nazarene was broached by Turnbull and Robertson.[113]

Blantyre. The church at Blantyre, which at one time had a Sunday evening congregation of 100,[114] and in 1911 a church membership of 50 and a Sabbath School membership of 90,[115] suffered a severe setback in 1912. Pastor George Dempsie, an able preacher, came into conflict with the denomination by his refusal to follow the prescribed course of study, and with the local congregation because of his refusal to take part-time work to supply his own salary until the debt on the building was paid off. Many of the congregation left for the latter reason[116] and before February 8th, 1913, he himself had resigned from the denomination.[117] For about eight months, Robert Purvis of the Parkhead church, took the oversight of the handful which remained.[118] By the Sixth Assembly, the Uddingston Church had made itself responsible for its sustenance.[119] The following year, J. A. Cunningham, a student at the Pentecostal Bible College, was pastor of the little flock,[120] which remained small until the time of the union[121] and for many years to come.[122]

Its Corporate Existence

Annual Assemblies. The annual Assemblies followed the pattern of the first. Proceedings were opened with religious exercises and the annual sermon was preached. Besides the Assembly sermon, it was usual for a presidential address to be delivered. The sacrament was celebrated in the opening session of the first four Assemblies. There is no reference to it in the fifth and sixth, but a communion service was held at the close of the seventh.

The Fourth Assembly fixed the constitution of future Assemblies as follows: the president, treasurers and secretaries were ex officio members of the Assembly in which they served and also the one in which they demitted office. Besides these the Assembly was made up of all acting pastors and others who had been recognised by the Assembly, teachers in the Bible School and representatives from the churches in the ratio of two for a membership of less than one hundred and one extra for every additional fifty. This was also the Assembly in which the delegates decided to ordain a woman to the ministry, Miss Olive M. Winchester. Only two others received ordination in the brief history of the Pentecostal Church of Scotland: John E. Watson, on June 5th, 1909,[123] and W. L. Telford, at the close of the Seventh Assembly.

The movement which began its career by protesting against Sabbath desecration delivered a parthian shot against the "Drink Traffic" by sending a resolution to the authorities urging "drastic measures" against "the country's greatest enemy, even to the point of prohibition."[124]

The Pentecostal Church of Scotland was formed by those who met together "to consider the best methods of propagating and preserving the work of holiness." There are four sides of its corporate life directly related to this purpose.

Evangelism. It has been stated that one of the committees formed at the First Assembly was that of Church Extension and Evangelism. This was merged with the Committee on Tent and Camp Meetings in the Second Assembly, which became the Home Mission Committee in the Third Assembly.[125] Its purpose was to investigate the applications of congregations desiring to join the Pentecostal Church of Scotland and to raise up new churches. It seems to have played a vital part in the establishment of the missions in Paisley Road, South Side, Glasgow, and at Shettleston. The tent under its jurisdiction was used to give impetus to the forming of the Gildersome church,[126] and was also employed to extend the churches at Parkhead[127] and Morley.[128] Tent meetings were planned in other places, but did not result in churches being formed. The corporate evangelism, therefore, of the movement was not outstandingly successful. It seems that the personality of Sharpe was to a considerable extent the magnet which drew other groups into fellowship with him and his associates, and the centre around which the movement revolved. The origin of most if not all the churches could be traced back in some measure to him.

Training. On the formation of the Pentecostal Church of Scotland, the Parkhead Holiness Bible School became its ministerial training institution.[129] The classes for the laity were continued and a correspondence course was commenced,[130] which by 1912 was serving about a dozen students.[131] The teaching staff was augmented by the addition of Olive M. Winchester (1909-13) and Rev. G. J. Kunz (1910-11).[132] The former took her A.B. degree at Radcliffe College, Harvard University, majoring in languages, with the emphasis on Arabic and Hebrew. In 1912, she became the first woman to receive the B.D. degree of the Glasgow University, and the Dean of the Faculty of Divinity, Professor Reid, honoured the Bible School with a visit while she was a teacher.[133]

From the inception of the denomination, the idea of a separate college building persisted, especially in Sharpe's mind. By the close of 1912, on his return from America, where he had received gifts for the purpose,[134] he secured a suitable building[135] on his own initiative, deferring, however, to the authority of the Educational Committee by asking them to name it. They approved its legitimacy by christening it, "The Pentecostal Bible College". (One of the names sub-

The Church of the Nazarene in Britain • 57

mitted by its father!)[136] The Fifth Assembly were informed that it was Sharpe's intention that they should adopt it, as soon as it was finished and occupied.[137] It cost £800.[138] On August 16th, 1913, it was officially opened by Dr. A. M. Hills, and the following September the 1913-14 session commenced there with "three resident students, three visiting students, and one correspondence student".[139] It was a big undertaking for such a small denomination. Miss Winchester returned to America in June, 1914. The country was on the eve of a war which would draw all available young men into the forces or the factories. Sharpe withstood the inevitable to the end, faithfully tutoring his last student until his call-up in June, 1916.[140] He was the chief mourner at the funeral of his untimely child.[141]

Magazine. Closely associated with the college was the official organ of the denomination, the *Holiness Herald.* Originally, the *Way of Holiness,* edited by Miss Crossley and Miss Hatch of Star Hall, Manchester, fulfilled this function, with space allotted for denominational articles and items. But there was a growing dissatisfaction with this arrangement, which became vocal in the Third Assembly,[142] and reached a climax in the Fourth.[143] With the purchase of the college premises and the gift of a printing press, the desideratum became a possibility. The *Holiness Herald,* so named by the Publication Committee,[144] commenced its course in September, 1913, with Sharpe as the editor and supervisor of the typesetting and printing, which were undertaken by the college students.[145] The identity of the college and the magazine in personnel and premises led to an amalgamation of the Educational and Publication Committees. Their careers also ran on parallel lines. The initial expenses of the printing equipment were met by the gifts of the churches and sympathisers. The first few editions showed only a slight deficit, and there was every prospect that the sale of the magazine would cover the cost.[146] But the churches did not find the sale of it to the general public an easy matter, and some delegates, while affirming "it was the best Holiness paper in the country", saw room for improvement.[147] Like the college, it was commenced too near August, 1914, and eventually became one of the casualties of war.[148, 149]

58 • *In the Steps of John Wesley*

Missionary Work. It is normal for those who stress complete dedication of the life to God to feel the missionary urge. The Pentecostal Church of Scotland was no exception. In its First Assembly it appointed a committee for foreign missions. But the recurring question, which was not answered until the Fifth Assembly, was through which channel the urge should find expression. The formation of its own missionary society was contemplated at first.[150] Then it was decided to affiliate with the Foreign Missionary Department of the American National Association for the Promotion of Holiness.[151] However, although negotiations were in progress for a considerable period, and at one time Sharpe's name appeared in the *Christian Witness* as one of the directors of the Association's Missionary Board,[152] the anticipated affiliation did not materialise. In the Fifth Assembly, a resolution was carried to "form a missionary society of our own".[153] It was also decided to "join with the Pentecostal Church of the Nazarene, and give through that source".[154] At the next Assembly, in the presence of Dr. E. F. Walker, it was unanimously decided to send all monies raised for foreign missions during the year to the missionary treasury of that church.[155]

UNION WITH THE PENTECOSTAL CHURCH OF THE NAZARENE

The union of the Pentecostal Church of Scotland with the Pentecostal Church of the Nazarene was the climax of a process which began before the former church came into existence. Sharpe was a product of the American Holiness Movement, and he never severed his ties with it. He frequently visited America, both before and after the foundation of a separate church in Britain. In seeking an avenue for missionary enterprise Sharpe turned characteristically to America. He looked to America for guidance in church polity and practice, and received help through the gifts and ministry of his American friends. Sharpe's first contact with the Pentecostal Church of the Nazarene is difficult to pinpoint. The man who led him into Holiness, L. Milton Williams, joined the church at Chicago in 1907.[156] Olive Winchester, a teacher in its Pentecostal Collegiate Institute, taught in his Bible School from 1909 to 1914. Timothy Smith declares that every major Holiness paper published in America carried some account of Sharpe's work between 1907 and 1909, and that Bresee reprinted in full in the *Nazarene Messenger* the record of the first Assembly of the Pentecostal Church of Scotland which he found in an English periodical.[157] The 1911 Nazarene General Assembly adopted a resolution that representatives should be sent to the next Assembly of the Pentecostal Church of Scotland.[158] At that time the British church was already contemplating changing its name to the Pentecostal Church of the Nazarene. The majority of the churches were in favour of the change, and, although it was announced that "our church had no official connection with the Pentecostal Church of the Nazarene at present",[159] some were already thinking in terms of union.[160] Aware of this sentiment, the American church appointed Dr. E. F. Walker, one of its three general superintendents, as its fraternal delegate. It was a happy choice, not only because of his previous contact with Sharpe, and his British ancestry,[161] but also because his expository preaching (he was an earnest student of the Greek New Testament) was particularly suited to British congregations.

He arrived in Britain in the winter of 1913-14,[162] and after conducting special services in several of the churches, he was received by the Executive Committee in the Parkhead Church on April 9th, 1914. He read the resolution of the Nazarene General Assembly relating to his visit, and proceeded to pass his observations on the situation. He touched on the close similarity in doctrine, spirit, government and general methods, and expressed the opinion that, in the event of affiliation, his church could be of considerable help.[163] His approach to the Assembly shortly after on the same day was on the same lines. He held out the hope that the Pentecostal Church of the Nazarene would furnish money for the support of a full-time district superintendent. "We have plenty of men and money", he said, "and such as we have we give unto you."[164] An apostolic offer, without the negative protasis!

A committee to consider the question of union was appointed, consisting of the president, the secretary, the treasurer and one represenative of each church.[165] In the fourth session, after Dr. Walker had conveyed the fraternal

60 • *In the Steps of John Wesley*

greetings of his church, and said something about its rise and progress, they laid the following proposals before the Assembly:

> 1. That the question of affiliation or organic relationship with the Pentecostal Church of the Nazarene be properly discussed in the Holiness Herald.
>
> 2. That the President of the Assembly visit the churches and present the question *pro* and *con* and that the law of the church be put in operation so that the church can consider and decide this question of organic union before June 30th, 1914.
>
> 3. Should the churches decide in favour of such union according to our law, that a provisional committee be appointed by the Executive Committee, to confer with the authorities of the Pentecostal Church of the Nazarene for the mutual adjustment of all matters involved in the said union and make their final report concerning such adjustments at the next Assembly.[166]

The report of the committee was adopted. In addition to the resolution to send to the Pentecostal Church of the Nazarene the monies raised for foreign missions during the year, the Assembly decided to circulate its missionary magazine, the *Other Sheep,* throughout the churches and to apply to its publishing house for samples of Sabbath School literature, including a catechism.

Everything seemed to be moving smoothly in the direction of union, when, at the Executive Committee Meeting on May 28th, letters were read from Watson and Schofield of the Morley church intimating that "the other churches could do as they liked but Morley Church would not join the Pentecostal Church of the Nazarene."[167] Neither Watson nor Pawson was enamoured at this juncture with the idea of joining an American church.[168] But the Executive Committee was strongly in favour of union, and it was agreed that Sharpe should write to Watson "and ask him if he realises what the attitude and finding of the Morley Church meant to him in his relationship to the ministry of the Pentecostal Church of Scotland."[169]

The next step was for Sharpe to visit the churches in order that they might give their decision concerning union. At the next meeting of the Executive Committee, 9-7-14, he reported the result: the eight churches had voted 176 in favour of union and 7 against.[170] On the surface it was an

The Church of the Nazarene in Britain • 61

overwhelming vote for union, but it was far from fully representative. Statistics for 1914 show a membership of 621.[171] So just over 28% voted for union. The occupations of the members hindered attendance at the meeting at Perth, and a thunderstorm at Morley,[172] but one may seriously question whether local conditions were altogether responsible for the poor attendance at these vital meetings, and whether the enthusiasm of the leaders was entirely shared by the rank and file.

At this point the question of property was raised, Watson informing the Executive Committee that the donor of the Morley church buildings had executed a trust deed, by which on his decease they were vested in a board of trustees, and that special provision was made for the disposal of the buildings "in the event of future contingencies".[173] The Executive Committee responded by appointing a provisional committee to "discuss the various matters pertaining to union." Both Watson and Pawson were included in the composition of this committee, but Pawson sent an apology for absence. The Provisional Committee met on 15-7-14, and settled the question of property to everyone's satisfaction, recognising

> that all Church Property held in the name of the Denomination in case of being sold for any reason, the proceeds therefrom to be reinvested again on behalf of Holiness work on this side;

and that church property, which was the gift of any individual or individuals, would exist in accordance with the trust deed under which it was held. The Committee also decided to ask the Pentecostal Church of the Nazarene that the British church might retain the names of its officials, and that a draft of obligations that would be laid on it in the event of union might be rendered.[174]

On October 2nd, 1914, the Provisional Committee met again, this time in the presence of Dr. H. F. Reynolds.[175] Discussion took place with regard to the name and election of church officers, and reference was again made to the difficulty Sharpe was experiencing in attempting to superintend the churches and pastor his own church. The two items were summed up in the following resolution:

> In view of the discussion to-night and the raising of the question of 'name' and 'election' we recommend that it be referred to the

churches, and provided that a solution be arrived at, Mr. Sharpe be asked to accept the appointment of Missionary District Superintendent.[176]

Now arose an unexpected problem—a problem of finance! Reynolds informed Sharpe that the General Missionary Board felt at liberty to allocate to the support of the work in the British Isles only such funds as were raised there for foreign missionary work and sent to the foreign missionary treasury of the Pentecostal Church of the Nazarene.[177] No wonder Sharpe "found it difficult to understand their attitude", and Reynolds called the Executive Committee of the Board to meet to see what further could be done.[178] A promise was made to grant £150 ($750), and the church in Kansas City, of which Dr. Reynolds was a member, pledged themselves to raise this amount for one year.[179] This solution also was unacceptable, as placing an undue burden on a local church and because of its temporary nature. Alternatively, Sharpe suggested that the Pentecostal Church of the Nazarene appoint a man from America to be district superintendent and guarantee his support; but this was not considered possible by the Executive Committee. Indeed, Reynolds's letter of 1-3-15, suggests it might be better "to allow matters to rest as they are" for the time being. Accordingly, the delegates came to the Seventh Assembly prepared to work on the old basis.[180] Even so, union was still "in the air", and, at the invitation of the Executive Committee of the Nazarene General Missionary Board,[181] the Assembly elected fraternal delegates to the forthcoming Nazarene General Assembly in the autumn: Mr. and Mrs. Sharpe and Mr. Pawson.[182]

Mr. Pawson was unable to make the journey, but Mr. and Mrs. Sharpe were warmly received, and given the opportunity of addressing the Assembly. A committee was appointed to consider the question of union between the two churches. In its report to the Assembly it gave a brief description of the British church, took cognizance of its identity in doctrine, its vote to unite with the American church and the fact that Britain presented a valuable territory for the propagation of the Nazarene doctrines. It recommended that the union of the two churches be consummated as soon as possible, that Rev. George Sharpe be appointed as district superintendent and that a sum of at least $1,000 a year be

The Church of the Nazarene in Britain • 63

appropriated to preserve and extend the work. The report was adopted in the afternoon session on Wednesday, October 6th, and Mr. and Mrs. Sharpe were besieged by well-wishers eager to clasp their hands.[183]

Back in Scotland, Mr. and Mrs. Sharpe gave an account of their visit to the delegates of the postponed meeting of the Seventh Assembly of the Pentecostal Church of Scotland, called at Parkhead for November 5th, 1915. The report of the Nazarene Committee on Union was laid before them, and after a period of discussion, the sixteen delegates registered their approval of union by a unanimous standing vote. A season of prayer and song followed. Outstanding items of business were dealt with, and at 10:15 p.m. the final session of the last Assembly of the Pentecostal Church of Scotland closed.[184]

The following day a cablegram conveyed the news:

Reynolds, 2109 Troost Avenue, Kansas City, Missouri
UNION CONSUMMATED WRITING
TURNBULL SECRETARY.[185]

THE BRITISH ISLES DISTRICT OF THE CHURCH OF THE NAZARENE

1916-19. The War Years

The first Assembly under the auspices of the Pentecostal[186] Church of the Nazarene was held in the Parkhead church on April 21st, 1916. Sharpe's report as the district superintendent was enthusiastic and optimistic. He touched on the benefits of working under a constitution which preserved the rights of the people and protected the preachers. Set-backs were recognised, but qualified. The college was to be given up,[187] but the large Nazarene colleges in America were open to prospective students. The war was hindering extension, but when it was over there was the hope that they would move from defence to advance.[188]

Twenty-five[189] were p r e s e n t at this Assembly.[190] Statistics[191] were slightly lower than at the corresponding Assembly in 1915: 622 members and 834 in the Sunday School, as against 655 and 841 respectively.[192] But there were 90 in the Young People's Societies as compared with 58 in the Bible Classes in 1915, a small group at Forfar had joined the church, and Edinburgh, "after a separation of fully a year", had returned to the fold.[193]

Before the next Assembly, Watson had transferred to Edinburgh, and H. E. Jessop, a young Baptist minister, especially gifted in expounding Holiness doctrine, took his place at Morley.[194] By the time Jessop was installed the membership had dropped to 116, which he purged to 90.[195] This fall from 200 to 90 was the main reason for a further decline in the church membership of the district, from 622 to 540.[196] The work in Forfar was closed, but groups at Ardrossan, Drysdale's previous pastorate, and Gray's, Essex, joined the church,[197] and the Sunday School and Young People's Societies figures were up at 1017 and 272 respectively.[198]

But war conditions were increasingly exacting their toll. At this Assembly, Sharpe announced that the publication of the *Holiness Herald* had been suspended for the time being.[199] No Assembly was held in 1918, and the statistical returns show a decrease in all sections: 464 members, 841 Sunday School enrolment and 118 in the Young People's Societies.[200]

To make matters worse, the church lost three of its leading ministers: Andrew Robertson, Junior, John E. Watson, who had never quite regained the prominence he enjoyed before his opposition to the union and joined the Baptist Church towards the close of 1917,[201] and H. E. Jessop who left to work with the International Holiness Mission in 1919, but remained an elder in the Church of the Nazarene.[202]

In his report to the Assembly which met in Parkhead Church on April 18th, 1919, Sharpe confessed that "the past two years have been fateful in losses." Edinburgh had ceased to exist and the little cause at Gray's had been disorganised. But in spite of the clouds there is no evidence of depression in the account of the proceedings.[203]

1919-24. The Post War Period

It was three years before the downward momentum of war was arrested in the sphere of membership, but by the 1920 Assembly matters took on a more hopeful complexion in personnel. James Jack was released from military service and took over the church at Ardrossan.[204] J. D. Lewis, a Faith Mission Evangelist,[205] stirred this Assembly with his preaching and was officially received as an elder at the next Assembly.[206] K. M. McRitchie and J. H. Hynd, both of Parkhead, were granted minister's licences. The Parkhead church consented to release Sharpe for the district work providing an associate pastor was appointed.[207] The choice fell upon James Jack, whose zealous ministry[208] brought a new lease of life to the mother church. He made a great impression upon the young people, many of whom were converted, among them George Frame.[209] In the 1922 Assembly, Mr. and Mrs. Frank Clark and James Macleod[210] represented the new church at Dunfermline, James B. Maclagan was given a licence to preach and Frame was continued in his studies.[211] The shape of things to come can be discerned.

In 1921, for the first time since its inception as a district of the Church of the Nazarene, a general superintendent presided at the Assembly: Dr. Reynolds, who played such a vital part in the events which led up to union. At this Assembly, the membership touched its lowest figure in the history of the church: 453. (Sunday School membership had dropped to 737 and that of the Young People's Societies to 281).[212] But the churches at Parkhead and Morley had been purged for greater fruitfulness, and Paisley under Lewis and Ardrossan under Purvis were on the verge of better things. The following year, Sharpe was able to report the greatest accession to membership in the church's history, about 150, and the addition of two churches, at Bellshill and Dunfermline.[213] In 1924 a further advance was made with the addition of a church at Cathcart Road, Govanhill, Glasgow, and the membership figures were 594, with 1063 in the Sunday School and 468 in the Young People's Societies.[214]

Progress was made in two other directions during this period. In 1920, Sharpe began what became the Nazarene Bible School in his own home, transferring it in 1922 to the

66 • *In the Steps of John Wesley*

Parkhead church. In 1923 it was officially recognised by the Assembly.[215] The *Holiness Herald* was also restored to its former ministry in 1922, with Sharpe as the editor.[216]

The church lost two of its early stalwarts through death: George Pawson, in 1921, who left the bulk of his estate to the Church of the Nazarene,[217] and the faithful Turnbull, who was taken away from a short but fruitful ministry at Blantyre in 1922.

1924-28. The Superintendency of Peter Clark

In 1923 the General Board had appointed Sharpe one of the three missionary superintendents, with jurisdiction in Africa, India and the Near East. It was an office midway between that of general and district superintendent.[218] Shortly after the 1924 District Assembly, he relinquished the office of district superintendent, and Peter Clark was appointed in his place.[219] Clark was the senior elder of the district, who had commanded the respect of his brethren by his initiative in the erection of a church building in his pastorate in Uddingston.[220] During his superintendency, churches were organised at Port Glasgow and at Kilmacolm.[221] At the 1926 Assembly the membership amounted to 678, an increase of 37 on the previous year. There was a decrease of 55 the following year, mainly owing to a drop of 72 in the membership at Parkhead, but statistics showed 635 members at the 1928 Assembly.[222]

Clark's was no enviable task. Owing to economic conditions, the office of missionary superintendent had to be discontinued.[223] Mr. and Mrs. Sharpe were given an impressive valedictory at the time of the 1925 Assembly. The following year they were present as "Elders without Charge."[224] However, a congenial work for Sharpe was close to hand. The Board of Education urged the 1926 Assembly to commence a Bible school.[225] The recommendation was adopted, and he undertook the task of establishing a British Nazarene college in Motherwell. But shortage of students,[226] lack of support from the district and sickness in his family conspired against the new venture. The college was opened in October, 1926, and closed in June, 1928.[227]

Meanwhile changes were taking place in personnel. J. H. Hynd, who had taken over the Morley pastorate in 1920, and

The Church of the Nazarene in Britain • 67

was elected district secretary in succession to Turnbull in 1923, moved away from "Nazarene orthodoxy" to more liberal theological opinions. Sharpe had a special regard for him, but to safeguard the ministry from heterodoxy he introduced a test relating to denominational orthodoxy and loyalty. Confronted by specific questions, Hynd tendered his resignation, and it was accepted with regret for he was a man of unquestioned morality and intellectual ability.[228] The district sustained other losses. Roach left to join the International Holiness Mission, before the 1925 Assembly.[229] Dr. and Mrs. David Hynd sailed as Nazarene missionaries to Swaziland, Africa, on May 22nd, 1925.[230] Telford went to assist his brother-in-law, Drysdale, at Emmanuel Training Home, Birkenhead before the 1926 Assembly.[231] But others were rising to take their places. The transfer of Rev. J. M. Cubie, an energetic and able Scotsman who had entered the Church of the Nazarene in America, was accepted at the 1925 Assembly.[232] Frame was ordained in 1926 and Maclagan in 1927. Macleod was given a minister's licence in 1928. McRitchie was elected editor of the *Holiness Herald* in 1925, district secretary in succession to Hynd in 1927 and he figured prominently in the election for district superintendent in 1928.[233]

In the 1928 Assembly, after nineteen ballots without anyone receiving the necessary two-thirds majority, the matter of appointing the district superintendent was put in the hands of the presiding general superintendent, Dr. Reynolds. Eventually he decided to appoint the one with the highest total of votes. The count revealed 386 for Sharpe, 362 for McRitchie and 203 for Clark. After asking for time to consider the matter, Sharpe accepted the appointment.[234]

1928-31. George Sharpe's Second Period of Superintendency

Sharpe never regained the supremacy he had enjoyed before leaving the district to take up his work of missionary superintendent.[235] This was probably partly due to the sympathy which some felt for Clark, who transferred to the Nazarene Alberta District, in Canada, shortly after the 1928 Assembly. But he probably was the man best fitted to lead the district for the time being. No great advances were made during this period. The number of churches remained at 14 from 1926 to the close of this period, with the exception of

68 • *In the Steps of John Wesley*

1930, when there were fifteen. Govanhill and Kilmacolm were closed, but churches were added at Troon and Edinburgh. By the 1931 Assembly, groups had been formed in Greenock and Leeds, which were later organised into churches. There was a net gain in membership of 39 over the three years, the statistics in 1931 being 677 members, 1626 Sunday School scholars and 205 in the Young People's Societies.[236]

At the request of the British Isles District Assembly, on May 23rd, 1929, Olivet College, Illinois, U.S.A., one of the leading Nazarene colleges, conferred the honorary degree of Doctor of Divinity on George Sharpe, in recognition of his service to the church.[237] There was an optimistic and militant spirit in the 1931 Assembly. Reports on evangelistic work in Greenock and Leeds were greeted with thanksgiving and prayer. J. D. Lewis, after seven years as pastor of the Parkhead church in succession to Jack, was appointed district evangelist. In view of "the increasing opportunities for a forward movement in our district", the Education Committee urged the establishment of a training centre in Glasgow.[238]

There were hands outstretched and eager to receive the torch. Shortly after the 1931 Assembly, Sharpe resigned the superintendency to accept the pastorate at Parkhead, and in August Robert C. Purvis, one of his sons in the Gospel, received a cablegram from Dr. Reynolds appointing him to the vacant office.[239]

1931-40. The Superintendency of Robert Purvis

Robert Purvis had shown marked ability as a pastor at Ardrossan (1920-26) and Morley, and he was content to remain a pastor. But on Sharpe's resignation he was the obvious choice. In the 1932 Assembly he was elected by 61 votes out of 64. A man of imposing appearance and attractive personality, he combined an acceptable pulpit manner with gifts of organisation and a shrewd mind. Between 1932 and 1940 the membership of the district increased from 744 to 1001, and the number of churches from 16 to 25. Every year until the last one, there was a gain in membership. The figures for the Sunday School and Young People's Societies fluctuated considerably. In 1940, the former showed a gain of 127 over the 1932 figure of 1829 (in 1939 the total was 2255), and the latter showed a loss of 2 on the 1933 figure

The Church of the Nazarene in Britain • 69

of 284 (in 1934 the total was 403). Churches were organised at Inverness, Irvine (these two by Sharpe) and Leeds (1932), Birkenshaw, near Gildersome, and Greenock (1933), Ayr and Twechar, in Dunbartonshire (1935), Govan (1936), Lurgan, in Northern Ireland (1937), Dundee, Viewpark, near Uddingston, Carlisle and Workington (1938), and Belfast (1939). The churches at Bellshill, Edinburgh and Birkenshaw were closed before the 1932, 1933 and 1936 Assemblies respectively.[240]

Throughout this period a spirit of advance is in evidence. Twice the target was set for a thousand members, in 1932 and 1938. In the 1935 Assembly Purvis was able to report advances at Coatbridge, Govan and Ayr, and at Lurgan, in Northern Ireland.[241] The tent campaigns conducted by Maynard James made a distinct impression on the British Nazarenes. There were demands for "a trekkers' band" (1933) and a "revival party" (1935), a healing service was held at the 1934 Assembly,[242] and tent campaigns figured prominently as a means of evangelism. In 1939 four successful campaigns were reported, in the new tent supplied by the General Missions Department.[243]

Besides the evangelistic campaigns, conventions for the edification of the members and other Christians were given due prominence. The local convention at Ardrossan had been made a district responsibility in 1922. By 1924 it had developed into a camp meeting and in 1934 the venue was moved to Ayr, as a result of which a church was organised there.[244] From 1931 the New Year Convention in the Parkhead church became an annual event.[245]

This period was fruitful in the promotion of fellowship between the Nazarenes and the International Holiness Mission and the Calvary Holiness Church, which was formed in 1934. J. D. Lewis was excused attendance at the Assembly to speak at the conventions of the former in 1933 and 1938 and at those of the latter in 1935 and 1937. Maclagan, Frame and Macleod were present with Lewis when Sharpe conducted the ordination service of Filer, Ravenhill and Ford of the Calvary Holiness Church on the Easter Tuesday.[246] In reciprocation, campaigns were conducted for the Nazarenes by the revival party of the Calvary Holiness Church[247] and prominent members of the International Holiness Mission spoke at their conventions.[248] Purvis sought to maintain friendly relations

70 • *In the Steps of John Wesley*

with evangelicals in all denominations.[249] In 1933, the district participated in the Worldwide Missionary Exhibition in Glasgow, and the 1936 Assembly adopted a resolution to "cherish and nurture the most benign . . . relationships with other religious bodies . . ."[250]

Cubie returned to the States before the 1938 Assembly. Sharpe retired from the Parkhead pastorate in 1938,[251] but continued an active pulpit ministry in the district and beyond. Death effected other changes. Collins, the district treasurer since 1919, died in 1935 and his place was taken by Frame. McRitchie, the district secretary, died before the 1938 Assembly and at the 1939 Assembly, Peter Clark, who had returned from Canada some two years previously, became district secretary.[252]

In 1934,[253] the name of the *Holiness Herald* was changed to the *Way of Holiness,* the magazine of that name having ceased publication in 1928.[254] Maclagan became the editor in 1937, after serving as sub-editor under McRitchie for two years.

1940-53. The Superintendency of George Frame

1940-45. The Second World War

At the 1940 Assembly, Purvis resigned as superintendent and refused to stand for re-election.[255] Nine ballots were cast before his successor was elected: George Frame. Frame had qualified for the office, not only by a successful, eight-year pastorate at Uddingston, during which a branch mission had been opened at Viewpark, but by taking his M. A. Degree at the Glasgow University and rendering keen and efficient service in the administrative work of the district. Among other offices, he had served on the Advisory Board since 1936. Upon his shoulders fell the responsibility of superintending the district during the difficult years of war.[256]

He was succeeded as district treasurer by Miss E. S. L. Baxter[257] and in the Uddingston pastorate by Rev. Arthur Fawcett, a leading minister in the International Holiness Mission, whose credentials were recognised by the Church of the Nazarene in 1941.[258]

For the first two years the membership figures remained steady. There was a drop from 996 in 1942 to 925 in 1943, but the decline was arrested the following year, and in 1945 there was a rise of 53 to 978. A similar fluctuation took place in

The Church of the Nazarene in Britain • 71

the Sunday School enrolment. Concern was expressed at "the serious situation in the Sunday Schools" (1942)[259] and the neglect of some churches in this direction (1943).[260] But the enrolment, after a fall of over 300 in 1941, gradually recovered, and in 1945 actually showed an increase of 134 on the 1940 figure of 1956. As may be expected, the Young People's Societies declined, but even they were on the increase in 1945 with a membership of 241.[261]

One of the many problems besetting the churches in the war years was that of man power. The Church of the Nazarene was fortunate to have no less than seventeen accessions to its ministry between 1940 and 1945: among them George Brown (1942), W. S. Tranter (1943), Ernest Eades, William Russell and Thomas Schofield (1944), Leslie Roberts and Sydney Martin (1945), all of whom were subsequently ordained.[262] Even with the restrictions of a country engaged in total war, some advance was made. The church at Inverness was disorganised in 1941, but three small churches were raised up in Birmingham in 1942, 1944 and 1945. In the latter year, a group at Ilkeston also joined the Church of the Nazarene.[263] An attempt was also made to minister to the needs of the areas devastated by aerial attacks, and by 1942 mobile canteens had been put into service in Scotland, England and Northern Ireland.[264] And, in spite of the difficulties confronting the work among children, 1941 was the year when an annual children's camp was inaugurated, which became a valuable institution in the Nazarene work among the children in Britain.[265]

During this period, the venue of the annual Assemblies was moved from Parkhead for five years; to Uddingston in 1942, Port Glasgow in 1943 and the Central Halls, Bath Street, Glasgow, from 1944 to 1946.[266]

Most important of all, what had been a desideratum for so long,[267] a building in West Hurlet, near Glasgow, was purchased in 1944, and a training college for the ministry was commenced.

1945-53. *Extension and Amalgamation*

It required no small degree of courage to make a third attempt at the establishment of a college.[268] And, indeed, in its early days, timorous souls could discern the ghosts of

72 • *In the Steps of John Wesley*

previous failures. Consideration was given to making it a joint college with the Calvary Holiness Church with shared responsibilities, but the General Board's offer, early in 1946, to give recognition to the new college decided the Assembly to maintain its denominational status.[269] Nor were they to regret such a decision. Besides a yearly grant in the region of £300 to £400 from headquarters, £1,500 was raised towards the wiping off of the debt by the General Nazarene Young People's Society in 1949.[270] Gradually, with disappointing fluctuations, the enrolment rose.[271] Throughout, Frame was the prime mover of the project. Combining the duties of acting principal and district superintendent, he fought through the difficulties and discouragements of the college's infancy, until it became a source of evangelism,[272] a centre of conventions[273] and a means of supply to the ministry of the district.[274]

Frame showed the same determination in the realm of advance. Out of the ten churches added during this period, only four had a membership of more than twenty: Chesterfield (23) and Speke Hall, in London (52), in 1950, Cosham, Portsmouth (35) in 1951 and Glenmore Street, Belfast (35) in 1952.[275] But often a diminutive centre had a valuable circumference of children in the Sunday School. The membership figures rose from 978 in 1945 to 1,407 in 1953. In 1950, the British Isles District had the second highest percentage increase in the whole Church of the Nazarene, with the addition of 113 members.[276] The Sunday School enrolment soared from 2,271 in 1945 to 3,293 in 1953. In the 1947 Assembly it was decided to inaugurate the Nazarene youth organisation, "The Pathfinders" and "The Trailblazers".[277] In the September, the first Nazarene Young People's Society Institute, a community holiday with a programme of study, was held at Biggar, near Galashiels.[278] The N.Y.P.S. statistics followed the pattern with an increase from 241 to 488.[279]

With all the sense of urgency in the matter of extension, there remained a consciousness of the importance of quality. The Committee of the State of the Church at the 1946 Assembly named among the "many deficiencies of the church" "a tendency to slackness, neglect, and a shelving of responsibility", and "the increased leaning towards worldliness in dress and manner of life".[280] In the 1949 Assembly, it

The Church of the Nazarene in Britain • 73

reminded the delegates of the danger of declension in "the second generation".²⁸¹ The importance of maintaining the traditions of doctrine and practice was emphasised in the 1950 and 1952 Assemblies by the same committee. There was a genuine concern that in its progress the church should keep to the old paths.

In this period, thirty-seven minister's licenses were issued, and sixteen were ordained. Two American Nazarene elders joined the district during this period: R. F. Tink (1947) and J. K. Grider (1951). And three ministers joined from other denominations: J. S. Logan and T. Ainscough (1949) and Neil Robertson (1953). All was not gain, however. John Dyson left to join the United Free Church of Scotland in 1946 and Peter Clark retired in 1952.²⁸² Arthur Fawcett resigned the Uddingston pastorate in 1949 to accept a research fellowship at the Glasgow University,²⁸³ and joined the Church of Scotland in 1951.²⁸⁴ Six years previously, in 1945, the district had suffered a severe loss in the transfer of James B. Maclagan to the superintendency of the International Holiness Mission.²⁸⁵ He had proved himself a successful pastor and pioneer evangelist. He had served on all the district boards and was a prominent candidate for the district superintendency in 1940.²⁸⁶ But his sympathies remained with the church which had nourished him, and he was an active supporter of the union between the two denominations which was achieved in 1952.²⁸⁷ Two of the first deaconesses died during these years: Miss Jenny S. Latta in 1949,²⁸⁸ and Mrs. George Frame in 1951.²⁸⁹ They were representative of the highest type of consecrated Nazarene womanhood. In March, 1952, J. D. Lewis also finished his course. He was an able convention speaker, sought after both inside and outside of his own communion and in America as well as in Britain.²⁹⁰

As part of the scheme of advance, the division of the district was discussed in the 1943 Assembly.²⁹¹ After mature consideration, it was decided in 1951 to concentrate on the raising up of churches in the South of England under Logan as district evangelist, with a view to making it a special home mission district, should the results justify it.²⁹²

Before the plan could come to fruition, negotiations, initiated by Frame, were entered into which resulted in the

74 • *In the Steps of John Wesley*

International Holiness Mission amalgamating with the Church of the Nazarene. The 1952 Assembly approved the recommendation of the Advisory Board that union between the two bodies should be effected. A division of the united group into a northern and southern district was envisaged, the denominational interests of the two movements such as the magazines[293] and the college were to be placed under a joint trusteeship, and suitable arrangements were to be made for the South African Mission Field of the International Holiness Mission.[294] On October 29th, 1952, at Leeds, General Superintendent Powers consummated the union.[295] The following May, the district was divided, George Frame being elected as superintendent of the North District and James B. Maclagan as superintendent of the South. They were called forward by General Superintendent Vanderpool, and stood with their wives[296] before the delegates. In his response to the ovation accorded them, Frame spoke of the time he went to Parkhead first, and found there James Maclagan, Jean Willox and Mary Tanner. He was now standing, he said, with these same three, for Jean Willox was now Mrs. Maclagan, and Mary Tanner was now Mrs. Frame, and James Maclagan was district superintendent of the British Isles South District.[297]

It was a high day for the Parkhead church, in which the founders would have rejoiced to share. But they were not permitted to see this climax to their labours. Mrs. Sharpe died on February 28th, 1943.[298] Her husband, to whom her gifted and consecrated service had meant so much, followed her to the grave in 1948. When too old to lead, he had continued to serve under men who had grown up under his tuition. He had taken an active interest in the church and up to the time of his death he was the senior member of the Advisory Board.[299] It was fitting that George Sharpe, the staunch advocate of parliamentary procedure in the church should breathe his last at the time the Assembly was in session.[300] Before the assembled delegates, General Superintendent Williamson described him as one of the great leaders of the Church of the Nazarene.[301] For their part, they acknowledged him as the Father and Founder of the Church in the British Isles, and resolved that his example should be their constant urge to more service for Christ.[302]

ASSIMILATION OF NAZARENE CHURCH ORDER

It was generally recognised during the negotiations concerning union between the Pentecostal Church of Scotland and the Pentecostal Church of the Nazarene that the polity of the two bodies was very similar. Nevertheless, it was to be expected that union would bring some minor changes in the administration of the former, especially in the realm of nomenclature.

Under the zealous leadership of George Sharpe, the 1916 Assembly lost no time in adopting Nazarene procedure. Of the eight district boards listed in the 1915 *Manual*, no less than seven were instituted. They were the District Advisory Board, the senior district board consisting of two elders and two laymen and the district superintendent, whose chief duties were to inform and consult with the district superintendent respecting the ministers and churches of the district and to confer with the general superintendent having jurisdiction over the district; the District Board of Church Extension, whose duty was to advance the cause of building houses of worship and parsonages; the District Rescue Board to establish, as far as practicable, homes for the redemption of fallen women; the District Committee of Real Estates and Titles, to attend to the legal side of church property; the District Board of Education, whose duty was to foster and guard the cause of education as represented by the Church of the Nazarene; the District Board of Examination, who were responsible for the examination of licensed ministers and deaconesses; the District Missionary Board, whose duty was to promote the cause of home and foreign missions. Besides these, the prescribed District Court of Appeals was formed, with authority to hear the appeals of church members who felt aggrieved by any action of their local churches and to adjudicate.[303] When the 1919 General Assembly created a mutual benefit system for ministers,[304] the British Isles District appointed a District Board of Ministerial Relief in 1920.[305]

Besides the Boards which were created at the 1916 Assembly, reports were heard from the Missionary Committee, the Home Mission Committee and the Publication and Educational Committee.[306] Having discharged their responsi-

76 • *In the Steps of John Wesley*

bility to the Assembly which had appointed them, they ceased to exist, their work being provided for by the newly created boards.

When the Pentecostal Church of Scotland became a district of the Pentecostal Church of the Nazarene, it forfeited its autonomy but gained a voice in the legislation of a much larger denomination. Each district was permitted to send delegates to the General Assembly, the supreme legislative court of the church. The British Isles District exercised its right to memorialise the General Assembly each quadrennium from 1923 to 1944 with the exception of 1940. With one or two exceptions some modification was made along the lines of all the memorials put forward by the British Isles District. At least eight of them were adopted, ultimately, if not immediately.[307]

There was, from the first, a consistent policy of consideration towards the needs and susceptibilities of the British section of the church. Unfortunately, P. F. Bresee died in 1915, so the British Isles District was deprived of the privilege of assembling under the founder's gavel. But all the other prominent general superintendents of the period presided at the District Assembly.

The general church was generous, too, in its financial support. In addition to the grant of $1,000 per year arranged at the time of the union in 1915, the 1919 General Assembly raised a special offering of $5,215[308] to create a home mission fund for the work in Britain. Mention has already been made of the assistance given by the general church towards the purchase of the building and the costs of the administration of the college at Hurlet. Canadian and American Nazarenes also shared in the provision of the mobile canteens in the 1939-45 War.[309] But the flow of finance was not all west to east. In common with other Nazarene districts, the British Isles District raised money for the general funds of the church. When Pawson died in 1921 the General Missionary Board was bequeathed half of his considerable estate.[310] The amount raised for Nazarene Foreign Missions by the time of the 1916 Assembly was £30.11.4.[311] In 1923, the figure was £480.14.11, and from then on it remained in the region of £400 to £600 until 1940 when it rose considerably.[312] The Budget system, the principle of ascertaining the financial requirements of the church's policy and apportioning them to the various districts and local churches, was gradually adopted by the Church of the Nazarene.[313] Before 1931 it was in force in the British Isles District. Emphasis was also laid on the system of tithing i.e. of every member giving a tenth of his or her income to the funds of the local church; but, though strongly and frequently pressed, it never was made a requirement of membership.[314]

One of the factors in the union between the Pentecostal Church of Scotland and the Pentecostal Church of the Nazarene was the outlet it promised for missionary enterprise. At first the missionary urge of the British church found expression in intercession and gifts for the Nazarene missionary work, and branches of the Women's Missionary Society were organised in the churches.[315] Later, in 1925, Dr. and Mrs. D. Hynd went as Nazarene missionaries to Swaziland, South Africa. By 1952, at least seventeen other missionaries from the British district had rendered missionary service on Nazarene fields.[316] Thus the union provided not only the opportunity of supporting like-minded workers on the mission field but also avenues of missionary service for British Nazarenes.

The work among children and young people was also affected by the union. The Nazarene Sunday School lessons were not made compulsory, but both General and District Assemblies constantly advocated their use. Branches of the Nazarene Young People's Society were started in increasing numbers as time went on, so that in 1952 only 9 out of 33 churches were without a branch of this society.[317] The Church of the Nazarene has sought to legislate as little as possible in matters of administration. Like-minded groups joining it have been expected to subscribe to its articles of faith, its standard of membership and its method of government. But the leaders have relied on education and exhortation rather than legislation in the adoption of its programmes and its auxiliary organisations.

As far as the ministry was concerned there was little change. The ordained minister was equivalent to the elder in the Church of the Nazarene, and the licentiate or pastor equivalent to the licensed minister. There was some misgiving in the British church over the substitution of the

78 • *In the Steps of John Wesley*

word "stewards" for "deacons" and "managers", and some apprehension about the introduction of an annual election for this office. The composition of the church board also made it likely that a young person, or at least a representaitve of the young people, would be a member of the governing body of the local church,[318] and, later, in 1928, the president of the Women's Foreign Missionary Society became an *ex officio* member of the Board.[319] But these innovations were found to work out quite well in practice and they became an accepted part of church life.

Similar in doctrine and government, the members of the Pentecostal Church of Scotland were also accustomed to the freedom and spontaneity which characterised the services of the Church of the Nazarene. Indeed, three and a half years after union, Sharpe, reporting on the work at Parkhead, said "we perhaps *used to have* more shouting."[320] In any case, as previously stated, it was not the policy of the Church of the Nazarene to insist on uniformity in everything. National and local traits and customs were respected. The chief concern was unity of heart and purpose in the faith, practice and proclamation of Holiness of heart and life. Being identical here, and raised up by one who had been cast in the mould of American Methodism and had been caught up in the spirit of the American Holiness Movement, the Pentecostal Church of Scotland experienced little difficulty in shaping itself into a district of the Church of the Nazarene.

NOTES ON CHAPTER 2

[1]The source for the above is George Sharpe's autobiography, *This Is My Story* (Glasgow: Messenger Publishing Co., n.d., c. 1948), chap. i, supplemented by conversations with Rev. J. B. Maclagan, 12 and 13-3-58.

[2]Sharpe, *op. cit.*, p. 13.

[3]*Ibid.*, p. 14.

[4]*Ibid.*, chap. iii.

[5]*Ibid.*, chap. iv.

[6]*Ibid.*, Ministerial Log, p. 143. His name first appears in the *Minutes of the Northern New York Conference* of 1889, where he is listed as "admitted on trial" and stationed at Gouveneur as assistant to S. T. Dibble.

The Church of the Nazarene in Britain • 79

⁷Sharpe, *op. cit.,* p. 143. All these particulars of his pastorates in the Methodist Episcopal Church I have checked in the records of the statistical office in Chicago.

⁸*Ibid.,* chaps. ix, x and xi.

⁹Jane Rose was born on April 2nd, 1865, in Motherwell. *Ibid.,* p. 36.

¹⁰*Ibid.,* chap. viii.

¹¹*Ibid.,* p. 55.

¹²*Ibid.,* p. 30.

¹³*Ibid.,* pp. 29-32.

¹⁴*Ibid.,* p. 56.

¹⁵Sharpe, *This Is My Story.* N.B. Pp. 59-79 of this volume are a reprint of Sharpe's *A Short Historical Sketch of the Church of the Nazarene in the British Isles* written c. 1926, pp. 5-26 and 32-33. Where the matter is identical, the later book is quoted as being more readily obtainable.

¹⁶The Evangelical Union Congregational Church.

¹⁷Sharpe, *op. cit.,* p. 63.

¹⁸*Ibid.,* pp. 62-63.

¹⁹*Ibid.,* p. 67.

²⁰The account of Sharpe's ministry in Ardrossan is taken from Sharpe, *This Is My Story,* pp. 65-68, and the *Centenary Souvenir, E. U. Congregational Church, 1837-1937,* pp. 10-12.

²¹Eighty new members were added in Sharpe's one-year pastorate compared with sixty-six from 1895 to 1904, and 94 from 1907 to 1913. Minute Book for the Parkhead Congregational Church Deacons Court, 1894-1913.

²²The deacons objected to the use of "heresy" and "blasphemy" in the letter, and Sharpe's signing himself "Yours in the blessing of a clean heart." *Ibid.,* 22-9-06, *loc. cit.* Cause 5th.

²³Sharpe, *This Is My Story,* p. 71.

²⁴Some of them, besides those mentioned in the above paragraph, were Sharpe's acceptance of a rise in salary of £40 (unanimously offered to him by the deacons!) and his "pushing the building of a manse" in preference to the building of new church halls, and his statement that he had been first on the short list for the pastorate of the Dalmarnock Road church, which one of the deacons, G. B. Henderson, declared was untrue. Deacon's Minute Book, 22-9-06, *loc. cit.*

²⁵Sharpe, *This Is My Story,* pp. 72-73.

²⁶Preface to the Minute Book of the Parkhead Pentecostal Church Sabbath School, 2-2-07 to 13-3-37. His account, written within a few weeks of the event, is in complete agreement with Sharpe's account in *This Is My Story,* pp. 71-77.

²⁷Interview with Rev. Peter Clark, 21-10-57.

²⁸Sharpe, *Short Historical Sketch,* etc., p. 27.

²⁹*Ibid.,* p. 28.

³⁰Of the four former officials who left the Congregational church to follow Sharpe, only one, William Barrie, a former Salvationist, had claimed entire sanctification under Sharpe's ministry. Mrs. Charles Hunter. Interview, 17-11-56.

³¹Sharpe, *Short Historical Sketch,* etc., p. 28.

80 • *In the Steps of John Wesley*

³²He was the superintendent of the Parkhead Congregational Church Sabbath School up to the time of his demission. Interviews with Dr. Mary Frame and Mrs. Hunter, 17-11-56.

³³Interview with Andrew Robertson, 17-10-57.

³⁴Minute Book of Deacons Meetings of the Parkhead Pentecostal Church (cited hereafter as MBDMPPC). The first meeting was attended by the pastor and the four deacons. After this the meetings are described as meetings of deacons and managers, and sometimes the trustees are included.

³⁵Particulars of the services have been obtained from the record of the offerings in the church Cash Book.

³⁶In the Great Eastern Road Halls "the altar" would probably be a form in front of the platform, facing the congregation, at which those seeking spiritual blessing would be invited to come forward and pray, while mature believers gathered round to assist in prayer and counsel.

³⁷Sharpe, *Short Historical Sketch*, etc., p. 25. Interview with Mrs. Charles Hunter, 17-11-56.

³⁸Sources for this paragraph are Sharpe, *This Is My Story*, pp. 77-79, MBDMPPC, *passim*, and Sabbath School Teachers Meetings, *passim*.

³⁹Parkhead Holiness Bible School Minutes, 22-10-08.

⁴⁰*Church Report, 1908.*

⁴¹Parkhead Holiness Bible School Minutes, April, 1909. There were 24 present at the closing meeting of the session on May 4th, 1909.

⁴²Sharpe, *Short Historical Sketch*, etc., p. 34.

⁴³See "The Holiness Movement in Scotland" by Rev. G. Sharpe. *Way of Holiness*, June, 1909, p. 27.

⁴⁴It is common in the Glasgow area to have a meeting, usually on a Saturday night, when a group of workers from some other church, called a "deputation", give addresses, testimonies and musical items.

⁴⁵Described as "an evangelistic choir". *Way of Holiness*, May, 1909, p. 21.

⁴⁶*Ibid.*, pp. 21 and 24.

⁴⁷Sources: Sharpe, *Short Historical Sketch*, etc., pp. 34-35. MBDMPPC, 14-11-08, Parkhead Holiness Bible School Report, April, 1909. Interview with Rev. J. E. Watson, 28-1-58.

⁴⁸Written statement, Miss M. K. Latta, M.B.E., 6-1-57.

⁴⁹*Way of Holiness*, Feb., 1910, p. 128.

⁵⁰Sharpe, *Short Historical Sketch*, etc., pp. 35 and 36. Parkhead Holiness Bible School Report, April, 1909. Statements, Latta, 6-1-57, Andrew Robertson, 17-10-57. *Way of Holiness*, May, 1909, p. 2, Jan., 1910, p. 116, Nov., 1910, p. 8.

⁵¹Sources: Sharpe, *Short Historical Sketch*, etc., p. 38. N. P. Grubb, *J. D. Drysdale, Prophet of Holiness* (London: Lutterworth Press, 1955), pp. 44-46. Written statement of Joan Reid, Jan., 1957. *Way of Holiness*, 1909: July, p. 45, 1910: Feb., p. 127, July, p. 12, Nov., p. 8, 1911: Jan., p. 8, Feb., p. 8, April, p. 13.

⁵²Sharpe, *Short Historical Sketch*, etc., p. 55.

⁵³A copy of the call is in the files of the Pentecostal Church of Scotland.

The Church of the Nazarene in Britain • 81

⁵⁴Minutes of the First Assembly. Minute Book of the Pentecostal Church of Scotland (cited hereafter as MBPCS), 8-5-09. The list was drawn up from cards handed out to the delegates present for the final meeting on the Sat. night. It does not tally completely with the names of those appointed to serve on the Assembly committees.

⁵⁵Others were present besides the delegates. In the account of the Assembly in the *Way of Holiness,* June, 1909, p. 27, it is stated that nearly 180 were present for the sermon and the sacrament.

⁵⁶MBPCS, First Session.

⁵⁷*Ibid.*

⁵⁸This was a *fait accompli* before the Assembly, no doubt as the result of an arrangement between Sharpe and Miss Crossley and Miss Hatch.

⁵⁹*Ibid.* and *Way of Holiness,* June, 1909, p. 32.

⁶⁰*Way of Holiness,* June, 1909, p. 32.

⁶¹There were Pentecostal League of Prayer centres at these two places.

⁶²It is not clear whether the items in this sentence were already in the Parkhead church's Declaration of Faith or adopted by this Assembly.

⁶³*Way of Holiness,* June, 1909, p. 32.

⁶⁴The Committee on Church Extension and Evangelism gave the following reasons for multiplying Holiness churches: "(i) It will unite the Holiness People. (ii) It will put the *true brand* upon those who have the Experience. (iii) It will save the violation of the Consecration made by many who know God. (iv) It will mean spiritual development unalloyed. (v) It will assure separation from all worldly entanglements. (vi) It will also provide for the clear teaching of Regeneration and entire Sanctification." In the files of the PCS, 1909.

⁶⁵MBPCS, First Assembly.

⁶⁶The Parkhead church appointed six immediately after the Assembly. It is doubtful whether the Paisley and Uddingston churches would furnish six more.

⁶⁷MBPCS, Fifth Session.

⁶⁸*Ibid.*, Executive Committee 26-11-10.

⁶⁹*Ibid.*, Fourth Assembly, Fourth and Fifth Sessions.

⁷⁰*Ibid.*, Fourth Assembly, Fourth and Fifth Sessions.

⁷¹*Ibid.*, Second Session.

⁷²*Ibid.*, Executive Committee 2-4-10.

⁷³*Ibid.*, Third Session.

⁷⁴Described as Gordon Halls, Paisley Rd. Toll, in the MBDMPPC, 6-12-10.

⁷⁵Sharpe, *Short Historical Sketch,* etc., pp. 52-53, and MBPCS, Fourth Assembly, Fifth Session.

⁷⁶MBPCS, Fourth Assembly, Fourth Session. Kunz's report.

⁷⁷In the *Holiness Herald,* May, 1914, p. 16 the address of the Edinburgh church is given as Mc'Donald Rd. and the meetings in Leith are in Water St.

⁷⁸MBPCS. "Pastor Sharpe spoke about the change in the Buccleugh (sic) Church and the formation of the Edinburgh Wesleyan

82 • *In the Steps of John Wesley*

Pentecostal Church. Bro. Jack was chosen pastor last October . . ." Fifth Assembly, First Session.

[79] See n. 77.

[80] Sharpe, *Short Historical Sketch*, etc., gives the date as Aug. 16th, but I have followed the account in *Way of Holiness* 1910: Aug., pp. 8 and 12, and Oct., p. 8.

[81] Sharpe, *Short Historical Sketch*, etc., p. 37.

[82] *Way of Holiness*, Feb., 1911, p. 8.

[83] Sharpe, *Short Historical Sketch*, etc., gives the date as Feb. 14th, but the *Way of Holiness*, Feb., 1913, p. 12, gives Feb. 15th.

[84] MBPCS, Fifth Assembly, First Session. Watson's report.

[85] MBPCS.

[86] *Way of Holiness*, Aug., 1911, p. 8. Sharpe, *Short Historical Sketch*, etc., p. 40. Interview with Watson 28-1-58.

[87] Minute Book of Gildersome Pentecostal Church, 12-1-14.

[88] The register at the beginning of the Minute Book of the Gildersome Pentecostal Church contains the names of 6 men and 29 women and 3 initials, up to and including Jan. 21st, 1914.

[89] MBPCS.

[90] Sources: Sharpe, *Short Historical Sketch*, etc., pp. 40-42. MBPCS. *Printed Minutes of PCS*, 1915.

[91] Meetings held in houses.

[92] Sources: MBPCS and interview with Mr. J. A. Cunningham, 16-10-57.

[93] MBPCS, Fourth Assembly, Fifth Session, 9-5-12.

[94] MBDMPPC, 4-7-11 and 19-3-12.

[95] *Ibid.*, 2-9-10.

[96] *Ibid.*, 19-3-12 (miscalled *William* Young). In 6-11-14 he was invited to consider a call to be pastor.

[97] *Ibid.*, 28-3-13.

[98] *Church Report*, 1911. MBPCS, Fifth Assembly, First Session and Sixth Assembly, First Session.

[99] *Church Reports*, 1914 and 1915-16. MBPCS, Seventh Assembly, First Session.

[100] MBDMPPC, 29-8-11, 29-12-11, 28-3-13, 2-9-12, 28-5-14, 26-1-15.

[101] *Church Reports*.

[102] E.G., *ibid.*, 1912. "Hardly a Sabbath evening has passed without souls seeking God."

[103] MBDMPPC, 2-7-14, 26-1-15. Church Reports 1910-1915-16. Cash Book 1910-13.

[104] *Way of Holiness*, May, 1910, p. 8.

[105] *Ibid.*, Dec., 1910, p. 9.

[106] MBPCS, Third Assembly 11-5-11, Fifth Session. Report of Executive Committee in Minute Book of Parkhead Holiness Bible School, 1910-11.

[107] He felt keenly that the Paisley church's request for his ordination before completing his studies was not granted (see full report in files of PCS) and he clashed with Sharpe on the exposition of I.John 1:7: Sharpe's letter to Miss Crossley 24-6-12 (in files of PCS).

The Church of the Nazarene in Britain • 83

[108] Statistics in files of PCS.
[109] First Session.
[110] In 1911 it was 27, and 33 in 1915, in which year the Sabbath School membership was 75: Statistics in files of PCS. Attendance on Sunday was about 30 in the morning and 50 to 60 in the evening. Home Mission Report, May, 1911. MBPCS, Fifth, Assembly.
[111] Wm. Turnbull 11-5-11 (Joint-Secretary with John Robb)—1922.
[112] Robert Latta, 8-5-09—1919.
[113] MBPCS. Postponed Meeting of Seventh Assembly, 5-11-15. Interview with Andrew Robertson, 17-10-57.
[114] *Ibid.*, Sharpe's statement, Fifth Assembly, First Session.
[115] Statistics in files of PCS.
[116] Statement by Joan Reid, 23-6-58.
[117] MBPCS, Executive Committee 8-2-13.
[118] Letter of Joan Reid c. Jan., 1957, and Fifth Assembly, First Session, MBPCS.
[119] MBPCS, First Session.
[120] MBPCS, Seventh Assembly, First Session.
[121] Church members 20, Sabbath School 50. Printed *Minutes of 1915 Assembly.*
[122] Letter from Joan Reid c. Jan., 1957. An account of the Blantyre Church is also given in *A Short Historical Sketch*, etc., pp. 38-39.
[123] Ordination Parchment in files of the PCS.
[124] The facts for the above two paragraphs are derived from the MBPCS.
[125] Sharpe formed the committee, "to which matters relating to new causes could be referred", naming its first members, and obtained the Executive Committee's endorsement in their meeting on 8-7-11.
[126] Interview with J. E. Watson, 28-1-58.
[127] *Church Report,* 1913.
[128] Interview with J. E. Watson, 28-1-58.
[129] Executive Committee, 23-10-09. Minute Book of Parkhead Holiness Bible School.
[130] *Ibid.*, 23-10-09.
[131] *Ibid.*, Education Committee Report 13-10-12.
[132] *Ibid.*, 23-10-09 and Report for 1910-11.
[133] *Ibid.*, Report for 1910-11.
[134] *Parkhead Pentecostal Church Report,* 1912.
[135] No. 1 Westbourne Terrace, Kelvinside, Glasgow.
[136] Minute Book of Parkhead Holiness Bible School. Educational Committee Report, 1912-13.
[137] MBPCS, Third Session.
[138] Report of the Committee on Education & Publications for 1913-14. Minute Book of Parkhead Holiness Bible School.
[139] *Ibid.*
[140] Interview with Cunningham, 16-10-57.
[141] Sharpe, *Short Historical Sketch,* etc., p. 53.
[142] MBPCS, Third Session.
[143] *Ibid.*, Second Session.
[144] *Ibid.*, Fifth Assembly, Third Session.

In the Steps of John Wesley

[145] Minute Book of Parkhead Holiness Bible School, *loc. cit.*

[146] *Ibid.*

[147] MBPCS, Sixth Assembly, First Session.

[148] Sharpe, *Short Historical Sketch*, etc., p. 54.

[149] The circulation was probably in the region of 1,500 to 2,000. In 1911 the PCS sold 1,824 copies of the *Way of Holiness* and in 1912 1,116 (Letters from Misses Crossley and Hatch in PCS file 4-7-11 and 29-4-12). The Holiness centres at Partick and Ardrossan, regarded as being in fellowship with the Pentecostal Church of Scotland, sold slightly over 1,000 more. In the 1915 Education & Publications Committee Report the income of the Publication Dept. is given as £96.17.9, which, even if it was all derived from the sale of the magazine, would be less than 2,000 copies at 1d each per month.

[150] MBPCS, Second Assembly, Third Session.

[151] *Ibid.*, Executive Committee, 8-7-10.

[152] MBPCS, Fourth Assembly, Fifth Session.

[153] I.e. to organise the raising of funds.

[154] MBPCS, Fourth Session. See also E. F. Walker's letter to H. F. Reynolds 13-4-14 (Church of the Nazarene Headquarters Archives, Kansas City).

[155] E. F. Walker's letter to H. F. Reynolds. According to the Foreign Mission Committee's Report for 1914 (in the files of the PCS), £13.5.6 was available for this purpose.

[156] Smith, *op. cit.*, p. 224.

[157] *Ibid.*, p. 239. Probably the *Way of Holiness*, June, 1909, p. 27.

[158] *Ibid.* and MBPCS, Sixth Assembly, First Session.

[159] Discussed in the Third Assembly, 11-5-11, Fifth Session, and deferred meeting of the Third Assembly, 2-9-11. MBPCS.

[160] Turnbull's statement to this effect in the Sixth Assembly, Fourth Session. MBPCS.

[161] His letter to Turnbull 24-4-15 in the files of PCS.

[162] Sharpe, *Short Historical Sketch*, etc., p. 56.

[163] MBPCS, 9-4-14.

[164] *Ibid.*, Sixth Assembly, First Session.

[165] MBPCS, Sixth Assembly, First Session.

[166] Files of PCS. Also Walker's letter to Reynolds, 13-4-14, in Church of the Nazarene Headquarters Archives, Kansas City.

[167] MBPCS.

[168] Interview with J. E. Watson, 28-1-58.

[169] MBPCS. Sharpe did so, in no uncertain manner, 1-6-14, and to Pawson also in similar vein, 1-6-14. Files of PCS.

[170] MBPCS.

[171] Printed *Minutes of Sixth Assembly*, in files of PCS.

[172] Letters from W. Stewart and John E. Watson, both dated 4-7-14, in files of PCS.

[173] Dated 4-7-14, in files of PCS.

[174] MBPCS.

[175] Reynolds was the one of the three general superintendents on whom the major portion of the administrative work fell. Dr. P. F. Bresee was 75, and in indifferent health (he died the following year),

The Church of the Nazarene in Britain • 85

and Dr. E. F. Walker was comparatively new to the church (he joined in 1908) and to the general superintendency (elected October, 1911).

[176] MBPCS.

[177] Reynolds's letter to Sharpe, 30-10-14. The Pentecostal Church of the Nazarene was essentially an American church at this time, and any other country was classed as a foreign mission field, though the distinction between the Christian and the heathen countries was clearly recognised. Later, especially under the influence of J. B. Chapman, it developed into a world church in polity and outlook.

[178] Reynolds to Sharpe, 8-10-14, in files of PCS.

[179] *Ibid.*, 22-12-14.

[180] Letter from Reynolds to Sharpe, 1-3-15, and Provisional Committee Report, 2-4-15 in files of PCS.

[181] Letter from Reynolds to Sharpe, 1-3-15.

[182] MBPCS, Seventh Assembly, Second and Third Sessions.

[183] *Proceedings of the Fourth General Assembly of the Pentecostal Church of the Nazarene*, Sept. 30th to Oct. 11th, 1915, pp. 25, 26 and 28.

[184] MBPCS.

[185] Files of PCS.

[186] See p. 27 of Introduction, n. 58.

[187] J. A. Cunningham was coached at the College until June, 1916. Interview, 16-10-57.

[188] District Superintendent's Report in the British Isles District Files (cited hereafter as BIDF).

[189] Counting all sessions.

[190] Printed *Minutes of British Isles District of the Pentecostal Church of the Nazarene* (cited hereafter as MBIDPCN. After 1919 cited as MBIDCN), 1916, in BIDF.

[191] Statistics (1916) in BIDF.

[192] These figures are taken from the printed *Minutes of the Seventh Annual Assembly of the Pentecostal Church of Scotland, 1st to 5th April, 1915*, statistical Report. In the *Proceedings of the Fourth General Assembly of the Pentecostal Church of the Nazarene*, p. 25, the number of members is given as 665, and in M. E. Redford's *The Rise of the Church of the Nazarene*, p. 164, the figure is 635. In both cases the Sunday School figure is the same, 841.

[193] District Superintendent's Report in BIDF.

[194] MBIDPCN (1916).

[195] Report by Jessop in BIDF.

[196] Statistics in BIDF.

[197] District Superintendent's Report (1917), pp. 2 and 3, in BIDF.

[198] Statistics (1917) in BIDF.

[199] District Superintendent's Report (1917).

[200] In BIDF.

[201] Turnbull's letter asking for the return of his ordination certificate is dated 11-12-17 in BIDF.

[202] MBIDPCN (1919).

[203] District Superintendent's Report (1919) in BIDF.

[204] *MBIDCN* (1920), p. 2.

[205] The *Way of Holiness*, June-July, 1952, p. 5.

86 • In the Steps of John Wesley

[206] MBIDCN (1921), p. 10.
[207] *Ibid.* (1920), pp. 4 and 7.
[208] Commenced October, 1920. See District Superintendent's Report (1921), p. 1, in BIDF.
[209] *Ibid.*, pp. 2 and 3. Interviews with J. B. Maclagan.
[210] Assembly Roll Call in BIDF.
[211] MBIDCN (1922), pp. xx and xxi.
[212] Statistical Reports (1921) in BIDF.
[213] District Superintendent's Report (1922), pp. 1 and 4, in BIDF.
[214] Official *Proceedings of BIDCN* (cited hereafter as PBIDCN) (1924), p. 35.
[215] Report of the Nazarene Bible School, *PBIDCN* (1924), p. 18.
[216] First issue July, 1922.
[217] District Superintendent's Report (1922), pp. 2 and 3, in BIDF.
[218] Church of the Nazarene *Manual*, 1923, par. 419, sec. 2, and pars. 238, 239. Sharpe, *This Is My Story*, p. 86.
[219] *PBIDCN* (1925), p. 7. Sharpe, *op. cit.*, p. 87.
[220] Sharpe, *Short Historical Sketch*, etc., p. 35, and interview, Peter Clark, Forfar, 21-10-57.
[221] The church at Motherwell was organised between the 1924 and 1925 Assemblies.
[222] Statistics in *PBIDCN* (1926 and 1927).
[223] Sharpe, *This Is My Story*, p. 95. Interview, Peter Clark, 21-10-57.
[224] *PBIDCN* (1926), p. 3. Mrs. Sharpe was ordained an elder at the 1917 Assembly. See *MBIDPCN* (1917), p. 18.
[225] *PBIDCN* (1926), p. 25. A special building to cater for full-time students was evidently in mind.
[226] There were about 3 boarders and 4 day and evening students. Letter from Mrs. I. R. Edwards, 18-7-58.
[227] *Ibid.* Sharpe, *This Is My Story*, p. 95.
[228] *PBIDCN* (1927). Interviews with R. C. Purvis, 21-10-57. George Frame, 22-9-58.
[229] *PBIDCN* (1925), p. 17.
[230] *Ibid.*, p. 43.
[231] *PBIDCN* (1926), p. 18.
[232] *PBIDCN* (1925), p. 7.
[233] *PBIDCN* (1925-28).
[234] *PBIDCN* (1928), "Election of District Superintendent", and Sharpe, *This Is My Story*, p. 95.
[235] In 1929 he received three votes above the necessary two-thirds majority, in 1930 eleven and in 1931 he was elected on the second ballot.
[236] The source for the above paragraph is *PBIDCN* (1928-31).
[237] *PBIDCN* (1927) and Sharpe, *This Is My Story*, p. 143.
[238] *PBIDCN* (1931), pp. 5, 21 and 36.
[239] Sharpe, *This Is My Story*, pp. 95 and 143 and letter from R. C. Purvis, 18-9-58.
[240] Sources for this paragraph are the relevant Assembly Minutes, letters from R. C. Purvis (18-9-58) and J. B. Maclagan (2-10-58), interview with Purvis (21-10-57) and my personal knowledge of him.
[241] *PBIDCN* (1935), pp. 21 and 22.

The Church of the Nazarene in Britain • 87

[242] *Ibid.* (1933), p. 30, (1935), p. 36, (1934), p. 11.
[243] *Ibid.* (1939), pp. 18 and 22.
[244] *Ibid.* (1935), pp. 22 and 27 and letter from Purvis 18-9-58.
[245] *PBIDCN* (1931), p. 37.
[246] The *Flame*, June-July, 1935, pp. 6 and 7.
[247] Notably in Coatbridge and Govan in 1935. *PBIDCN* (1935), pp. 21 and 22.
[248] District Superintendent's Report in 1939 mentions visits by President Wain and Rev. Arthur Fawcett. *PBIDCN* (1939), pp. 18 and 19.
[249] Interview with Frame, 22-9-58.
[250] *PBIDCN* (1933), p. 18 and (1936), p. 28.
[251] *Ibid.* (1938), pp. 16 and 23.
[252] *Ibid.* (1935), pp. 3 and 19, (1938), p. 29, (1939), p. 3.
[253] The change was recommended at the 1932 Assembly, *PBIDCN* (1932), p. 24.
[254] Interview with Miss E. K. Crossley, Crowborough, 26-11-58.
[255] Interview with Frame 22-9-58. Letter Maclagan 18-9-58. At the following Assembly, he resigned from the Nazarene ministry. *PBIDCN* (1941), p. 9.
[256] Interview with Frame 22-9-58 and relevant Assembly Proceedings.
[257] *PBIDCN* (1940), p. 1. She was succeeded by Rev. David Anderson in 1948. *PBIDCN*, p. 12.
[258] *Ibid.* (1941), p. 6.
[259] *Ibid.* (1942), p. 9.
[260] *Ibid.* (1943), p. 9.
[261] Statistics are from relevant *PBIDCN*.
[262] Orders and Relations Committees in *PBIDCN* for these years.
[263] Statistics in *PBIDCN* for these years.
[264] *PBIDCN* (1942), p. 10.
[265] *Ibid.* (1951), p. 16. "For *ten years* now our children's camp has gone from strength to strength. . . ."
[266] Relevent *PBIDCN*.
[267] See *PBIDCN* (1931), p. 36, (1932), p. 29, (1934), p. 31, (1935), p. 31, (1937), p. 32, (1938), p. 22, (1939), p. 25, (1944), p. 13.
[268] The *Way of Holiness*, Jan.-Feb., 1950, p. 18.
[269] My notes of a meeting between representatives of the Church of the Nazarene and the Calvary Holiness Church, Dec. 7th and 8th, 1945 at Hurlet College and *PBIDCN* (1946), p. 16.
[270] *PBIDCN* (1949), p. 17, (1950), pp. 16, 17 and statistics supplied by Rev. Hugh Rae, M.A., 22-10-58. The British Nazarene churches also supported the college and the Bellahouston Trust donated £1,000.
[271] It fell as low as 5 in 1950, but rose to 16 in 1953. Statistics supplied by Rev. Hugh Rae, 19-10-58.
[272] *PBIDCN* (1949), p. 17, (1952), p. 18. The *Way of Holiness*, Aug.-Sept., 1951, p. 13.
[273] *PBIDCN* (1947), p. 18, (1948), p. 17, (1951), p. 22.
[274] *Ibid.* (1950), p. 17, (1951), p. 16. The *Way of Holiness*, July-Aug., 1949, p. 13.
[275] The others were in Bromley (9) and West Norwood, London (11) in 1951. Donegel Rd., Belfast (15), Dromore, Northern Ireland (8),

88 • *In the Steps of John Wesley*

Houghton-le-Spring, Co. Durham (12) and Derbyshire St., Leeds (16) in 1953.

[276]*PBIDCN* (1951), p. 16.

[277]*Ibid.* (1947), p. 15, (1948), p. 14.

[278]Conversation on the phone with Hugh Rae, 16-10-58.

[279]The statistics are taken from the relevant *PBIDCN*.

[280]*PBIDCN* (1946), p. 19.

[281]*Ibid.* (1949), p. 16.

[282]The source for the facts in this paragraph is the relevant *PBIDCN*.

[283]The *Way of Holiness*, Nov.-Dec., 1949, p. 15.

[284]*PBIDCN* (1951), p. 18.

[285]Executive Council of I.H.M. Minutes 27-6-45 and 16-10-45.

[286]Relevant *PBIDCN*. Letters from Maclagan, 18-9-58 and 2-10-58. Interview with Clark, 21-10-57.

[287]*PBIDCN* (1953), p. 21.

[288]The *Way of Holiness*, July-Aug., 1949, p. 15.

[289]*Ibid.*, March-April, 1951, p. 13.

[290]*Ibid.*, June-July, 1952, pp. 5 and 6.

[291]*PBIDCN* (1943), p. 6.

[292]*Ibid.*, (1949), p. 13, (1951), p. 20.

[293]Maclagan was editor of the *Way of Holiness* in association with Macleod from 1939-42. The magazine was edited by an editing committee consisting of Macleod, Frame and Anderson from 1943 to 1947. In 1948, Fawcett was editor, and from 1949 onwards D. J. Tarrant (Relevant *PBIDCN*). The circulation rose from about 5,000 to the region of 8,000 in 1950. The *Way of Holiness*, July-Aug., 1950, p. 13.

[294]*PBIDCN* (1952), pp. 21 and 22.

[295]The *Way*, Jan., 1953, p. 3.

[296]Frame married again in November, 1952.

[297]*PBIDCN* (1953), p. 21.

[298]Sharpe, *This Is My Story*, p. 37.

[299]Every year after his resignation of the superintendency he was elected to this office, with one exception; the year 1937, when, ironically enough, he was replaced by Peter Clark, on his return from Canada, on the fourth ballot.

[300]*PBIDCN* (1948), p. 11.

[301]*Ibid.*, p. 10.

[302]*Ibid.*, p. 18.

[303]1915 *Manual*, pp. 51-57 and 71 and MBIDPCN (1916) in BIDF.

[304]*Proceedings of the Fifth General Assembly of the Pentecostal Church of the Nazarene*, p. 107.

[305]1915 *Manual*, p. 56 and 1919 *Manual*, p. 61, and *MBIDCN* (1920), p. 2.

[306]MBIDPCN (1916), pp. 4-5, 7.

[307]Sources for this paragraph are the memorials recorded in the *PBIDCN* and the corresponding sections in the *Manuals* for this period.

[308]*Proceedings of the Fifth General Assembly of the Pentecostal Church of the Nazarene*, p. 32. At that time the amount was equivalent to about £1,000.

309*PBIDCN* (1942), p. 10.

310District Superintendent's Report, 1922, in BIDF.

311Missionary Committee Financial Report, March, 1915 to Feb. 1916, in BIDF.

312Financial statements in relevant *PBIDCN*.

313*Manual*, 1928, pars. 36, sec. 3, and 425.

314*Manual*, 1915, p. 28 and 1923, par. 463.

315The first mention of the Women's Missionary Society in the Assembly Minutes is in 1921, p. 17. By 1923 (see Reports in the Minutes) there were only one or two branches of it, but by 1925 "practically all churches" had branches. *PBIDCN* (1925), pp. 24 and 25.

316*Way of Holiness*, April-May, 1952, p. 9, and *PBIDCN*.

317*PBIDCN* (1952), statistics.

318The president of the Young People's Society was an *ex officio* member of the Church Board. 1915 *Manual*, p. 41.

3191928 *Manual*, par. 98.

320MBIDPCN (1919), p. 6. Italics mine.

CHAPTER 3

The International Holiness Mission

ITS ORIGIN AND FORMATIVE YEARS

Reader Harris

It is impossible to understand David Thomas and the International Holiness Mission which he founded without a knowledge of Reader Harris and the Pentecostal League.[1]

Richard Reader Harris was born at Worcester, on July 5th, 1847. His father, after whom he was named, was made the first Chief Constable of Worcester at the age of 19, and later was called to the Bar. At the age of twenty-three, Harris was appointed Engineer-in-Chief to the Bolivian Government,[2] and later made Financial Commissioner for Bolivia to represent them in the Bolivian Bonds case,[3] which was carried through to a successful conclusion on May 30th, 1879.[4] Deciding to remain in England and study law, Harris was called to the Bar on November 16th, 1883,[5] and made a Queen's Counsel on November 19th, 1894.[6]

Although he was brought up with a religious background, Harris became an agnostic and for a time was a disciple of Charles Bradlaugh.[7] But he became restless in agnosticism. In the solitudes of Bolivia the stars seemed to speak to him

The International Holiness Mission • 91

of the Creator, and events, notably a remarkable escape from death, strained his scepticism to breaking point.[8]

While dealing with the Bolivian Bonds dispute, he met Mary Griffin Bristow, the daughter of the senior partner of the firm which later represented the bondholders.[9] Partly through her influence and partly through the ministry of Rev. Aubrey Price, the vicar of St. James Church, Clapham Park, which they attended and where they were married on August 10th, 1880, Harris became a believer in Christ.[10]

After his marriage, Harris began to take part in Sunday evening services at a mission room in Lillieshall Road, Clapham, although as yet he had not an inward assurance of salvation. While on a train journey to Ealing reading Dr. H. C. G. Moule's *Union with Christ* he opened his Bible at John 20:22: "Receive ye the Holy Ghost . . ." He promptly knelt in the compartment and claimed the fulfilment of the promise. Harris told the ticket collector what had happened and immediately there came an assurance that the Holy Spirit had been given to him. He later interpreted this as his experience of the New Birth, believing that previously he had been converted when he had turned to Christ in faith.[11]

In 1884, he was one of the three superintendent stewards in the Moody and Sankey Mission in South London. On October 25th, 1885, he commenced a week's special mission in Speke Road Hall.[12] Eventually, in 1887, he bought it and the adjoining house for £3,100. Soon the 1,400 seats were filled for the Sunday evening services. A powerful evangelistic work was maintained, supplemented by a programme of social work.[13]

The Pentecostal League

In the year 1889, Harris entered into the religious experience which was to make him one of the outstanding leaders of what may be called the Holiness Movement in Britain. Two American preachers, Rev. G. D. Watson and Rev. F. D. Sanford, were invited to hold a series of Holiness meetings in Speke Hall. During these, both Mr. and Mrs. Harris claimed the experience of entire sanctification.[14] This led, by 1891, to the formation of what became the Pentecostal League.

Previously, missions, independent of the churches, had been established at Long Ditton, Hook, Hampstead, Kingston and Hull in association with Harris and Speke Hall. They constituted the Speke Hall Mission.[15] But Mr. and Mrs. Harris became doubtful whether this was the most effective way of spreading the teaching of full salvation and reviving religion in Britain. At the close of 1890 they decided to rename the Speke Hall Mission the "Pentecostal Mission" and to form in connection with it the interdenominational Pentecostal Mission Prayer Union, which in February, 1891, was given the name of the "Pentecostal League". Harris announced these innovations in *Tongues of Fire* produced by him in January 1891.[16] In it he defined the special objects of the Prayer Union as

> (1) That the members may pray for one another; (2) for the work of the Pentecostal Mission; (3) the filling of the Holy Spirit for all.[17]

He declared

> We seek to spread Scriptural Holiness by unsectarian methods broadcast through this and other lands.[18]

In the May issue he offered

> ... to send Holiness Evangelists to conduct Missions anywhere in England or Wales.[19]

Before the close of the century there were over 150 centres in Britain and about a dozen overseas, excluding the American branch which began about 1896.[20]

David Thomas heard Reader Harris speak early in 1890, at a meeting for the Sunday School teachers of Milton Hall Congregational Church, held in a private house in Lavender Road, Battersea. He had already become aware of a spiritual lack in a meeting conducted by Moody and Sankey in the Exeter Hall. After Reader Harris had spoken on John 1:12, stressing the positive side of regeneration, he raised his hand with others to confess his spiritual hunger and his acceptance of God's provision. On his return home, he told his brother, John, of the step he had taken, and immediately he felt an "assurance of the Holy Spirit coming into his heart." Though he remained a business man, from that evening the service of God became the dominant purpose of his life.[21]

David Thomas

David Thomas was born on September 29th, 1860, in a little farmstead known as "The Gors", in Llanllanddog, Carmarthenshire. His parents, John and Rachel Thomas, were staunch members of the Congregationalist Church, of which his father was a deacon. David attended the British School in the adjoining village and made the most of its limited educational facilities. Leaving school at the age of fourteen, he spent the next three years on his father's farm. At seventeen he became apprenticed to a cousin named Lewis, a draper in Morriston, a suburb of Swansea. At the age of twenty, he went to London, and eventually found work with Hull and Son, Kingsland Road. Some four years later, he set up in the drapery business with a partner named Friend, in a small shop at 55 Falcon Road, Clapham Junction. Owing to weak health, his partner withdrew from the partnership after only a year, but Thomas remained to build up a prosperous business. In May, 1885, he married Elizabeth Lowth, whom he had met as a fellow-employee at Hull and Sons. Five sons and four daughters were born of the marriage.[22]

Speke Hall and the Pentecostal League

Mindful of his upbringing, even before he met Harris, Thomas was upright in business, a member of Milton Hall Congregational Church, Cabul Road, Battersea, and a teacher in its Sunday School. But the experience he received as a result of the preaching of Harris brought with it an enthusiasm which revolutionised his life. Within six months, every lad in his Sunday School class was led by him to confess Christ as Saviour. But his enthusiasm aroused opposition, and Thomas soon found a more congenial sphere of service in Speke Hall. Here he entered into a yet deeper spiritual experience. His hasty temper caused him sorrow and shame. When, therefore, in 1891, he heard G. D. Watson speaking on entire sanctification as an experience of cleansing and power, he went forward to the penitent form to claim it by faith. He found the deliverance he sought, and from that time the preacher's text, Romans 6:6, became to him the essence and touchstone of sound Holiness doctrine.[23]

For the next fifteen years, he served wholeheartedly under the leadership of Reader Harris, whom he greatly admired and respected. He became leader of the Young Men's Bible Class, leader of one of the three open air bands, a Pentecostal League Missioner and one whom Harris consulted concerning the conduct of the work.[24] It came, therefore as a severe blow to his leader,[25] when, after much prayer and thought, he broke the news that he felt that he could no longer subscribe to the principle of confining his work within the existing churches.

The Parting of the Ways

Thomas's experience as a Pentecostal League Missioner had convinced him that many of those entering into spiritual blessing in the missions which he and his fellow-missioners had conducted had "backslidden" as a result of the unsympathetic attiitude of the churches to which they belonged.[26] Harris's vision was of a nucleus of Spirit-filled believers who would spread revival throughout the Church. But Thomas was concerned about providing a suitable environment for those in a newfound faith, that they might be nourished with Holiness teaching and training to serve.

After three weeks of earnest discussion Harris is reported to have said, "Thomas, I will set you free if you still feel the Lord is calling you to work outside the churches. Whatever you decide to do in after years, never say I hindered you from doing the will of God."[27]

It was a bowing to the inevitable, but far from an endorsement of Thomas's vision. The first hint of the difference of views appeared in the January issue of *Tongues of Fire* in 1907:

> A minor difficulty has lately arisen in the action of a few of the League workers who have resigned their connection with the League on the sole ground that they desire to be free to work in opposition to the churches.

When Thomas commenced meetings in his shop, which was in the vicinity of Speke Hall, and as other League members joined him in his venture, Harris's tone became sterner:

> . . . recently a few of the Head Centre Band missioners (Mr. David Thomas and some others employed in his business) have left the work in order that they might be free to carry on holiness work in opposition to the churches. While their action is deeply to be regretted, it is hoped that the League Centre Secretaries and

members generally will show no sympathy with such a course of action, which is directly contrary to the whole principle of the League as well as the plain statements of Scripture.[28]

The Commencement of the Holiness Mission

David Thomas saw things in a different light from his leader. Although he had been a member of the League for many years, he had first attended Speke Hall when it was the headquarters of a small group of missions, working independently of the churches. He had been welcomed there as a member of a Congregational church. In spite of the League principle that its members should stay within the churches, Speke Hall remained an independent congregation, with an unordained member of the Church of England celebrating communion in spite of episcopal protest.[29]

Nor could Harris deny that Thomas's concern for those who sought blessing under League missioners was well founded. Indeed, in the same article in which he deplores Thomas's resignation he admits that, with some bright exceptions, the League has "encountered the determined opposition of the churches."[30]

It was in such circumstances that Thomas took his decision to raise up centres of Holiness teaching outside the framework of the churches.

The First Meetings

Thomas's first meeting independent of Speke Hall was in the open air, early in December, 1906, at the end of the railway arch in Falcon Road, near Clapham Junction Station. He was the leader, his "workers" were his wife and his children, and a woman pressed through the crowd and asked him to pray for her.[31] Shortly afterwards, some twelve or fifteen men and women, mostly, if not all, members of the Pentecostal League and employed in his shop, met in a room on his business premises for a Sunday morning service. Here was the nucleus of what was to become the International Holiness Mission.[32]

In February, 1907, the meetings were transferred to Sydney Hall, York Road, Battersea, previously a venue of the Fabian Club, where Bernard Shaw is reputed to have written some of his early works. The ground floor was used for the adult services on Sundays and every night during the week except Friday. The upper floor accommodated the Sunday School, some two hundred strong. Full scope was given to those who showed any preaching ability to minister in the meetings. Testimony played a large part in the services, which were usually concluded with a short address.[33] It was a layman's movement both in conception and practice. Plain buildings and unsalaried workers was the founder's ideal.[34] But this did not mean that the ministry of sound Holiness preachers was not valued. G. D. Watson had led both Harris and Thomas into the experience of entire sanctification, and he and those like him were looked up to as authorities.

Early Features

In Thomas's break with Harris and the League there was only one point at issue: whether Holiness should be propagated inside or outside the existing churches. Apart from this, Thomas was a loyal and admiring disciple of the man who had led him into spiritual blessing. The League had its headquarters in the slums, and so had the Holiness Mission.[35] By April, 1908, the *Holiness Mission Journal*,[36] an eight-page monthly, made its appearance as the official organ of the Holiness Mission. It was virtually a small edition of *Tongues of Fire*, printed by the same firm and consisting of an editorial by Thomas, testimonies, articles, a children's story and reports of meetings. If it lacked the breadth of outlook of its archetype, it emphasised with vigour the League doctrines of the New Birth and entire sanctification on the shortened front on which it elected to fight.

By the time the *Journal* was published, the congregation at Sydney Hall had been joined by the Holiness missions at Penn, in Buckinghamshire, at Southampton and at Carmarthen. Thomas believed he was called of God to lead a movement of Scriptural Holiness throughout the land. His conception of this movement is revealed in his editorial in the first copy of his magazine. He entitles it "The Holiness Mission. Its Aims and Objects." He writes:

> The object of the Holiness Mission is to proclaim to a lost world the truth of Full Salvation, Regeneration for the sinner and the Baptism of the Holy Ghost and Fire as the privilege of every believer, and that it shall be done effectually in every town and village throughout the land.[37]

The International Holiness Mission • 97

He invites anyone who shares his vision to inform him of buildings, however plain and humble, which can be engaged in their locality, and he undertakes to "send workers who are filled with the Spirit, to conduct the services free, without salary, simply to the glory of God."[38]

The Difference from the League

Here is the burden of Reader Harris to bring revival to Britain, and the Holiness Mission workers are the counterpart of the Pentecostal League Missioners. But there is an important difference. Thomas makes it clear in his editorial that his field of operation is outside the existing churches. "Evangelise the churches?" he asks; "Never!" is his answer. Apart from "those thousands among them who are praying for liberty . . . [they are] hopeless as a body."[39] Thus is the League principle dismissed with an exasperated gesture. It is obvious that he is not only a man writing with a sense of commission but also in the centre of conflict. He accepts the charge that "the Holiness people divide the Churches" with the bold assertion that "the word of God tells us, and history confirms it, that if there is to be a Pentecostal revival there will be a split." He quotes Paul, Luther and Wesley as precedents for necessary division and believes that he and others who believe the truth of full salvation are faced with a similar decision.[40] But by the next editorial he adopts a more conciliatory attitude: "We know the cry will be that we are antagonistic to the Ministers and the Churches, but it is not the case. We love them and pray for them."[41] At the head of the editorial we are informed that the Holiness Mission is "for the spread of Scriptural Holiness outside (but not antagonistic to) the Churches." This kind of dialectic can be traced throughout the history of the Holiness Mission.

Optimism and Responsibility

The note of optimism, characteristic of all three movements under review, is prominent in this editorial. Difficulties are recognised, but they are not to be compared with those which confronted the early disciples and they "turned the Roman Empire, which had been established over 700 years, topsy turvy in a few months". "The Holy Ghost will manu-

98 • *In the Steps of John Wesley*

facture men and women all over the land to proclaim this glorious truth."

Withal there is a deep sense of responsibility. Beneath the title "The Holiness Mission Journal" there are the words: "The Holiness Movement; or, God's Last Call to a Lost World."

Personnel

David Thomas, the undisputed leader of the Holiness Mission, was ably supported by four lieutenants who shared his vision. His right-hand man was Leonard Wain, like his leader a countryman who had come to London to seek his fortune. Active, virile, shrewd, he was at the same time manager of his business and second in command in his religious enterprise. Harry Seekings, tall, fearless, with a distinct streak of humour and a flair for doctrinal discussion, was regarded as something of a theologian by his fellows. W. S. Milbank, whose cultured voice and facile pen commanded respect and forwarded the cause, was a regular writer in the *Journal*. B. H. Dunning, of Frome, Somerset, an able worker among children and young people, was already showing promise which was to find its fulfilment in his work as the secretary of the South African Branch. These four, all members of his business staff, became known with David Thomas as "The Five Men of the Holiness Mission."[42]

Besides these, two others were prominent in the early days, both cast in a radical mould and of a courageous and determined bearing: George Wooster, a Buckinghamshire farmer, who was led to claim the experience of entire sanctification by David Thomas, and Frank Lucas, an engraver in Southampton, who claimed the same experience under the guidance of Leonard Wain. They owed their prominence partly to the fact that they were both pioneers of Holiness missions independent of the churches.

Lucas, a Strict Baptist, was informed by the minister and deacons of the church to which he belonged that they regarded as error the Holiness teaching which he had embraced. Faced with the choice of complete silence on the subject or leaving the church, he chose the latter alternative and was followed by a group of like-minded believers, who, in the absence of

The International Holiness Mission • 99

indoor accommodation, held all their meetings in the open air. At last, after five years,[43] temporary accommodation was found in St. Andrews Hall. About a year later, on March 28th, 1908, the dauntless band entered settled quarters in St. Mary Street, David Thomas acting as guarantor and donating two hundred chairs.[44]

Wooster remained in the Methodist Church for about two years after he had claimed the blessing of entire sanctification on January 28th, 1904, in a Pentecostal League Mission, conducted by David Thomas, in the chapel which he attended. Frustrated by the opposition which he encountered from the chapel leaders to his testimony and his weekly Holiness meeting, in November 1905, Wooster withdrew from the Methodist chapel, and within a few weeks commenced meetings in his home, Pennbury Farm. In October, 1906, he met Rev. Charles H. Stalker of U.S.A., who readily consented to his invitation to open a mission in Penn. A building was secured and the opening services took place on January 3rd, 1907.[45]

Missions

It has been mentioned that these two missions with a house meeting in Carmarthen and the headquarters at Sydney Hall were the sum of the Holiness Mission by the time the first *Journal* was published in April, 1908. In 1909, seven more missions were added:[46] at Long Ditton,[47] at High Wycombe, at Hitchin, at Hammersmith, at Luton, at Perth in Scotland, and at Bargoed in Wales. The following year missions were added at Forfar in Scotland, at Eastbourne, at Bradford, at Allerton near Bradford, and at Heacham.[48] By the close of 1911, the total had risen to twenty, with additional missions at Carstairs in Scotland, at Seven Kings and at Hull. The twentieth was a mission established in Krugersdorp, South Africa, by a former member of Sydney Hall, David B. Jones. In 1912, missions were added at Leicester, at Bridgewater, at Leeds, at Cleethorpes and at Stockton, but the missions at Perth,[49] at Hammersmith and at Heacham were withdrawn. In 1913, missions were added at Hoylake and at Neston,[50] but four withdrew: at Carstairs, at Allerton, at Forfar, and, one of the original four, at Carmarthen. In 1914, there were further additions at Newick and at Taunton. The year 1915

100 • *In the Steps of John Wesley*

saw the addition of missions at Birkenhead, at Bootle, at West Kirby[51] and at Ilford, but the withdrawal of the mission in Little Neston. In 1916, only one mission was added, at Portslade near Brighton, but the missions at Penn, another of the original four, at High Wycombe and at Leicester withdrew.

Three Categories

The origin of some of these missions is obscure, but they could be broadly placed in one of three categories: those brought into existence by the direct efforts of David Thomas and the workers connected with Sydney Hall; those which were in existence prior to their alliance with the Holiness Mission; and those raised up by an individual working in some kind of an association with the Holiness Mission.[52]

Thomas worked mainly on the lines laid down in his editorial in the first issue of the *Journal*, when he invited

> anyone who has got the burden of souls on their heart, and *know*, or *want to know*, this experience [i.e. entire sanctification], to write to us, and let us know of suitable plain buildings in which to hold meetings, and we will send workers who are filled with the Spirit, to conduct the services free.

But he did not hesitate to take the initiative, and in some places held convention services and open air meetings where he had received no invitation from local sympathisers with his cause.

In the second category, there were some missions which allied with the Holiness Mission because of an identity of belief and purpose and a desire for fellowship, which considerably antedated it in origin. Typical of these were the missions at Long Ditton, which has already received comment, and at Leeds.

The mission at Leeds was commenced by Alfred Place, a miner, who was converted about 1886 as a result of open air services conducted by the Hunslet Carr Wesleyans. Taught to read by one of the members, he became not only a zealous witness but anxious for service. Feeling that the Wesleyan chapel in which he had been converted was too "worldly", he commenced house meetings in Roxburgh

Road.⁵³ About 1889 he transferred his meetings to a former coal store and stables in Hunslet Moorside, and within about a year he made a further move into premises above a bakehouse in Selbourne Place, which were named "The House of Prayer". Place taught "the blessing of a clean heart", regarding John Wesley as his chief authority, but influenced also by Mr. Huskinson of the Holiness Church in Albion Street. About 1901, the little company, now increased to between fifty and sixty, moved into larger premises in Dewsbury Road. Here, in conjunction with small Holiness missions at Hull and Dewsbury, doctrine and rules were drawn up, evangelical in character, embodying articles on full sanctification and triune baptism, and with special emphasis on divine healing.⁵⁴ Place failed in both business and health, and before 1912 John Dyson, who had been converted in the House of Prayer in 1894, was elected leader. The membership remained in the region of sixty. In 1911, W. G. Anderson, a regular contributor to the *Journal,* associated himself with the mission. At his suggestion contact was made with David Thomas. This led to alliance with the Holiness Mission by February, 1912.⁵⁵

Of the third class of missions, those raised up by George Wooster and George Dempsie are the outstanding examples.

On August 26th, 1908, a tent campaign was commenced by Wooster at High Wycombe, resulting in the building of a mission which was opened by Charles Stalker on January 6th, 1909.⁵⁶ In 1911, a campaign was held in Leicester, resulting in the renting of a hall in Mere Road, which was opened as a Holiness mission by Rev. George Kunz on January 6th, 1912.⁵⁷ Both these missions were added to the list in the *Journal.*⁵⁸

Dempsie was similarly successful in raising up missions for the Holiness Mission. After resigning from the Pentecostal Church of Scotland at the beginning of 1913, he eventually made his way to England and by the close of the year had raised up missions at Hoylake and Neston, which were included in the list in the *Journal* in December. From these two centres he conducted services in the surrounding district, and, although the mission at Neston (or Little Neston) is omitted from the list in June, 1915, in the same issue missions under his jurisdiction appear at Birkenhead, at Bootle and at West

102 • *In the Steps of John Wesley*

Kirby. He continued active in the work until he left the country on February 14th, 1917,[59] and he is described in the *Journal* for February, 1916, as "Superintendent under God of the work of Holiness at Hoylake, Bootle, Birkenhead, and West Kirby, also all around Liverpool."[60]

Friends of the Holiness Mission

On March 30th, 1909, Reader Harris died, never recovering consciousness after a stroke four days previously. David Thomas paid tribute to him as "one of the most wonderful men of God we have been privileged to know" and prayed that "out of his death may arise a spiritual revival, that will end in meeting together once more in yonder clouds . . ."[61] The hope of future reunion out of time was all that was now left.[62]

But if Harris and the Pentecostal League felt they could offer no encouragement to Thomas's enterprise, there were others of repute in the Holiness Movement who were glad to do so. Among these[63] were Rev. George Kunz, Dr. A. M. Hills[64] and Mrs. and Miss Crossley and Miss Hatch of Star Hall, Manchester. David Thomas was in charge of the intermediary meeting on Thursday, October 7th, 1909, at the Star Hall Autumn Convention;[65] and Miss Crossley subscribed £5 towards the new Holiness Mission Tabernacle in Battersea.[66] These are but some of the indications of the bond of sympathy which existed.

The Easter Convention

It was probably from Star Hall that Thomas derived the idea of an Easter Convention in Battersea, to which contingents from the various centres of the Holiness Mission should rally. The Holiness convention, a coming together of preachers and hearers interested in the subject of Holiness, had been employed as a method of inaugurating Holiness missions and strengthening those already established from the inception of the Holiness Mission. Special services were held at the main religious festivals and on public holidays at Battersea, Southampton, Penn, High Wycombe and at other Holiness missions. But the Easter Convention held at Sydney Hall from the Good Friday to the Easter Monday of 1914 was

The International Holiness Mission • 103

more widespread in its appeal and representation, and it was regarded as a new step in the history of the Holiness Mission. It exceeded Thomas's highest expectations, over 300 being present for the Easter Monday afternoon and evening services.[67]

Thus the pattern was set for the succeeding years: an annual Easter Convention, with large congregations, swollen by visitors from the London district and the provinces, special preachers and testimonies, enthusiastic singing, seekers for spiritual blessing at the penitent form, and a special offering for the missionary work in South Africa.[68]

Steps to a Superintendent Ministry

Within four months of the first Easter Convention, the nation was engulfed in the 1914-18 war. It laid its restrictions on the young denomination and took its toll of its members.[69] But it did not damp its enthusiasm nor divert its course. Thomas saw in it the failure of human attainments and especially of what he called the "Laodicaean Church". He interpreted it as a challenge and a call to the individual believer in full salvation to witness to the truth as never before.[70]

But there were forces within the movement which were modifying its structure more determinatively than the pressure of external events. The laymen's movement with its scorn of organisation was evolving to find a place for the full-time minister and a more clearly defined basis of alliance.

The discerning student of its early days can trace the beginnings of the first-mentioned change shortly after its inception. An honorary evangelist is very limited in the number of campaigns he can conduct, if he must earn his living in secular employment. David Thomas was the most generous of donors to the work he loved, not only in finance but also in the service of his employees. Even so, key men like Wain, Seekings, Milbank and Dunning could not be spared too often from his growing business. A solution was sought in the financing by Thomas of those who showed ability as preachers and winners of converts. Among the earliest of these were Esther Rees,[71] Lizzie Davies[72] and Harry C. Best.[73] These would still be classed as laity, but they gave

104 • *In the Steps of John Wesley*

up their secular employment to devote all their time and energies to religious work.

A more positive step towards an ordained as well as a separated ministry was the association of George Dempsie with the Holiness Mission in his work in the Birkenhead and Liverpool area. He had previously been a candidate for ordination in the Pentecostal Church of Scotland. He regarded himself as a minister in his work in association with the Holiness Mission, and by November, 1915, he was described in the *Journal* as "Pastor George Dempsie".

The way was paved for an ordained, full-time minister to be appointed to superintend the work. A man was already in mind. In the early part of 1913, shortly after his induction to the pastorate of St. James Road Baptist Church, Watford, W. J. Willis had attended a Holiness meeting[74] and subsequently claimed the experience of entire sanctification. On February 22nd, 1914, he spoke at the Sunday services in Sydney Hall, and in April, 1915, he was one of the speakers at the opening services of the Holiness Mission Tabernacle in Battersea Rise. Between then and the close of the year 1916 twelve and a half weeks were taken up with evangelistic campaigns for the Holiness Mission. His testimony appeared in the *Journal* April and May issues, 1916, and long articles by him on aspects of Holiness were printed in the last four issues of the same year. In the January issue, 1917, the announcement was made that he had been appointed as "the first Superintendent Minister of the International Holiness Mission", with "practically a free hand to go as the Holy Ghost leads him to proclaim this great truth of Bible Holiness".[75]

The International Holiness Mission

In the same issue the name of the Holiness Mission is changed to "the International Holiness Mission".

The change had its origin in the work begun in South Africa by David B. Jones, who arrived there in 1908.[76] In conjunction with two American missionaries, Rev. and Mrs. Roy Bendinger, he raised up a Holiness mission adjoining the mine compound at Ferguson in Krugersdorp.[77] The three worked together under the name of the International Holiness Union.[78] When Mr. and Mrs. Bendinger were recalled,[79] Jones allied the mission with the Holiness Mission and it was listed in the *Journal* for December, 1911, as "the Ferguson (Native) Holiness Mission". Shortly after this, Jones felt called to preach to the natives on other mine compounds, and he approached the owners for permission to build mission stations near them. The owners were willing, but wished to draw up the agreement with a legally constituted body. This caused Jones, who had gone out to Africa on his own initiative, albeit with the good wishes of David Thomas and his co-workers, to apply to the Holiness Mission for official recognition. This was granted and in 1914 his work became the South African Branch of the International Holiness Mission.[80]

An undated, printed document[81] which appears to have been drawn up at this time indicates that a Board of Council, consisting of the "Five Men", Thomas, Wain, Seekings, Dunning and Milbank with Lucas and Harry Trigg of Southampton, George Walker of London and William Tyler of Luton[82] was created to control the work in consultation with a Field Council, acting in an advisory capacity.[83] Articles of Faith are embodied in the document, evangelism rather than educational activities is stressed as the purpose of the work and strong emphasis is laid upon separation from "worldliness", upon total abstinence from alcohol and smoking and upon the importance of entire sanctification.[84] Thomas is named as president and Wain and Lucas as vice-presidents.

About two and a half years later, a meeting was held on September 18th, 1916, "of those upon whose hearts the burden and needs of the work in connection with the Holiness movement in this country have been laid",[85] and a constitution was drawn up for the home side of the Holiness Mission, now to be known as the International Holiness Mission. The missions allied to it were invited to apply for "affiliation". A self-perpetuating Executive Council was formed with power to "decide as to whether individual Missions should be received or retained in affiliation with the International Holiness Mission" and also to decide "at any time" "whether individual members, either of the Executive Council or of the General Council, shall be retained".[86] Apart from this power of "excommunication" vested in the Executive Council, affiliated missions were to be "entirely self-governing and self-supporting" and their leaders were to form a General Council, in conjunction with the Executive Council, which would meet annually.[87]

Article 4 declared that "a Superintendent Minister shall be appointed and paid by the Executive Council", which had "the power to appoint other paid workers as the need arises". In the letter sent out over the president's signature to the leaders of the allied missions Willis's appointment is announced and his services offered. It appears that, among other things, he would be a liaison officer between the Executive Council and the missions.

The Articles of Faith and the emphasis on Holiness and the separation from worldliness are the same as in the South African Constitution.

In sponsoring such a Constitution Thomas conceded that the loose organisation of the past left room for improvement and that there was a place for a separated and supported ministry.

These innovations were more than the independent stomach of George Wooster could digest. Already, with missions raised up by him and looking to him for leadership, in which circulated a magazine of his own editing, he was virtually the leader of a movement with greater coherence than the Holiness Mission with which he was associated. Strongly opposed to anything in the nature of a "paid ministry", he could but view the advent of the closer affiliation and the superintendency of Willis with misgiving. No doubt discerning the shape of things to come, he withdrew from the Holiness Mission with his associated missions before November, 1916. John D. Drysdale, who had left Ardrossan in October, 1915, and taken the pastorate of the Birkenhead Holiness Mission in February, 1916,[88] also declined to enter the closer affiliation, feeling called to work on an undenominational basis, and the Birkenhead Holiness Mission no longer appears in the list in the *Journal* after December, 1916. The missions at Hitchin and Newick are also missing from the January, 1917, list, so the International Holiness Mission began its career with a total of nineteen missions, five less than the total in October, 1916.

The International Holiness Mission • 107

DEVELOPMENTS AND DEVIATIONS

The Blending of the Old and the New, 1917-29

The appointment of Willis as superintendent minister was a decisive step in the direction of a separated ministry. His superintendence was undefined and largely inoperative, except in limited areas, but the conception of a permanent official ordained to preach the gospel and administer the sacraments had come to stay.

The Place of Ministers

The success which attended his preaching ministry caused David Thomas and the Executive Council to invite other ministers to join the movement. Rev. H. E. Jessop, who had been led to claim the experience of entire sanctification under David Thomas at a Pentecostal League meeting in Sheffield in May, 1906,[89] left the Pentecostal Church of the Nazarene, at Morley, to become the superintendent of the work of the International Holiness Mission in South Wales in March, 1919.[90]

Willis, who had been appointed to the pastorate of the Manchester Holiness Mission Tabernacle on October 4th, 1919,[91] resigned in February, 1920, to go as a missionary with the Oriental Missionary Society to Korea,[92] and Jessop was appointed immediately to his pastorate and his superintendency in the Midlands and North of England.[93]

At almost the same time, on May 1st, the recognition services of Rev. E. A. J. Bolt as pastor of the Bristol mission of the International Holiness Mission were held. It was through the witness of this mission that Bolt had claimed the experience of entire sanctification toward the close of 1918. He was at that time the curate of St. Silas. Exception was taken to his forthright testimony and preaching by members of the congregation, his vicar and, finally, the Bishop of Bristol. This led to the termination of his curacy and an inhibition from preaching in the diocese. He was received with warmth into the ministry of the International Holiness Mission as a champion of the truth, and a pamphlet was published giving an account of the controversy.[94] His sudden death on June 15th, 1924, was universally mourned throughout the International Holiness Mission.[95]

Two of the next ministers to be added to the International Holiness Mission had both previous connections with Star Hall, Manchester. Joseph E. Griffiths had been on the Star Hall staff from January 1st, 1910, until October 24th, 1918.[96] He was appointed to the pastorate of the Holiness Church, Hull, on November 30th, 1920.[97] The church flourished during the six years of his ministry, and many were led into a profession of full salvation. He vacated the pastorate on September 21st, 1926,[98] to take charge of the mission in Luton and his place was taken at Hull by Edmund Roach on October 26th, 1926.[99] Roach was a previous member of the Star Hall congregation, who had entered the ministry of the Pentecostal Church of Scotland (q.v.). In the *Journal* for January, 1925, he was listed as a member of the International Holiness Mission ministerial staff, and until his appointment to Hull he ministered with acceptance in evangelistic campaigns throughout the movement. He returned to the Church of the Nazarene in the autumn of 1930.

Roach was preceded on the ministerial list by James Bedwell, whose name appears on it in June 1922. He joined the Baptists at the age of 15 and was converted in his late teens. Shortly after, he joined the Primitive Methodists in South Cerney and became a lay preacher. He claimed the experience of entire sanctification under the ministry of Reader Harris in Liverpool. He began a League centre in Ellesmere Port about 1903, which became an independent congregation about 1907,[100] and joined the International Holiness Mission in 1919.[101] A forceful preacher, Bedwell was frequently engaged in evangelistic work, but for the first fourteen months on the ministerial staff he exercised supervision in the South Wales area.[102]

Dan Phillips of Manchester was the first member of the International Holiness Mission to become one of its ministers. He prepared for the ministry by a course at Cliff College, the Wesleyan Methodist college for training evangelists.[103] Phillips was a lively, evangelistic preacher and an attractive singer. He was accepted as a probationary minister at Easter, 1926,[104] and was engaged in an evangelistic itinerary with considerable success until he was appointed to the pastorate at Grimsby on June 26th, 1928.[105]

Phillips was followed as a probationary minister by Thomas Food, whose name was included on the list in August, 1927. Food was a native of Leicester and had been a worker under George Wooster for about six years.[106] At the suggestion of Thomas, Food took charge of the Holiness Mission, 6 Teakwood Buildings, Bradford, on March 29th, 1921,[107] but at the beginning of 1922 he was removed from leadership by the Board Meeting because of his presentation of holiness. He built up another congregation and, by December, 1923, erected a place in which to meet in Caledonia Street, Wakefield Road.[108] From the end of 1925, Food was in demand in other missions as a preacher and a singer.[109] His case is interesting as combining in itself the evolution from the full-time lay worker, such as H. C. Best and Esther Rees, to the ministerial office.

Incorporation

Although the period under review witnessed the growth numerically and in prestige of a separated ministry, the control of affairs remained firmly in the hands of the laity. The incorporation of the Mission on November 3rd, 1920, as a limited liability company under the Companies Act, 1908 to 1917, put a legal stamp on the authority of the Executive Council.

The document drawn up for the purpose of incorporation is entitled "Memorandum and Articles of Association of the International Holiness Mission". It is basically the 1916 Constitution in legal language. For the purposes of incorporation the membership of the International Holiness Mission is limited to twenty, and all the twenty named are members of the Executive Council.[110] The subscribers to both the Memorandum and the Articles of Association are the "Five Men": Thomas, Wain, Milbank, Dunning, Seekings, and two others: Sydney H. Strong, of Seven Kings, and Herbert Lane, of Surbiton. The thirteen other members of the Mission named in the Articles of Association were all active members of the missions affiliated to the International Holiness Mission with the exception of George Walker, a Baptist minister, and George Longley, a Methodist.[111] All the sixteen members of the 1916 Executive Council are included with the exception of Willis and Dempsie.

110 • *In the Steps of John Wesley*

More power is given to the Executive Council than in the 1916 Constitution. An "Annual General Meeting" of the members of the Mission is specified,[112] but this evidently refers to the twenty men already on the Executive Council and not to the General Council of the 1916 Constitution. Therefore it in no sense limits the power of the Executive Council, which is given authority

> from time to time to make any bye-law, rule or regulation and to alter or amend the same, for appointing, constituting, directing or regulating any Mission which forms part of the International Holiness Mission, and to appoint, dismiss or remove any Leader or Officer of any such Mission.[113]

The provision most pregnant with consequences was "that no member of the Council of Management or Governing Body of the Mission shall be appointed to any salaried office of the Mission".[114] This precluded the ministers of the Mission from a place in the Executive Council, although, to complete the anomaly, ministers drawing their salaries from other denominations, like George Walker, could be given the privilege which they were denied. It was not long before this became a point of contention. Jessop and Willis pressed for the ministers to have a say in the government of the Mission, and eventually, about 1923, the Executive Council admitted the ministers to their meetings, in an advisory capacity. Some years later they conceded the right of ministers to vote on all but certain financial matters, especially those relating to their salaries. A Finance Committee was created to deal with these, on which ministers were not permitted to sit.[115]

A further widening of the area of consultation during this period was the institution in 1919, of a conference of workers on the Saturday morning before Easter Sunday in the Holiness Mission Tabernacle, Clapham Junction. From Easter, 1921, it was divided into a Leaders Conference at 10 a.m. and an Open Conference at 11.15, and from Easter, 1923, only the leaders met. At Easter, 1929, the meeting was announced for Ministers, Mission Leaders and Workers.[116]

Development of the Existing Pattern

Apart from some innovations the International Holiness Mission adhered to its previous pattern during the period under review.

The International Holiness Mission • 111

Missions were added[117] by the same methods as previously, except that there was no counterpart to the role filled by Wooster and Dempsie in the early days. Willis and Jessop were given a certain freedom in exploiting opportunities of raising up new missions, but there was not the undefined relationship to the movement, as was the case with Wooster and Dempsie.

The convention continued to be the chief method of gathering together a nucleus to establish a mission. Conventions were also held as before to give fresh impetus to existing missions of the movement. The Easter Convention in London increased in size and importance, and from Easter, 1920, the Easter Monday services were held in the Battersea Town Hall.[118]

The *Journal* continued on its course with certain modifications. In January, 1917, notes for the International Sunday School Lesson were introduced. G. D. Watson remained a favourite writer, and articles which he had written continued to appear frequently even after his death on February 28th, 1924. The laity, notably T. Lamb Scott, a chemist in Trimdon Colliery, Milbank and Misses M. Waldron and E. L. Manning,[119] continued to contribute articles, but as was to be expected, articles were now coming from the pens of the ministers, especially Jessop and Willis. "Uncle Nebo" (Dunning) continued his "Letter to the Children", reports of the missions and conventions remained a feature, testimonies to full salvation were still given a place, though not quite such a prominent place as in the previous period, and the growth of the South African Missionary Work was reflected in the space devoted to it. For most members of the Mission the Editor's Notes if not *mandata* were at least regarded as paternal *consilia*. They alternated between anticipations of widespread revival and the doctrine of the remnant, but persistently the readers were urged to live out the experience of Scriptural Holiness and were warned to beware of worldliness, and of substitutes for spiritual experience such as education, ecclesiasticism and culture.

At the beginning of this period there were only two International Holiness Mission missionaries in South Africa: Mr. and Mrs. D. B. Jones, the pioneers. By the close they

112 • *In the Steps of John Wesley*

had been joined by ten more missionaries and three auxiliaries. The fact that almost all of the fifteen were members of missions of the International Holiness Mission indicates how firmly the South African work had embedded itself in the hearts of the rank and file. In this fertile soil it was destined to maintain a steady growth, with portentous consequences for the work at home.

Innovations

The purchase of the Brunswick Street Presbyterian Church as a centre of Holiness witness in Manchester[120] was something of a new departure. Its stately spire, stained glass windows, pipe organ and ordained minister were far removed from the original vision of plain buildings and unsalaried workers.[121] Moreover, its architectural splendour was openly admired, and a block of it appeared regularly in the *Journal* from October, 1919, until the style of the *Journal* was altered in January, 1924.

The innovation was more than architectural. There was now a northern centre as well as a southern one. In some measure it entered into the inheritance of Star Hall,[122] from which most of its foundation members came. It became the seat of the superintendent minister, and his "Manchester Letter" became "Our Superintendent's Letter". To some this came to be as authoritative as the Editor's Notes, laying a more ample and informed conception of Holiness before the readers. It was the Superintendent's Letter which commended the move in 1927 towards a closer union among the Holiness movements of the land. There was a more cordial approach to the other churches: "One pleasing feature of the work at the moment", wrote Jessop in 1923,[123] "is the stream of blessing that is flowing to other churches." Ernest Hampden-Cook, who edited Weymouth's Translation of the New Testament, often attended the Sunday morning service at the Tabernacle.[124] Principal Samuel Chadwick preached at the pastor's anniversaries, and Jessop was invited to preach at Cliff College and at the Southport Convention.[125]

The growth of a separated ministry made itself felt in another way. In November, 1922, the following notice appeared in the *Journal*:

The International Holiness Mission • 113

A system and course of training for a limited number of *single* young men who have the call of God upon them to be Holiness workers has been decided upon. For particulars apply to Mr. David Thomas....[126]

It was stated in the *Journal* for January, 1923,[127] that nine or ten had applied, but only four of the most suitable could be selected. The Committee would meet to consider the applications at Easter, or earlier, if possible. Nothing further was heard of this scheme, but the idea of providing training for prospective Holiness workers was revived by the advent of the Trekkers.

The Holiness Mission Trekkers were perhaps the most dramatic innovation of the entire period. Although they appeared in these years, and their originator grew up in this period, he and they belong to the next brief cycle, in which they might have changed the course of the Mission.

A Break Between the Old and the New, 1929-34

When Jessop resigned in the autumn of 1929[128] responding to an invitation to become Guest Pastor for one year at the Northwest Gospel Tabernacle, Chicago,[129] Maynard G. James was appointed to take his place in Manchester.[130] The appointment was an acknowledgement of the past and prophetic of the future. Within the space of five years, James was to rise from a promising young man to be the outstanding personality in the Mission: a dynamic pioneer, a centre of controversy and a leader of revolt.

The Holiness Mission Trekkers

James was converted in the Bargoed Holiness Mission as a boy, restored to faith as a youth of seventeen under the ministry of Wain in January, 1920, and led to claim the experience of entire sanctification at the Battersea Easter Convention of the same year. By the time he was twenty-one he was made the leader of the Cardiff Holiness Mission. When he was given the opportunity of going to Cliff College in January, 1927, Samuel Chadwick, the principal, recognised his gifts of leadership, making him chairman of the students in the October, and asking him to remain an additional two terms.[131]

114 • *In the Steps of John Wesley*

At Cliff College he saw the possibilities of trekking. He communicated his vision of a band of Holiness Trekkers to three of his fellow-students: William Henson, William J. Maslen and Albert E. Hart, receiving encouragement in the enterprise from George D. Holmes, a prominent member of the International Holiness Mission Executive Council and a personal friend of Samuel Chadwick.[132]

After a preliminary campaign in the Fenton Holiness Mission, commencing on June 27th, 1928,[133] James and his three companions conducted a mission in the headquarters of the International Holiness Mission at Battersea, where they were joined by a fifth, the son of Pastor James Bedwell, Kenneth. In both places they met with outstanding success. From this auspicious beginning, they set out on an itinerary throughout the Mission, which began in August, 1928, and was not completed until September[134] the following year. Almost every mission was visited; everywhere a great impression was made.[135]

The Holiness Mission Trekkers, as they were named, were the counterpart of Cliff College's Methodist Friars. Like the Friars, they tramped from place to place with their sleeping bags and the bare necessaries of life on a two-wheeled trek cart, subordinating everything to the main purpose of winning the uncommitted to a decision for Christ. Their ministry included more indoor meetings than was customary with the Friars, and they had more opportunity of emphasising the experience of Holiness for believers.

Such was the enthusiasm aroused among the young men of the Mission, that the following year two trek parties were formed: one touring the North and Wales, and the other concentrating on the South. In 1931 also there were two parties: one trekking from Manchester across to Sunderland and the North-East, and the other engaging in the Bolton tent campaign. In the summer of 1932, a trek party participated in the Manchester tent campaign, then, emulating the first trek, it continued its activities throughout the winter, not breaking up until October, 1933. There was one trek in 1934, which devoted its activities partly to campaigns in existing missions in Lancashire and Yorkshire, and partly to the pioneer campaign in Dewsbury.[136]

Revival and Healing Campaigns

James, having initiated the trekking movement in the International Holiness Mission, turned his attention to the responsible pastorate committed to his care. For the next six months, with Henson and Pastor J. H. Farmer to assist him, he roused the members to renewed evangelistic activity and intense prayer. The numbers, which had declined after the close of Jessop's ministry there, increased rapidly in all the services. James was given the additional opportunity of writing the letter in the *Journal* formerly the privilege of Jessop.[137]

For some years James had been impressed by the success of the Revival and Healing Campaigns conducted by Stephen and George Jeffreys, in raising up churches for the Pentecostal Movement. By October, 1930, he succeeded in persuading the Executive Council to permit a preliminary reconnaissance in the Potteries.[138] On July 11th, 1931, in a large tent at the Daubhill Crossing, Bolton, a revival campaign was commenced by James and Dan Phillips, assisted by a team of Trekkers, with the express purpose of raising up a Holiness mission. In two and a half months about one thousand decisions were registered, and there were some cases of faith healing.[139] A prefabricated building, accommodating about four hundred, was erected, and Rev. Norman G. Dunning deputised for Samuel Chadwick at the dedication ceremony in October.[140]

A campaign at Farnworth, near Bolton, the following year, proved to be a damp squib,[141] but, undaunted, James planned a similar campaign in Leeds. An intensive revival and healing campaign was held in which two hundred decisions were recorded and the Holiness mission there was filled to overflowing.[142] Almost immediately, the tent was erected in Oldham for a campaign in which all previous records were broken. At the close of it, premises accommodating seven hundred chairs were engaged and officially opened as the Holiness Tabernacle on September 3rd.[143] James and Michael Keeley were put in charge of the new work in Oldham.

The International Holiness Mission had arrived at the cross-roads.[144] There were those who felt that a pause should be made to consolidate the gains of the past two years. But

116 • *In the Steps of John Wesley*

James forthrightly declared "we dare not go back to the old state of things. If we do, God will remove our candlestick from its place..."[145]

The tent was erected in Salford towards the end of July, 1933. A modest beginning gave place to a spate of crowded meetings and decisions, culminating in the establishment of another Holiness tabernacle, in a disused mill in Lissadel Street.[146] About the same time, the Trekkers, under the leadership of J. T. Henson, commenced a campaign on August 12th in a hired hall in Atherton, near Bolton. They met with remarkable success, and a strong church was formed.[147]

The year 1934 was outstanding in the realm of pioneer revival and healing campaigns. It began with a small church being opened in Shaw, near Oldham.[148] At Easter, the Executive Council yielded to James's demands by setting aside three ministers specifically for revival work: James, Keeley and Jack Ford.[149] As the result of a campaign led by them, commencing on April 30th, a strong church was formed in the village of Queensbury, near Bradford.[150] In some ways the peak was reached in the Dewsbury campaign which followed. Commencing on June 9th, it gathered such momentum that the final Sunday evening, August 5th, the Playhouse Cinema was packed with about two thousand people, and a further thousand overflowed a simultaneous meeting hurriedly arranged in the tent.[151] The Keighley campaign was hard in comparison, but here, too, a good centre was established.[152]

But 1934, the year of the greatest advance, was a year of contention and division. It closed with the International Holiness Mission bereft of its revival party and two of its new churches, at Salford and Oldham.

Tension and Division

On Monday night, June 16th, 1930, David Thomas died.[153] He had lived with one object in view: to devote time and money to the spread of Scriptural Holiness. His views changed little with the passage of time. He was quite content to see ministers coming into the structure of the layman's movement which he had founded, providing they justified their place by preaching full salvation and winning converts to the truth. He enthusiastically welcomed the advent of the Trekkers with their evangelistic zeal.[154] To the end, he remained suspicious of organisation. Though he valued and respected the men who made up the Executive Council, it is said that before his death he regretted calling it into being. It was easier to create than to control.

David Thomas was succeeded in the presidency by Leonard Wain, marked out from the beginning as his second in command and eventual successor. A man of more logical frame of mind than Thomas, he was better equipped to preside over the Executive Council. Friendly and with a quick sense of humour, but firm and determined, it had been said of him in the February *Journal*, 1925, "with such a leader the Holiness movement looks into the future without fear . . ."[155] He made a good beginning, holding the confidence of both the old and new elements in the Mission.[156]

On Wain's promotion to the presidency, George D. Holmes was made a vice-president. A man of considerable business energy, he had raised himself from a bargeman to a position of wealth and influence in the town of Goole. As a young man, he had been led to claim the experience of full salvation by his uncle, a fellow-bargeman, Daniel Wildblood, an illiterate but devout member of the Hull Holiness Mission, which Holmes joined. He won the esteem of those with whom he served on the Executive Council, his sincerity and success combining to bring him promotion. He was a warm-hearted and generous man, a home-spun evangelist and with some natural gifts of leadership. He became more prominent than Frank Lucas, his senior in the vice-presidency, partly because he could spare more time from his business and partly because of Lucas's natural reserve and austerity. B. H. Dunning, who now became head of David Thomas Ltd.,[157] came into increasing prominence, and George Walker, the secretary, had a quiet influence which could count at critical moments.[158]

The five years under review witnessed a steady increase in the number and influence of ministers. At the beginning of the period there were six ministers; at the close, before the resignation of James and his companions, there were sixteen.[159] This increase was almost entirely due to the advent of trekking. It might have been even greater if the appeal for a Bible Training School in the May *Journal*, 1929, had been taken up. Arising directly out of the enthusiasm engendered by the first trek, it seemed at first as if the project would receive warm support. A fund was opened, but the response was poor.[160]

Noteworthy with regard to the entry of ministers into positions previously held by laymen was the appointment in July, 1932, of Jack Ford, a young probationary minister, to the editorial chair of the *Journal*.[161] The editing of the *Journal* had come to be regarded as a concomitant of the president's office, but Wain felt neither the inclination nor the ability for it; indeed, it was he who took the initiative in Ford's appointment. When Ford left the Croydon pastorate at Easter, 1934, to engage in revival campaigns, another young probationary minister, Arthur Fawcett, was made editor,[162] and for the rest of its history the *Journal* remained in ministerial hands.

During this period, ordained ministers continued to sit on the Executive Council as previously, being permitted to vote on all matters except those aforementioned, relating to finance. But, as time went on, some, notably James, felt increasingly that the evolution taking place in the Mission should be reflected in its legal status, and that the constitution should be changed to give the ministers a legal seat and vote on the Executive Council. What gave further point to James's contention was a division of opinion between some of the members of the Executive Council and himself regarding revival campaigns.

This extended, as we have seen, to the pace of advance. It included also the method. There was complete harmony concerning the method of trekking. Holmes gave it his unqualified support and was regarded as "the Chief Trekker". But when faith healing was introduced into the pioneer revival campaign at Bolton and in subsequent campaigns, Holmes expressed disapproval. His past experience had led him to treat it with caution, conscious that it could be taken to fanatical lengths. Moreover, though he and others on the Executive Council did not deny that faith healing was scriptural,[163] the revival and healing campaign smacked too strongly of Pentecostalism for their liking.[164] When, in 1933, Phillips declared that he had spoken in tongues and had embraced the belief of some Pentecostalists that it was the authentic evidence of the baptism of the Holy Spirit, they saw a confirmation of their fears. Phillips had to resign; James wrote an editorial affirming the Mission's tenet that the baptism of the Spirit is received by faith;[165] but misgivings remained.

Division

In 1934 matters came to a head.

James met the Executive Council on January 26th with a view to discussing the points at issue. He was already thinking in terms of resignation, in which he was supported by Keeley, Leonard Ravenhill and Clifford Filer, and would probably have been joined by the churches at Oldham and Salford.[166] The Executive Council, aware of the stimulus that James had given to the Mission, was anxious to meet his demands, but felt there was a limit to the concessions it could make. The crisis was postponed until Easter. By then their attitude had hardened. In deference to James's request, a revival party was appointed; but in spite of his strong opposition, the name was changed from Pilgrim Revival Party to "Revival Campaigners". When the question of the constitution was reached, discussion was cut short by a motion from Dunning inviting all the legal members of the Council to vote that the constitution should stand and the question of its alteration should never be raised again. The motion was carried.[167]

When the Executive Council met at the Manchester church on October 9th and 10th, the issue of Pentecostalism was before it. A letter to Wain declared that some Pentecostalists had spoken in tongues in some of the meetings connected with the Keighley campaign. This caused a motion to be put to the meeting calling upon those in charge of missions to forbid this practice; a motion which James and Ford declared they could not support as it seemed to them to be in direct contravention of I Corinthians 14:39. After prolonged discussion, involving an extra day, an uneasy agreement was reached. The lay members of the Executive Council, detained from their businesses and taxed in patience, dealt with the remaining items of the agenda swiftly and firmly. To James and Ford this appeared as but another evidence of where the real authority lay, upheld by a constitution,

120 • *In the Steps of John Wesley*

immutable and unassailable. Hearing that Ravenhill and Filer had refused to give the assurance to forbid speaking in tongues, James and Ford decided that the time had come for them to resign and to launch out into aggressive evangelism untrammelled by outmoded administration. The four of them resigned together.[168] On being informed of their action, Filer's church at Salford and Ravenhill's church at Oldham elected to join them in leaving the International Holiness Mission.

The Resultant Synthesis, 1934-52

The resignation of James, Ford, Ravenhill and Filer created a crisis in the International Holiness Mission and at first there was considerable apprehension concerning the proportions it would assume. When they were joined first by the missions at Oldham and Salford, then by the new mission at Queensbury and the old established mission at Bradford, it became clear that a new movement was being formed which might well constitute a challenge to the old. But here for the time being the transfer of allegiance ceased.

Those who remained settled down to the task of shaping the policy of a society linked to the past but leavened with new ideas. The history of the International Holiness Mission between 1934 and 1952 is the account of the interaction and harmonisation of the old and the new elements which remained together to form the resultant synthesis.

The gap created by the resignations confronted the International Holiness Mission with three immediate questions: whether the Constitution should remain unchanged; how Forward Work should continue; and who, if anyone, should take James's place as the leading minister.

The Constitution

It became evident to the ministers who remained that, having suffered loss through an unbending resistance to equal, legal voting powers for laymen and ministers, the Executive Council were in a mood for concessions. The ministers took advantage of this mood to draw up a new administration and present it for consideration at the Easter meeting of the Executive Council on April 23rd, 1935. Not only did they receive the assurance that it would be given priority at the

The International Holiness Mission • 121

next half-yearly meeting, but further scope was given for united action by the institution of half-yearly ministerial conferences to be convened about a month before the Executive Council meetings.[169]

The suggested administration was a revolutionary document. It vested supreme authority in an Annual Conference composed of the Executive Council, all the accredited ministers, and elected delegates from the missions in the proportion of one for the first fifty or fewer members and one for each additional fifty.[170] The Executive Council were given the right to elect the president and the treasurer from their number, while the one elected by the ministers as the superintendent minister was to act as the Conference vice-president and the ministers were given the right to elect the secretary. The election of all officers was to be annual.[171]

This administration was considered and modified at the Executive Council Meeting in October, 1935, but it did not pass beyond this stage. The following Easter a committee of seven[172] was appointed to draw up a form of administration to be submitted to the missions for their consideration, after which the whole matter was to be dealt with at the October Council meeting.[173]

The Constitution as amended by this committee, submitted to the missions and approved by the Executive Council in October, 1936, bears only a slight resemblance to the one presented by the ministers. It is a virtual reversion to (or establishment of) the *status quo*. The governing body is the Executive Council, with which the Council of Ministers sits, having equal voting powers in all matters except finance. The Annual Conference, which was the supreme authority in the ministers' administration, is a resurrection of the former Ministers, Leaders and Workers Conference. Its composition is more clearly defined[174] and its powers are greater. It could discuss and pass resolutions "on any matter regarding the general conduct of the work". But the resolutions, which must be passed by a two-thirds majority, must then be submitted to the Executive Council for confirmation or otherwise.[175]

Evidently the mood for concessions had passed. The Executive Council remained the governing body and the equal

122 • *In the Steps of John Wesley*

voting powers of the ministers were granted, and could be withdrawn, by them. But the 1935 Administration gave expression to an ideal which persisted and was favourably considered at the Easter Executive Council Meeting in 1952. Those who drafted it were sixteen and a half years in advance of their time.

Forward Work

When James and his companions left the International Holiness Mission the tension eased but the pace of advance slackened. The spearhead was broken off. Nevertheless, there was a genuine concern among those remaining that Forward Movement Campaigns should continue and efforts made in this direction at first met with some success.

A tent campaign, led by Fawcett, Maslen, Yeo and Food, on the lines of the previous campaigns but with less emphasis on faith healing, resulted in a mission being established in Tower Street, West Hartlepool, in 1935. The following year a similar campaign in Sunderland resulted in a considerable accession of converts to the existing mission in Kyall Road, and a mission was established in a former warehouse as the result of a tent campaign in Batley under the leadership of Lown in 1937.[176] Here, however, the founding of new missions by the campaign method came to an end. The new phase of evangelism begun in 1931 virtually ended in the International Holiness Mission with the sale of the campaign tent for £10 in 1940.[177]

With trekking the story was almost the same. From June 25th, 1935, to November, 1936, three main itineraries were made, all commencing at Manchester. They reported many seekers for spiritual blessing in their reports in the *Journal* and as a result of their campaign in Farnworth a mission was established. It was not until fourteen years later, in the summer of 1950, that trekking reappeared in the International Holiness Mission. Thirteen missions were visited and again a number of seekers were reported.[178] W. Henson, one of the original Trekkers, was responsible for the organisation of the trek, and in this blending of the old and the new the Trekkers made their last appearance in the International Holiness Mission.

The International Holiness Mission • 123

Leaders

The mantle of James in pressing the claims of the ministry and the continuance of Forward Work was taken up mainly by the probationers, led by Fawcett. He was largely responsible for the presentation of the new administration[179] at the Executive Council Meeting in October, 1935. For a whole year, from Easter, 1935, he shared the responsibility of Forward Work with Holmes, and he remained a member of the Forward Work Committee until it ceased to function with the advent of war. In addition, he was editor of the *Journal* until Easter, 1938. When he left the Mission in 1940, Lown and Maslen having previously left in August, 1939, there was no distinctive leader of the ministers, although Keeley had the full confidence of the president and W. Henson was respected for his experience and reliability. Five years later, Rev. J. B. Maclagan, a leading minister of the Church of the Nazarene was installed as the superintendent minister at Bolton in October, 1945, and throughout the remaining years of the Mission's history he exercised a greater authority than any of his ministerial predecessors.

Among the members of the Executive Council, Wain, Holmes, Dunning and Lucas continued to exercise a dominant influence. Holmes died in 1942 and Dunning in 1945. Wain began to feel the strain of leadership in 1941, and a committee was appointed to assist him. Eight years later a severe illness undermined his strength, and in 1951 the Board of Trade rule stipulating the retirement of executives over 70 deprived him, Lucas, Lane, Evans and Seekings of their official positions on the Executive Council.[180]

Throughout this period, George Walker increased in prestige, and influence. He was invited to be full-time general secretary in 1941,[181] elected vice-president in 1949 and elected president in succession to Wain at Easter, 1951. His sagacity and sincerity, coupled with a gracious and brotherly bearing, won the esteem of ministers and laymen alike. It was a grievous blow to the Mission when he died unexpectedly on May 23rd, 1951.[182]

The Development of the Former Pattern

The Holiness Mission Journal. Although the format of the *Journal* was changed several times in the period under review and it inevitably reflected the different emphases of the succession of editors, there was little alteration in the main pattern of previous years.

Wain,[183] Lucas[184] and Ford[185] all took the *Journal* as created by David Thomas as their model, Lucas following him closely in radical Holiness editorials and Ford seeking a wider application of the Holiness ideal. Fawcett[186] was more disposed to introduce innovations and imparted some of his energy and drive to the *Journal*. Under Food,[187] a devoted disciple of Thomas, it reverted closely to the master's pattern, with a Thomasian editorial, a stress on definite testimony and a fair flavouring of American Holiness articles. William Henson[188] aimed at keeping the *Journal* a Holiness magazine, which would nevertheless be attractive to readers outside the Mission. Lown[189] was perhaps the best all-round editorial writer of them all, striving in the editorials and in the *Journal* generally to relate the recognized Holiness standards to current affairs and to give a lead to the Mission in denominational matters.

The circulation of the *Journal* fell from 8,000 in 1939 to between 5,000 and 6,000 in 1943, and it remained at that figure until the *Journal* was amalgamated with the *Way of Holiness* in the *Way* in January, 1953.[190]

Sunday School and Youth Work. Sunday School work was a feature of the International Holiness Mission from its earliest days in Sydney Hall. From as early as 1917 the teachers in its Sunday Schools were encouraged to follow the course of the International Sunday School Lesson by the notes on it published in the *Journal*. From its commencement the Sunday School of the Manchester Tabernacle was graded into a primary and main school.[191]

Between 1934 and 1952 attempts were made to further the effectiveness of work among children by the use of modern methods.[192] Fawcett published in the *Journal* a series of articles on the psychology of Sunday School Teaching by Sydney M'Caw, the superintendent of the Manchester Tabernacle Sunday School.[193] The organisation of a denominational Scripture examination in 1942 by P. Gladwin, a school teacher on the Executive Council, met with an encouraging response[194] and became a feature of the Mission's Sunday School work. At the Easter Executive Council Meeting in

1952, it was reported that there were approximately 2,121 children and 250 teachers and youth leaders connected with the Mission.

The attempts to organise Youth work on a denominational basis, especially among those in the thirteen to sixteen age group, made comparatively little progress. The Minutes of the Executive Council make reference to the Government's plans for promoting Youth Work in 1942, but no effective action was taken. The Executive Council elected a Sunday School and Young People's Board in 1947 to deal with the matter and in 1948 suggested that the Mission's youth groups should be affiliated with the Covenanters' Union.[195] The fear of sanctioning anything which might be interpreted as compromising the Holiness standard of separation from the world was constantly before the Executive Council. Eventually they recorded a suggestion of the Youth Board "that Youth Meetings be arranged for the 'teen-agers' (Quizzes, hobbies and rambles)",[196] but they went no further and organised nothing more definite and by this time the Mission's separate existence was virtually at an end.

Local Preachers' Courses. During the period under review further encouragement was given to lay preaching in the provision of a postal training course for lay preachers.[197] In 1948 it was reported to the Executive Council that nineteen were participating in the scheme. Women were permitted to take the course, and the first lay preacher successfully to complete it was a woman, Miss Armitage of Dewsbury.

Developments in the Ministry. At the beginning of this period a further year's course of studies after the completion of the probationer's course, leading to ordination and permission to use the title "Reverend", was instituted.[198] The ministers remained under the jurisdiction of the Executive Council, with whom a service agreement was drawn up in 1942,[199] by whom their salaries were paid and who had jurisdiction over where they should be stationed.[200] Nevertheless, by the close of the period, the Executive Council recognised the advisability of giving freedom to pastors and churches to make their own decisions about the length of the pastorate and the number of preaching appointments in other churches.[201]

126 • *In the Steps of John Wesley*

Conventions. Conventions continued to be held as a medium of propagating the Holiness message and as a means of fellowship between those of different missions. The Easter conventions were maintained at Battersea and Manchester, and from Easter, 1941, a convention was held in Dewsbury, which eventually rivalled that at Manchester for attendance. Up to 1938, the main autumn convention continued to be held in the Manchester Tabernacle. In 1939 it was suspended because of the uncertainty of war conditions.[202] Subsequently it was held in Dewsbury (1940), Manchester (1941-44 and 1949-50), Bolton (1945, 1946 and 1951), Keighley (1947) and Leeds (1948).

STEPS TO UNION

South Africa

Between the years 1929 and 1952 the International Holiness Mission work in South Africa so extended that it outstripped the work in Britain. By Easter, 1952, thirty missionaries were directing operations on eleven mission stations and 195 outstations. There were 1,863 members and fifty native evangelists, while attendances at meetings were reported as 6,788.[203] There was also a Bible School, commenced about 1922,[204] for the training of native evangelists, in addition to which a secondary school and a hospital were commenced about 1931.

David B. Jones remained in charge of the mission field until his death on January 14th, 1950. An Advisory Council was created by the missionaries to assist him in 1940,[205] and a Field Council was set up in 1943,[206] which took charge of the work when Jones died,[207] H. C. Best succeeding him in the superintendency. Throughout its history the South African Field loyally accepted the decisions of the Executive Council and looked to the home church for support.

As the work grew so the financial problem of its support increased. The members in the home missions responded generously, and their gifts were supplemented by the wealthier members of the Executive Council, who gave liberally in their lifetime and remembered the South African work in their wills.[208] For a time generous legacies diverted attention from the gap between the regular income and the monthly expenses.[209] Between 1946 and 1950 twelve new missionaries were sent to the Field. Then, with legacies exhausted and the monthly budget at £520 compared with £210 in 1945, the Executive Council were faced with a monthly deficit of £120.[210] The solution seemed apparent to them. "The branches over the wall" had overgrown the root which bore them. There must be an extension and strengthening of the work in Britain.[211] But within a year another solution was presented: the amalgamation with a larger denomination with the same missionary vision and ampler resources.

Relations with the Calvary Holiness Church[212]

The thought of union with a sister Holiness denomination was not new in the International Holiness Mission. Within the first four years of its existence David Thomas had been present at a meeting at which C. J. Fowler, the president of the National Holiness Association of America, had broached the subject of a National Holiness Association of Britain.[213] Jessop had written in 1927, "Why cannot the 'Eradicationists' of England come to some mutual understanding and each work to some recognised plan of campaign . . ."[214] In 1930 Wain wrote with approval of a prayer conference at Old Jordans Hostel attended by representatives of Holiness groups.[215] When the National Holiness Association (of Britain) was forming in 1942, the International Holiness Mission was present and participating.

After the schism of 1934, it was impossible for the International Holiness Mission or the Calvary Holiness Church to think of Christianity unity without considering a reconciliation with each other. An approach by James to Wain and Dunning in 1938[216] and a motion by Fawcett and Lown in the Executive Council Meeting at Easter, 1939, brought the matter before the Executive Council and issued in a meeting between representatives of the two movements at Bolton on October 30th, 1939, at which a reconciliation was effected.[217]

After a setback in 1941[218] and a fruitless meeting in the Manchester Tabernacle on February 7th, 1946,[219] a complete reconciliation was effected at a meeting between the representatives of the two movements in the Battersea Tabernacle on September 27th, 1946.[220] Reunion seemed a possibility, and, at the invitation of James and the Executive

128 • *In the Steps of John Wesley*

Council of the Calvary Holiness Church representatives of the two movements met again in the same place on March 4th, 1948, for a full discussion of the subject.[221] A further meeting was envisaged,[222] but the International Holiness Mission decided to postpone the question of fusion, nevertheless maintaining happy fellowship with the Calvary Holiness Church.[223]

Union with the Church of the Nazarene

There was much in common between the International Holiness Mission and the British Isles District of the Church of the Nazarene. They both originated in the year 1906. Their founders were both for a time members of the Pentecostal League, and both came under the censure of its official organ when they launched movements independent of the churches.[224] They both were welcome visitors at Star Hall, Manchester. The two movements were close enough in purpose and method for ministers to pass from one to the other without any change of doctrine.

On the other hand, there was originally a sharp difference in outlook and organisation. Sharpe was convinced that to be effective the propagation of Holiness required a thoroughly organised church, while Thomas was just as convinced that for the Spirit to work unhampered there should be a minimum of organisation. But, as indicated above, the International Holiness Mission gradually moved away from its founder's ideal of unsalaried workers and undefined administration until by 1952, besides an Executive Council and a Delegates' Conference, there were twenty ministers on the home staff and seven ordained missionaries on the South African Field.

In the appointment of Maclagan as superintendent minister the International Holiness Mission took a step with far-reaching consequences. Converted as a youth in the Church of the Nazarene, Maclagan's mind was steeped in its ideals and procedure. A sincere advocate of the union of the Holiness denominations of Britain, he accepted his appointment with the intention of working to that end. He was a moving spirit behind the conversations between the International Holiness Mission and the Calvary Holiness

The International Holiness Mission • 129

Church, and he played an important part in the union of the International Holiness Mission and the Church of the Nazarene. From the time of his entry into the Mission, Nazarene terms and methods appear in the legislation,[225] which, whatever the motive for introducing them, certainly smoothed the way to union. Besides the efforts of Maclagan and providing a favourable context for them, there was a growing desire and demand in the Mission for a more democratic form of government which had its origins in the days of Willis and Jessop, found disruptive expression in the Calvary Holiness Church schism, persisted in the suggested administration of 1935, and, after sundry reverses, emerged to prepare the International Holiness Mission for the ecclesiastical democracy of the Church of the Nazarene.

The visit of George Frame, the district superintendent of the British Isles District of the Church of the Nazarene, to the October Convention of the Mission at Bolton in 1951 brought the process to a climax. At his request the Executive Council granted him an interview at their autumn meeting and listened with favour to his suggestion that the two movements should come closer together. Exploratory Committees were appointed by both movements in Britain and South Africa, and their reports favouring union were considered at the Executive Council Meeting on 15th and 16th April, 1952. After a period of prayer, Dr. Hardy C. Powers, a general superintendent of the Church of the Nazarene, and Frame were received by them, and they gave them an insight into the administration of the Church of the Nazarene. When they withdrew, the Executive Council came to its decision. Many factors must have been at work at that critical moment; the need of the South African Field; the desire for a more democratic form of government; Maclagan's influence; the advantage of belonging to a larger denomination; the vacant presidential chair.[226] The decision was almost unanimous: by twenty votes to one the Executive Council endorsed the reports of the Exploratory Committees.[227] It remained for the individual churches to be consulted. Their vote was as emphatic as the Executive Council's: all, with the exception of the church at Southampton, voted in favour of union.

On October 29th, 1952, in the Zion Methodist Church, Leeds, the International Holiness Mission formally united

130 • *In the Steps of John Wesley*

with the Church of the Nazarene, seeking the fulfilment of its mission in the context of an international church with a Holiness emphasis and a missionary vision.[228]

NOTES ON CHAPTER 3

[1]The name of the Pentecostal League was amplified to the "Pentecostal League of Prayer" in the October issue of *Tongues of Fire* in 1911. It was later abbreviated to the "League of Prayer" in 1946 and it exists under that name at the present time.

[2]Mary Reader Hooker, *Adventures of an Agnostic* (London: Marshall, Morgan & Scott, 1959), p. 21.

[3]*Ibid.*, pp. 68-69. See also the entire chapter.

[4]*Ibid.*, p. 92.

[5]*Ibid.*, p. 96.

[6]*Ibid.*, pp. 118-19.

[7]*Ibid.*, pp. 19-20.

[8]*Ibid.*, pp. 97-98.

[9]*Ibid.*, pp. 76-77.

[10]*Ibid.*, chaps. x, xi and p. 95.

[11]*Ibid.*, pp. 99-100.

[12]*Ibid.*, 101, 102.

[13]*Ibid.*, chap. xvi.

[14]*Ibid.*, p. 109.

[15]*Tongues of Fire*, Jan., 1891, p. 3.

[16]Pp. 1 and 3.

[17]P. 3.

[18]P 1.

[19]P. 8.

[20]Hooker, *op. cit.*, chap. xvii and lists of centres in *Tongues of Fire*, 1899.

[21]David Thomas (London: International Holiness Mission, n.d., c. 1933), pp. 19-22.

[22]*Ibid.*, chaps. i and ii.

[23]*Ibid.*, chap. iii.

[24]*Ibid.*, pp. 23-25, 36-39, 42, and conversation with Rev. H. C. Best, London, 25-11-58.

[25]Conversations with Mrs. M. R. Hooker at Ridgelands Bible College, 20-6-55, 23-11-58, 3 and 4-2-59.

[26]*David Thomas*, pp. 42, 43, 99, 100.

[27]*Ibid.*, p. 100.

[28]*Tongues of Fire*, March, 1907, p. 6.

[29]*Ibid.*, Feb., 1899, p. 6, and letters in Harris's files: Bishop of London, 31-12-98, Bishop of Rochester, 6-1-99 and 12-1-1900.

[30]*Ibid.*, March, 1907, p. 6.

[31]*David Thomas*, pp. 106-7, and interview with Rev. H. C. Best, London, 25-11-58.

³²*Ibid.*, p. 43. Shortly after claiming the New Birth, Thomas commenced meetings on his business premises for his employees. Most of them professed conversion, and were active in Christian service. But meetings on Sunday during the hours of church services were a new departure.

³³*Ibid.*, pp. 46-48. Interview with Rev. H. C. Best, London, 25-11-58.

³⁴*The Journal*, April, 1908, p. 4.

³⁵Less than a mile separated the one from the other. This aggravated the division, but it was probably not an intentional challenge to Speke Hall. It was near Thomas's shop, where most of his early followers lived, and accessible to his residence.

³⁶Hereafter referred to in the text of this chapter as the *Journal* and cited in the footnotes as *HMJ*.

³⁷*HMJ*, Apr., 1908, p. 4.

³⁸*Ibid.*

³⁹*Ibid.*

⁴⁰*Ibid.*

⁴¹*Ibid.*, May, 1908, p. 12.

⁴²I was personally acquainted with all these men. The paragraph is the fruit of personal knowledge and many conversations concerning them with others, and checked by reading *HMJ*, *David Thomas* and other relevant matter.

⁴³Accommodation was found during this period for a few weeks in a Wesleyan Church and "a place which stood for Holiness." *HMJ*, Nov., 1911, pp. 122-23.

⁴⁴Sources for this paragraph are *HMJ*, 1908, May, p. 16, June, pp. 17 and 23; 1911, Nov., pp. 122-23 and conversation with Frank and Harold C. Lucas in Battersea, 8-7-59.

⁴⁵The main source for this paragraph is G.W., *The Work of the Holy Ghost*, pp. 2-21. See also *HMJ*, Nov., 1912, pp. 121-22.

⁴⁶The words "added" and "withdrawn" refer to the missions being included in and excluded from the list at the back of *HMJ*.

⁴⁷One of the original missions of the Speke Hall Mission before Reader Harris inaugurated the Pentecostal League as an interdenominational movement.

⁴⁸A house meeting.

⁴⁹Transferred its allegiance to the Pentecostal Church of Scotland, apparently with Thomas's consent, or, at least, without his opposition.

⁵⁰Described as Little Neston Holiness Mission from February, 1914.

⁵¹Probably a house meeting.

⁵²The mission at Hitchin was the result of the activities of the Luton mission and the mission at Ilford was similarly an extension of the Seven Kings mission, but this hardly constitutes a fourth category.

⁵³"Proposed Deed-poll for the legal binding of the Holiness Church, Hull and Leeds", (undated, c. 1906), Item (1) states "Alfred Place of Leeds, a local preacher of . . . the Methodist New Connexion, having received sanctification, began to preach and teach the same, and being rejected by the Ministers and people of the said connexion, withdrew . . ." H. Saville, who joined Place in 1894, states Rev. W. H. Bainbridge of Methodist New Connexion was preaching in the open air when Place

was converted. His son, John Place, says his father had fellowship with the Hunslet Methodist New Connexion. Whether he joined them after leaving the Wesleyans is uncertain.

[54] *Doctrine and Rules of the Holiness Church* (Leeds: W. Davy, 1902).

[55] *HMJ*, Feb., 1912, p. 24. Other sources for this paragraph are interviews with Mr. and Mrs. John Place, son and daughter-in-law of Alfred Place (6-10-57), and with Mr. H. Saville and Mr. and Mrs. H. Pickles (7-10-57), at Leeds, and with Mrs. John Dyson (15-10-57), at Carnock, near Dunfermline.

[56] *HMJ*, Feb., 1909, p. 15.

[57] G. W., *op. cit.*, pp. 28-32.

[58] Besides establishing these missions, Wooster was active in promoting evangelistic and Holiness campaigns in about twenty other places before he left the Holiness Mission at the end of 1916.

[59] *HMJ*, June, 1917, pp. 45 and 46.

[60] P. 14.

[61] *Ibid.*, May, 1909, p. 48.

[62] Thomas visited Harris the evening before he died. Although Harris was able to do no more than acknowledge him, he spent some time in fellowship with Mrs. Harris and met other members of the family. Interview with Rev. H. C. Best, (8-7-59), London.

[63] Full use was made of articles by Rev. G. D. Watson, apparently with his whole-hearted consent, in *HMJ*, and in the July, 1914, issue (p. 76) a letter of personal greeting from him was published.

[64] Preached at the mission at Southampton (*HMJ*, Nov., 1908, p. 64) and in the tent at High Wycombe (*Ibid.*, Dec., 1908, p. 70).

[65] *Way of Holiness*, Nov., 1909, p. 87. See also Nov., 1912, p. 8.

[66] *HMJ*, May, 1915, p. 58.

[67] *HMJ*, May, 1914, p. 54.

[68] See report in *Ibid.*, p. 55, and reports of subsequent Easter Conventions.

[69] I have seen no evidence that many belonging to the Holiness Mission lost their lives in the 1914-18 War, but a number would be diverted to wartime duties. Thomas's eldest and third sons, David and Stephen, were in the Forces, and Dunning was directed into Munition Work. Wain and Lucas were above recruiting age and Milbank was exempt for health reasons. Letter from Rev. H. C. Best, 20-7-59.

[70] *HMJ*, Sept., 1914, p. 102 and subsequent issues during the war.

[71] Stationed at Eastbourne, apparently from Feb. 13th, 1910—Nov., 1916. See *HMJ* for the period. But James remembers her in charge of Bargoed early in 1916.

[72] Conducted an evangelistic campaign at King's Lynn from Nov. 19th—Dec. 21st, 1911. Leader of the Holiness mission there from May to Sept., 1912. *Ibid.*, Dec., 1911, p. 142; May—Sept., 1912.

[73] Stationed at Taunton, June, 1913—Dec., 1914. *Ibid.*, Aug., 1913, p. 95 and subsequent issues. Interview with Rev. H. C. Best, 8-7-59.

[74] Probably at the home of George Longley of Apsley Lodge, Watford, a prominent man in the Holiness Mission.

[75] P. 1.

The International Holiness Mission • 133

⁷⁶*HMJ*, 1908, June, p. 21, Sept., p. 43. Mrs. D. B. Jones *et al., David Jones* (Kansas City: Beacon Hill Press, 1955), pp. 23, 24.

⁷⁷Mrs. Jones *et al., op. cit.,* pp. 31-33.

⁷⁸Letter from Mrs. D. B. Jones to Rev. R. E. Jones, 29-7-59.

⁷⁹Mrs. Jones *et al., op. cit.,* p. 37.

⁸⁰*Ibid.,* pp. 44-45; *David Thomas,* pp. 81-82; letter from Mrs. Jones to R. E. Jones, 29-7-59.

⁸¹*International Holiness Mission. Constitution of South African Branch.*

⁸²*Ibid.,* p. 1

⁸³*Ibid.,* arts. 9 and 10.

⁸⁴*Ibid.,* arts. 7 and 8.

⁸⁵Undated printed letter to accompany *Constitution.*

⁸⁶*International Holiness Mission. Constitution,* art. 3.

⁸⁷*Ibid.,* art. 7.

⁸⁸Grubb, *J. D. Drysdale,* p. 62. His name first appears in charge of the mission in the list in *HMJ* in April, 1916.

⁸⁹*HMJ*, July, 1926, pp. 4 and 5.

⁹⁰*Ibid.,* Feb., 1919, p. 13.

⁹¹*Ibid.,* Oct., 1919, p. 77.

⁹²*Ibid.,* April, 1920, p. 43.

⁹³*Ibid.,* p. 37. Willis returned to this country, and re-entered the International Holiness Mission in April, 1922. Jessop, however, remained superintendent, and Willis was appointed pastor of Trinity Hall, Grimsby, on April 29th, 1922. He left the staff of the International Holiness Mission finally on August 31st, 1925. (*Ibid.,* June, 1922, p. 69 and Sept., 1925, p. 4.)

⁹⁴*Ibid.,* May, 1920, pp. 49, 50; and E. A. J. Bolt, *From the Church of England to the International Holiness Mission* (London: International Holiness Mission, 1920).

⁹⁵*HMJ*, 1924, July, p. 4, and Sept., p. 4.

⁹⁶Interview with Rev. J. E. Griffiths, 49 Golborne Rd., Lawton, 6-10-59.

⁹⁷*HMJ*, Dec., 1920, p. iii.

⁹⁸*Ibid.,* Nov., 1926, p. 3.

⁹⁹*Ibid.,* Feb., 1927, p. 3; cf. Oct., 1926, p. 8.

¹⁰⁰Facts for the preceding part of the paragraph were obtained in an interview with James Bedwell at 42 Magdalen Rd., London S.W. 18, 27-11-58.

¹⁰¹List of missions in *HMJ*, July, 1919 onwards.

¹⁰²"South Wales" appears in brackets behind his name on the ministerial list in *HMJ* for this period.

¹⁰³*Ibid.,* Aug., 1928, p. 4.

¹⁰⁴*Ibid.,* May, 1926, Ministerial List, p. 7.

¹⁰⁵*Ibid.,* Aug., 1928, p. 4.

¹⁰⁶Letter from Thomas Food, 3-12-59.

¹⁰⁷*Ibid.,* and *HMJ*, May, 1921, p. 53.

¹⁰⁸*Ibid.,* and *HMJ*, Dec., 1923, p. iv.

¹⁰⁹See meetings announced in *HMJ* for this period.

¹¹⁰Articles of Association, par. 4.

134 • *In the Steps of John Wesley*

[111] *Ibid.,* par. 10.
[112] *Ibid.,* par. 14.
[113] *Ibid.,* par. 11 (j).
[114] 'Memorandum of Association, par. 5.
[115] I am indebted to Rev. J. E. Griffiths for this information. He was not able to recollect the exact time when the two concessions were made to the ministers. Interview at 21 Taunton Rd., Ashton-u-Lyne, 7-1-60.
[116] These facts are adduced from the announcements of the London Easter Convention in *HMJ* for the relevant years. See also *Ibid.,* May, 1923, p. 52.
[117] Missions were added and withdrawn at the following places during this period.

Year	Added	Withdrawn	Total
1917	Earlestown, Cefn Ruabon, Bolton (2) and Cardiff	West Kirby, Ilford and Portslade	21
1918	Cosham	Bootle	21
1919	Keighley, Westhoughton, Fenton, Ellesmere Port, Manchester, Swinton and Bristol	None	28
1920	Bradford, Lancaster, Grays and Morecambe	None	32
1921	Gloucester	Bolton (2)	31
1922	Darlington and Grimsby	Grays and Morecambe	31
1923	None	Cefn Ruabon & Bridgewater	29
1924	None	Stockton	28
1925	Kettering and North Watford	Hoylake	29
1926	Carcroft	Gloucester	29
1927	Nelson	None	30
1928	Abergavenny, Denton and Scunthorpe	Nelson and Swinton	31
1929	None	Brockhurst	30

These statistics are compiled from the lists at the back of the relevant copies of *HMJ*.

[118] *HMJ,* May, 1920, p. 54. It is stated that nearly 1,000 were present at the final meeting.
[119] On substituting the *Journal* for the *Holiness Herald,* which they had previously edited and sold, when their mission at Kettering joined the International Holiness Mission, David Thomas gave them the right to contribute a monthly article.
[120] *HMJ,* Editor's Notes, Nov., 1919 and Feb., 1920.
[121] *Ibid.,* April, 1908, p. 4.
[122] Handed over to the Salvation Army on October 24th, 1918.
[123] Oct., p. 109.
[124] Interview with Jessop, Emmanuel Bible College, Birkenhead, 1-8-57.
[125] *HMJ,* Aug., 1926, p. 4. Jessop was first invited while Phillips was a student at Cliff College. Above, p. 108.
[126] P. 129.
[127] P. 6.

128Announced in *HMJ*, Dec., 1929, p. 4.

129Letter from Rev. H. E. Jessop to Ford, 21-7-62. He later accepted the pastorate of Austin Nazarene Church, Chicago.

130He was in charge in October. See "Manchester Letter", *HMJ*, Jan., 1930, p. 5.

131Conversation with Rev. Maynard G. James at 27 College Rd., Oldham, 31-10-57, and previous conversations.

132*Ibid*. Also conversation with Rev. Wm. Henson at British Isles Nazarene College, Didsbury, Manchester, 11-8-61. Also *HMJ*, Aug., 1928, p. 5.

133*HMJ*, July, 1928, p. 8.

134*Ibid.*, Oct., 1929, p. 3.

135*Ibid.* for this period.

136The sources for this paragraph are *HMJ* for the period, the writer's personal knowledge and a letter from Rev. A. J. Lown, dated 7-9-61.

137Conversation with Henson, 11-8-61, and *HMJ*, 1930, Jan., p. 5 and Feb., p. 5.

138Entry in writer's diary, 7 and 8-10-30.

139*HMJ*, Oct., 1931, "Great Revival Tent Campaign" by A. Fawcett, and "The Challenge of the Hour" by Maynard G. James. Writer's diary, 19—26-9-31.

140*HMJ*, Dec., 1931.

141*Ibid.*, 1932, Mar., p. 8, and June, p. 5.

142*Ibid.*, July, 1932, "What the Lord did in Leeds".

143*Ibid.*, 1932, June, p. 8, Aug., p. 5, Sept., p. 5, Oct., p. 5.

144The writer recorded in his diary on 16-8-32 that both James and Wain used these words.

145*HMJ*, Feb., 1933, p. 5.

146*Ibid.*, 1933, Sept., p. 3, Oct., p. 5, Dec., p. 5, and 1934, Feb., p. 8.

147*Ibid.*, 1933, Oct., p. 2, Nov., p. 5, and conversation with Rev. J. T. Henson at the British Isles Nazarene College, Didsbury, Manchester, 30-9-61.

148*HMJ*, 1934, Feb., p. 6, April, p. 5.

149*Ibid.*, May, 1934, p. 1.

150*Ibid.*, 1934, June, p. 5, July, p. 3, and the writer's diary, 30-4-34, 4 and 5-5-34.

151*HMJ*, Sept., 1934, p. 3, and the *Dewsbury Reporter*, 14-7-34 and 11-8-34.

152*HMJ*, Oct., 1934, p. 3, and the writer's diary, 13 and 14-8-34.

153*HMJ*, 1930, July, p. 4, Aug., pp. 1 and 2.

154*Ibid.*, Sept., 1928, p. 4.

155P. 1.

156The writer was well acquainted with Leonard Wain, acting as his assistant at the Headquarters, Battersea, from October 30th, 1930, to March 8th, 1931, and being in close contact with him until he left Croydon in April, 1934.

157Wain had left the business some years before this to take over a draper's shop previously managed by two of David Thomas's sons.

158All these men were personally known by the writer. This paragraph is the result of his personal knowledge and of research done by him in the *HMJ*.

159Cf. Ministerial lists, *HMJ*, Jan., 1929, p. 7, and Sept., 1934, p. 8.

160In the May *HMJ*, 1929, £50-7-0d was acknowledged; in the Dec., *HMJ*, £144-3-6d; but by Feb., 1930, it had risen to only £155-11-9d.

161*HMJ*, July, 1932, p. 4, and writer's diary, 23-5-32.

162*HMJ*, May, 1934, p. 4.

163See *HMJ*, May, 1931, p. 2.

164Holmes and those like-minded objected to people being invited to come forward to be prayed over and anointed for healing. They insisted that in the chief proof-text for faith healing, James 5:14, 15, the sick person is told to call the elders to pray over him and anoint him, not vice versa. James and his colleagues contended that this applied to pastoral practice, but that in the evangelistic itinerary of the apostles it seems that they took the initiative (cf. Mark 6:13).

165*HMJ*, July, 1933, p. 4.

166Writer's diary, 26-1-34.

167Writer's diary, 3-4-34.

168Writer's diary, 9 and 10-10-34, and personal recollections. Also conversation with James and Henson at British Isles Nazarene College, Didsbury, Manchester, 22-9-61.

169Executive Council Meeting 23-4-35. Apparently these half-yearly ministerial conferences were promised the ministers at an Emergency Conference in November, 1934.

170The Conference had the power to co-opt others, not exceeding seven, to act in an advisory capacity.

171"A Suggested Administration", opposite Minute 11, 18-3-35, Minutes of the I.H.M. Ministerial Conference.

172Wain, Lane, Dunning, Walker, Fawcett, Yeo and Waterson.

173Executive Council Minutes, 14-4-36. Cited hereafter as IHMECM.

174It is composed of the Executive Council, the ministers, probationers and leaders of the missions, and lay representatives of the missions in the ratio of one for fifty or fewer members, and one for each additional fifty.

175A Suggested Administration for the International Holiness Mission, adopted at Manchester, Oct., 1936. With this the following year an administration for the missions was incorporated and adopted in Oct., 1937.

176Relevant copies of *HMJ*.

177IHMECM, 22-10-40.

178*Ibid.*, 17-10-50.

179He was assisted in the formation of it by Lown, Yeo and some of the other ministers.

180They were made honorary vice-presidents, and invited to attend Executive Council Meetings and to report. IHMECM, 27-3-51.

181He declined the invitation.

182The main sources for the above section are the relevant IHMECM.

183July, 1930 to April, 1931.

The International Holiness Mission • 137

[184] May, 1931 to June, 1932.
[185] July, 1932 to April, 1934.
[186] May, 1934 to April, 1938.
[187] May, 1938 to May, 1941.
[188] June, 1941 to April, 1946.
[189] May, 1946 to December, 1952.
[190] IHMECM, 13-10-39, 27-4-43, 11-10-49, 17-10-50. The circulation of the *Journal* was as high as 15,000 in 1934, when the strength of the Mission was increasing owing to the Forward Movement Campaigns. *HMJ*, Jan., 1934, p. 4.
[191] Conversation on the phone with Sydney M'Caw on 20-12-61.
[192] See Sunday School Constitution in Minute Book of the IHM Ministerial Conference opposite items 17 to 20, 6-3-36.
[193] Between Jan., 1935 and Nov., 1936.
[194] At the Easter Executive Meeting, 1947, 604 entries were reported.
[195] Apparently the suggestion was not generally followed and in the Executive Council Meeting of 12 and 13-10-48 it was made clear that each mission was free to make its own decision in the matter.
[196] IHMECM, 15 and 16-4-52.
[197] First suggested at the Executive Council Meeting, 30-3-37 and commenced under the supervision of Winterburn and J. T. Henson in 1944 (IHMECM, 10-10-44).
[198] Suggested at the Executive Council Meeting, 23-4-35 and put into the hands of D. W. Lambert, M. A., of Cliff College at the Executive Council Meeting, 14-10-35. A revision of the probationers' course was proposed in the Executive Council Meeting, 12-10-37, and in the Executive Council Meeting, 8 and 9-4-47, Maclagan introduced "a comprehensive new four year course of study for Probationer and Ministers' Examinations".
[199] IHMECM, 13-10-42.
[200] "All appointments of Pastors shall be decided by the Executive Council in conjunction with the local church." Suggested Local Administration, October 1937, Item 7.
[201] IHMECM, 15 and 16-4-52.
[202] Actually the International Holiness Mission suffered comparatively little in the way of material loss during the war. No mission was destroyed, neither was any minister or member of the Executive Council killed, and even among the members of the missions the loss sustained was not large. War restrictions inevitably hampered the work, and they were the cause of the closing of the mission at Eastbourne. (See IHMECM, 22-10-40.) But the Mission survived the Second World War, as it had done the first, scarred but in no sense disabled.
[203] International Holiness Mission. Overseas Missionary Department. Numerical Statistics I. Presented at the Executive Council Meeting, 15 and 16-4-52.
[204] H. Kenneth Bedwell, *Black Gold* (Cape Town: Cape Times Ltd., n.d. [c. 1936]), p. 45.
[205] IHMECM, 22-10-40.
[206] *Ibid.*, 27-4-43.

138 • *In the Steps of John Wesley*

²⁰⁷*Ibid.*, 11-4-50.
²⁰⁸Notably G. D. Holmes, who was always ready with several hundred pounds to meet a need and included a £6000 legacy for the South African work in his will.
²⁰⁹In 1946 a credit balance of £4,124-15-8d was reported.
²¹⁰IHMECM, 16-10-51.
²¹¹*Ibid.*, 17-10-50.
²¹²The name which James and his companions gave to the denomination which they formed.
²¹³Interview with Miss E. K. Crossley, Crowborough, 26-11-58. C. J. Fowler spoke at Star Hall, Manchester, at Easter, 1910. (See *Way of Holiness*, March, 1910, back page.)
²¹⁴*HMJ*, Aug., 1927, p. 5.
²¹⁵*Ibid.*, Dec., 1930, p. 4.
²¹⁶Reported in the Executive Council Meeting, 11-10-38.
²¹⁷*HMJ*, Jan., 1940, p. 11, and the *Flame*, Jan., 1940, p. 13.
²¹⁸IHMECM, 14-10-41.
²¹⁹Writer's diary, 7-2-46, and Calvary Holiness Church Executive Council Minutes, 7-2-46.
²²⁰IHMECM, 15-10-46, p. 4.
²²¹Calvary Holiness Church Executive Council Minutes, 16-2-48 and 3-3-48.
²²²Calvary Holiness Church Ministers' Meeting, 31-3-48, Minute 2.
²²³IHMECM, 11-10-49, pp. 3 and 4.
²²⁴*Tongues of Fire*, March, 1907, p. 6, and Oct., 1909, p. 6.
²²⁵In 1947 a Sunday School *Board* was elected and a *Board* of Examiners was appointed. (IHMECM, 14 and 15-10-47.) "Board" is a Nazarene, not an International Holiness Mission term. The question of infant baptism was raised at the Easter Executive Council Meeting, 1948, and it was conceded in the autumn Executive Council Meeting that water could be used at the dedication of an infant providing the parents requested it. At Easter, 1952, a resolution concerning baptism almost identical with Article 18 in the Nazarene Manual was recommended to the Executive Council from the Delegates Conference.
²²⁶J. Place was elected as chairman of the Executive Council at the meeting held on October 16th, 1951, but the office of President was left vacant.
²²⁷The facts in this paragraph are gleaned from the relevant Executive Council Minutes.
²²⁸Twenty-seven churches with about 1,000 members and twenty ministers constituted the home section of the International Holiness Mission which joined the Church of the Nazarene. (The churches are given by name in the *Way*, Jan., 1953, p. 12. The Nazarene *Manual*, 1956, p. 22, states about twenty churches. The Nazarene *Manual*, 1960, p. 20, states twenty-eight churches, over 1,000 constituents and thirty-six missionaries. The *Other Sheep*, Jan., 1953, p. 1, implies twenty-five churches. I have arrived at the figure of twenty ministers by research in the Executive Council Minutes.)

CHAPTER 4

The Calvary Holiness Church

ITS ORIGIN AND FORMATIVE YEARS 1934-1939

Founders

Though not forgetful of their debt to the International Holiness Mission in which they had found enriching fellowship in faith and service, the dominant sentiment of Maynard James and his companions in the days immediately following their resignations[1] was a mixture of relief for the ending of tension and restraint and of hope and anticipation for the future.

The thirties were young men's years. Mussolini and the Fascists had captured Italy; Hitler and the Nazis were rising to power in Germany; and Mosley and his uniformed followers were marching the streets of Britain. More to the point was the success of comparatively young men in raising up religious groups by the method of revival and healing campaigns. The brothers Stephen and George Jeffreys and Stephen's son, Edward, were all young men when they launched their campaigns. With these precedents, James and his companions felt their youth to be more of an asset than a liability. To them the world presented a field of conquest rather than a testing ground of experience and caution.

140 • *In the Steps of John Wesley*

Maynard G. James was the only one of the four over thirty years of age, and the only married man. Reference has already been made to him in the history of the International Holiness Mission. Born[2] and brought up in the small mining town of Bargoed in South Wales, James lost his father while still a boy and hard times were not unknown at No. 2 Cross Street. Leaving the Higher Elementary School at the age of fourteen, he found employment first at the Powell Duffryn Company, Bargoed, then at the Llan Bradach Colliery. Later, in 1920, he took a job at the Mental Hospital in Cardiff as a junior research chemist. There was a period of nine months unemployment during the national coal strike. From his background he derived the conservatism of the Welsh Valleys, leavened by experience of a great, howbeit Welsh, city, and a sympathy for and understanding of the working class.[3] His parents were Baptists, but from his conversion at the age of thirteen he attended the Bargoed Holiness Mission.[4]

Jack Ford was the youngest[5] of the four, though next to James in seniority in the ministry. The son of a Hull business man who retired on his capital at the age of fifty-five, he attended Hymers College as a fee-paying pupil. He left school at the age of fifteen and a half and took life leisurely as a junior clerk in a corn merchant's office. A casual contact with a zealous tract distributor in the summer of 1927 stimulated a desire in him for a conscious relationship with God and an assurance of personal salvation. Receiving the desired experience in a time of private prayer, Ford threw himself wholeheartedly into evangelistic activities. Although brought up and confirmed in the Anglican Church, he was introduced to the Holiness Church of the International Holiness Mission in Coltman Street, where he lived, by the lady responsible for his conversion.[6] Here through addresses and testimonies he heard about the experience of entire sanctification, and he eventually claimed the experience at the Japan Evangelistic Band Convention at Swanwick in June, 1928. Here, too, he met James and the Trekkers when they visited Hull in May, 1929, and he was invited to join the trek party.[7] When the trek finished in the September, Ford entered Cliff College, serving as chairman for the final term. After leading the southern trek in the summer of 1930, he was appointed to assist Wain at the headquarters in the November. In less

The Calvary Holiness Church • 141

than six months he was inducted to the pastorate of the Addiscombe Mission Church, where he remained until he joined James and Keeley on the revival party in May, 1934. A close friendship developed between James and Ford in which the younger looked up to the elder for vision and leadership and James leaned heavily on his lieutenant's judgment and advice.

Leonard Ravenhill was also a native of a large Yorkshire city. Born in Leeds, he attended the Cross Flatts Council School there until the age of thirteen. Two years later he entered the employment of Montague Burton's tailoring works to learn to be a cutter. Ravenhill attended the Methodist New Connexion church with his parents. His father had a remarkable conversion from a life dominated by alcohol; Leonard was converted at the age of fourteen. As a young man he began to attend the services of the Leeds Holiness Mission and to seek the experience of entire sanctification, which he eventually received under James's ministry in 1929. He joined Ford's southern trek in 1930. After a year at Cliff College and a further period on trek, he spent the next two years as assistant pastor to Fawcett at Bolton, becoming James's assistant at Oldham in the autumn of 1933. He took part in the revival campaigns at Oldham (1932) and Salford (1933). When James left Oldham for the summer campaigns of 1934, Ravenhill remained in charge and for the next two years he exercised a dynamic evangelistic ministry there. Ravenhill devoted himself to a ministry of preaching and prayer. A colourful personality, he could catch the imagination of the crowd, and, although he held no major administrative office[8] in the Calvary Holiness Church, he undoubtedly exercised a considerable influence in the early days of the Church.[9]

Clifford Filer, Ravenhill's close friend, was a miner. He was born in Bedwas, a small mining community, about eight miles from Bargoed. His father, also a miner, was respected as one of the trustees of the local Methodist chapel and a local councillor for thirty years. Clifford showed some degree of both mental and athletic ability. He passed the test for grammar school but was unable to go for economic reasons. He was converted at the age of eighteen in an evangelistic campaign in Tre-Thomas conducted by Rev. Wm. Jones, a

142 • *In the Steps of John Wesley*

Presbyterian minister. In December, 1928, he claimed the experience of entire sanctification, largely through the influence of Maslen, who was also a member of the Bedwas Methodist Chapel. Again through Maslen's influence, he joined the Trekkers in 1931, and he took part in the Bolton campaign. After a year at Cliff College, he became a member of the revival party in the Oldham campaign (1932), and in the autumn he joined Phillips as assistant pastor in Manchester. Participating also in the Salford campaign in the summer of 1933, he remained as Keeley's assistant at the close. When Keeley joined the revival party in 1934 Filer took charge of the Salford church. Filer was essentially a man's man. He gave the impression of strength and ruggedness, and he was no mean debater in a rather narrowly logical style. His ability as a leader was shown in his pioneer work on the mission field, but before he left in 1937 he contributed a virility and strength to the leadership of the new Movement in its formative years.[10]

Inauguration

Within a short time of their resignations the churches at Salford and Oldham decided to join James and his colleagues and the one at Queensbury applied to do the same.[11] This confronted them with the challenge of leadership and compelled a decision concerning the commencing of a new denomination. Such an idea was not absent from their minds, but there were other possibilities. Their evangelistic gifts were valued by the Church of the Nazarene, which was concentrating on a forward drive, and the months immediately after their leaving the International Holiness Mission were spent in Nazarene campaigns at Uddingston, Coatbridge and Govan.[12] But the pressure of events called for a swift decision. And so, on November 8th, they met to form themselves into an Executive Council of four to legislate for the two churches which had joined them and to state the terms on which they were prepared to receive the application of the church at Queensbury. A further meeting on January 15, 1935, gave a name to the new Movement and accepted the church at Queensbury and the church at Bradford, formerly affiliated with the International Holiness Mission.

The items dealt with in these first two Executive Council

The Calvary Holiness Church • 143

Meetings give an important insight into the priorities of the new Movement. After the election of James as president and Ford as secretary, it was decided that the name of the party engaged in pioneering work should be the "Pilgrim Revival Party".[13] Here then was a Movement committed to extension at the laying of its foundation stone. It was to be a Movement with central government in the form of an Executive Council,[14] with an official ministry,[15] an annual Easter Convention,[16] an official magazine named the *Flame* and with Holiness embodied in its name, the Calvary Holiness Church.[18] The emphasis of James on prayer is reflected in item 6, 8-11-34,

> It should be made a rule in all the centres connected with the Movement that a week of prayer should be held at the beginning of every year, a day of prayer and fasting should be held once a quarter, and a half night of prayer should be held the first Saturday of every month.

The pattern is familiar. So much of the old Movement is reproduced in the new that one might well question its *raison d'etre*. No mention is made of the gift of tongues, which had been made such an issue by the Executive Council of the International Holiness Mission. The doctrine of the new Movement is assumed to be identical with the old. Indeed, until Articles of Faith were drawn up in the middle of 1936,[19] the churches at Oldham and Salford used International Holiness Mission application for membership forms, complete with the International Holiness Mission Articles of Faith, with the simple substitution of "Calvary Holiness Church" for "International Holiness Mission"! This does not mean that there was no difference in the attitude of the two Movements to the gifts of the Spirit. But it is questionable whether it would have become a point of division if it had not been made a point at issue.

On their return from Scotland for the Easter Convention at Oldham, James and Ford set about the task of extension. After a campaign in the Church of the Nazarene, Morley, during May, a revival and healing campaign was held in the Movement tent, New Street, Barnsley, in June and July, in which a real impact was made on the non-church-attending population.[20] Ford remained in charge of the work when the tent and most of the team moved on to Bradford. Sunday

144 • *In the Steps of John Wesley*

evening congregations of between 250 and 300 continued to meet in the Temperance Hall, Pitt Street.[21] As a result of the Bradford campaign in Westgate in August and September the existing church there was increased from an average attendance of fifty to 250, and moved into larger premises in Kirkgate.[22]

The winter months were spent in consolidation. The following year witnessed a forward move which was never to be surpassed in the history of the Calvary Holiness Church. On February 24th, 1936, a revival and healing campaign was commenced in the Co-operative Hall in the conservative market town of Skipton. Before the close the two largest Methodist churches were filled on successive Sundays to hear the Pilgrims, and a church was formed with a congregation of about 200.[23] A campaign was held in the Welfare and Cooperative Halls in Thornaby[24] followed by two tent campaigns: the first on the Market Ground, Colne,[25] and the second on the Cattle Market, Burnley.[26] Churches were raised up in the three places with congregations of 150,[27] 250,[28] and 300,[29] respectively. The year was brought to a close with a short campaign in the West End Liberal Club, Pudsey, where a small church was formed with a congregation of about sixty. Besides the churches established as a result of the campaign method, a small church numbering about thirty was formed about the middle of the year in Rochdale, consisting in its inception mainly of those residing there who previously attended the church in Oldham. Campaigning in 1937 opened in Barnoldswick, near Colne. An unresponsive campaign followed in Haworth, near Keighley, and in the summer a tent campaign in Eccles resulted in a church being formed with a congregation of about 100.[30] In 1938, two churches were established in Yorkshire: one as the result of a tent campaign in Sheffield,[31] with a congregation of 180,[32] and the other in the small town of Hebden Bridge,[33] after a campaign notable for its Sunday evening rallies, with a congregation of about 100.[34]

Under gathering war clouds, five campaigns were held in 1939. Gillingham, in Kent, was visited in February[35] and a church with a congregation of about forty was formed. In Middleton, near Manchester, a tent campaign was held during the months of June to September, culminating in a church

The Calvary Holiness Church • 145

with a congregation of about 170,[86] and a tent campaign commencing in August, held in connection with Trinity Hall, Grimsby, resulted in an increase in the congregation to about 130.[87]

Colleagues

It is obvious that this programme of extension could not have been effected without a considerable accession of workers. When the four founders left the International Holiness Mission, John McMullen and George Thomas were already on campaign with James and Ford in Keighley, and within a few weeks H. E. Lewis and the church at Queensbury elected to join them. Further reinforcements came: in 1935, eight; in 1936, seven; in 1937, ten; in 1938, four; and in 1939, six.

They came from different denominational backgrounds. Twelve came from the International Holiness Mission and twelve were Methodists. Of the remainder, six came from the Pentecostal Movement, three from churches of the Calvary Holiness Church, one from the Church of England and there were two Baptists. Understandably, the appeal was strongest to those belonging to denominations which stood in the Wesleyan tradition and emphasised a second experience of cleansing and power.

Most of them had had previous experience in full-time Christian work,[38] and at least sixteen of them had attended some Christian training institution.[39] Probably no more than six had attended grammar school, and most of them were manual workers before entering full-time Christian service. Although there was still a good deal of unemployment during these years, it is worthy of note that almost without exception those who were not already in full-time Christian work or training gave up employment to offer themselves for the work of the Calvary Holiness Church.

Church Life

The churches raised up by James and the revival party inevitably reflected the mind of their founders. Those who composed the churches of the Calvary Holiness Church were

146 • *In the Steps of John Wesley*

for the most part active in service and wholehearted in their support of the work. Some who had been attracted by the novelty of the campaign soon lost interest, which accounted to some extent for the sharp decline in the congregations of the new churches during the first year or two of their existence. But those who remained participated in a weekly programme of prayer, Holiness and testimony meetings and sought further to extend the work by open air meetings[40] and the Sunday evening evangelistic service.[41]

The campaign emphasis on faith healing was maintained in proportion to the outlook of the pastor appointed to take charge of the local church. It was made clear, however, by the Delegates Conference in 1938 that invitations should be given to the sick in the distinctive Sunday evening revival and healing service, and that a weeknight meeting should be appointed as a suitable time when Christians might make a personal request to the Pastor for anointing.[42] There was little in the way of speaking in tongues in the churches. It was permitted, when the occasion was considered appropriate, as being biblical, rather than encouraged as being desirable, and as only a minority of the pastors (and none of the founders) claimed ability to exercise the gift, the laity were for the most part content to hold belief in it as a little understood tenet of faith rather than seek it as a *desideratum* for the full-orbed Christian life.

Children's meetings were a part of the pioneer campaigns, and Sunday School work was organised as a feature of the newly formed church. In most campaigns young people made up a substantial proportion of the congregation, sometimes being in the majority. While they attended most of the other meetings in the local church, once the campaign was over a meeting was organised specially for them in which they were encouraged to take part on similar lines to the Christian Endeavour societies. Missionary meetings came to be held monthly[43] after the organisation of the Calvary Holiness Church Missionary Society, and boxes were made available for both the Missionary Society[44] and the Forward Work,[45] while local secretaries were appointed to stimulate interest in both phases of the new denomination's outreach.

Several months were allowed to elapse after the conclusion of a campaign before members were made.[46] At first all authority was vested, under the Executive Council, in the local pastor, and members' meetings were called at his discretion.[47] As soon as practicable a treasurer and secretary[48] were appointed. The main layman was the lay delegate who was elected by the church to represent it at the Delegates Conference. He was the one appointed to be the vehicle of any appeal on the part of the members of the local church to the Executive Council.[49] Later deacons were appointed. The Delegates Conference laid down the rule that they should be selected by the pastor and submitted to the church for election, with the proviso that in the case of a new church the first time deacons were to be appointed their names should be submitted to the Executive Council for approval.[50] In 1943 the Delegates Conference defined their function as being to advise and assist the pastor in the government of the church.[51]

Baptism by immersion upon confession of faith was held as an article of faith and administered at the request of worthy applicants.[52] It was not made a condition of membership. The sacrament of the Lord's Supper was generally, though not universally, observed every Sunday morning, often as the central act of worship.

Administration

Like most Christian sects, the Calvary Holiness Church evolved; it organised itself as it grew, much of its organisation being a response to the stimulus of need. James carried over from his contact with David Thomas an apprehension of over-organisation. In his conception the Calvary Holiness Church was meant to be an evangelising agency with only sufficient organisation to conserve the gains of revival campaigns and provide an environment for spiritual development and service for the new recruits. At the same time he had a deeply ingrained esteem for order and authority which forced him, sometimes with uneasy after-thoughts, into the role of legislator.

James, Ford, Ravenhill and Filer had made the Constitution of the International Holiness Mission a matter of principle, and they were aware that the attainment of power brought with it a test of their good faith. Accordingly, in

148 • *In the Steps of John Wesley*

their second Executive Council Meeting in January, 1935, they came to the following decision:

> The existing Council should remain in office for two years, counting from Easter 1935. At Easter 1936, three laymen should be elected by the delegates from the various churches of the Movement. At Easter 1937, the entire Council should stand for re-election, and the elected members should remain in office for three years.[53]

By October, 1935, however, they had changed their minds:

> After consideration, prayer, and consultation with experienced leaders[54] in Christian Churches, it was decided that the constitution of the Executive Council should be altered.
>
> Bro. James proposed that the policy outlined to the Delegates Conference and unanimously endorsed thereby should be adopted viz. the Founders of the Movement i.e. Bros. James, Filer, Ravenhill and Ford, should be made trustees and permanent members of the Executive Council providing they maintain their spiritual experience, doctrinal belief, and membership in the Movement; at Easter 1936 two lay members of the Delegates Conference should be nominated by the present Executive Council for election by the Delegates Conference[55] to sit on the Executive Council for one year, at the end of which the entire Executive Council, excluding the permanent members, should stand for re-election or change for a period of three years. This proceedure (sic) to continue until and after the maximum number (i.e. nine) of Council Members is completed. The maximum number of nine Executive Council Members is to consist of five ministers and four laymen with one of the ministers as President.[56]

In its favour it could be said that the laymen were given a vote equal in all respects to that of the ministers, even though the ministers retained a majority of one. Against it could be levelled the criticism that apart from the founders only one minister had the opportunity of a seat on the governing body of the Movement and that the founders had secured their position on the Executive Council for life. The logic of the former criticism made itself felt and eventually the number of the Executive Council was increased to thirteen. It is impossible to say how far their own security entered into the decision of the founders but their reply to the latter criticism would have been that as founders they had a right and duty to see that the Movement they founded continued on the lines of their commission.[57]

The Calvary Holiness Church • 149

If James and his colleagues were concerned to keep power in their own hands while the Movement was taking shape, they showed an equal concern to consult their coworkers and the churches. As early as Easter, 1935, they called together "An Informal Conference between Ministers and Workers of the Calvary Holiness Church, Who Met at the Invitation of the Executive Council, to Help It Find Out the Mind of the Churches Associated Therewith."[58] This was the forerunner of the Delegates Conference which was convened in Bradford the following October.[59] The Delegates Conference was composed of the Executive Council, the pastors of the churches and a lay delegate from each church, elected to attend two half-yearly Conferences. At first its decisions were subject to the confirmation of the Executive Council, but it increased in power in the course of time and from Easter, 1942,[60] it ceased to be a recommending body and became a legislative body.[61] Every major issue was brought before it and its endorsement was obtained before anything of primary importance became law. And it elected the members of the Executive Council.

Missionary Work:

For the first months of the new Movement the question of an outlet for missionary enthusiasm was a matter of concern. The churches at Oldham, Salford and Bradford had been encouraged to support the missionary work of the International Holiness Mission in South Africa, and there was an understandable reluctance to take any action which would weaken a cause which commanded the sympathy of those who knew it. But in autumn, 1935, the Delegates' Conference decided that the best course was to inaugurate the Calvary Holiness Church Missionary Society.[62]

Candidates were soon forthcoming for the new society. At the Executive Council Meeting in October, 1936, Filer and his fiancée, Elenor Gregory, with George Thomas and his fiancée, Edith Moore, applied and were accepted as the first missionary candidates.[63] Norman P. Grubb, the secretary of the Worldwide Evangelisation Crusade, who was a speaker at the Bradford Convention held at the same time as the aforementioned Executive Council Meeting, offered the infant missionary society the benefit of his experience and the co-operation of the Worldwide Evangelisation Crusade. His offer was gladly accepted and the first step was taken in the direction of united service in which Grubb became the missionary secretary of the Calvary Holiness Church and the Worldwide Evangelisation Crusade became a testing centre for its missionary candidates and a springboard for its missionary enterprises. Filer and Thomas sailed for Colombia in April, 1937, and were followed by Miss Gregory. After a period of preparation at the headquarters of the Worldwide Evangelisation Crusade in Bogota, they set out in March, 1938,[64] for Santa Marta to establish the first Calvary Holiness Church mission field. In 1939 Miss Moore and Annie Noble joined them, and a national worker, Francisco Martinez, was also received on the missionary staff.[65]

Unum Corpus

The fact that the Calvary Holiness Church was a unit rather than a loose association of independent churches was an important factor in its forward drive both in the homeland and overseas. This sense of unity was fostered in several ways, one of which was Movement conventions of the International Holiness Mission pattern. The Easter Convention was always held in Oldham, where, until the Bible College was established in Stalybridge, was the official headquarters of the church.[66] An autumn convention was inaugurated in 1935 with Bradford as its venue in pre-war years. At each convention it became customary to ask converts in recent campaigns to testify, which added a sense of expansion to the feeling of fellowship. Testimonies and addresses were expected to give prominence to the Movement's emphasis on the experience of full salvation, and as each member was required to subscribe to the Movement's Articles of Faith the ideal of a common faith was another unifying element. A distinctive badge to be worn only by members emphasised the uniqueness and unity of the brotherhood, and the *Flame*, the official organ of the Calvary Holiness Church,[67] was at the same time a rallying point and an evangelising agency.[68]

This consciousness of unity led to the demand for a Calvary Holiness Church Sunday School Union. It was first put on the agenda of the Delegates Conference at Easter, 1937,[69]

The Calvary Holiness Church • 151

and, after consideration by the Delegates[70] and a conference of Calvary Holiness Church Sunday School workers and the Executive Council,[71] the Union was authorised. Its function was defined as the holding of annual conferences and the appointing of an examination committee to arrange examinations. It was resolved that each Sunday School should contribute to it.

Ministry

The ministry played an important part in the corporate life of the Movement. Suitable applicants were received by the Executive Council as probationary ministers on a term of three years probation, during which time they were expected to pursue a set course of study and pass annual examinations.[72] During their probation they were given the title of "Pastor" and were permitted to take charge of a church and conduct the sacraments. On the successful completion of the three years' probation, which involved satisfying the Executive Council regarding their spiritual experience, their mental attainments and pastoral ability, they were ordained with the laying on of hands by the ministers of the Executive Council and other ordained ministers, and they were given permission to use the title of "Reverend"[73] and to wear the ministerial collar.[74] The Executive Council fixed the salary of the ministers and no church was allowed to alter the scale of remuneration without its permission.[75] The salaries rose with the cost of living, but remained at a comparatively low level, and if the finances of the local church were low there was no guarantee that even this slender allowance would be received.[76]

To promote fellowship and to facilitate pulpit exchanges, the ministers met in circuit meetings about once every five weeks. The circuit meetings played an important part in maintaining the close-knit structure of the Movement. But if the ministry was a vital link in the bond of unity, under the authority of the Executive Council and representing the authority of the Executive Council in the local churches, it was also an indication of the fluidity of the Movement. In the period under review, of the thirty-two who joined the Movement as full-time workers (excluding the founders), fourteen resigned. These frequent changes of personnel,

152 • *In the Steps of John Wesley*

which persisted throughout the history of the Calvary Holiness Church, gave the impression of instability to the thoughtful observer. But such changes are not without parallel in other movements with similar ideals and methods.

By the close of the period the pattern of leadership was set. James was made president of the Movement for life, with Ford as vice-president and his successor to the presidency for life.[77] James was established as the undisputed leader of the Movement, universally respected as a man of vision and prayer, whose gifts as an evangelist had been the main factor in the raising up of the new churches. Ford came into increasing prominence as an administrator, his appointment as general secretary giving at the same time recognition and scope to what ability he possessed in this direction. Ravenhill resigned as a member of the Executive Council and a permanent trustee at Easter, 1938, and Filer was absent in Colombia from 1937 to 1945. Opportunity was given in the Delegates Conference and in the Executive Council for free discussion and expression of opinion, but the fact remained that if James and Ford both gave their support to a measure it was more than likely to be adopted.

THE WAR YEARS, 1939-1945

Reaction to War

The Munich Crisis brought at least one benefit. It helped to prepare the nation for war, not only in the realm of arms and men but also in the realm of ideas. Special prayer meetings were held as the crises heightened both in 1938 and 1939, and from the pulpit and via the medium of the *Flame* the infant society sought, in its limited sphere, to speak to the nation's need.[78]

The threat of war also caused the Movement to look to its own affairs. In January, 1939, the registration of the Movement at the Supreme Court of Judicature was effected to give it legal constitution in the eyes of the Government,[79] and shortly after the outbreak of war steps were taken to define the position of probationary ministers and evangelists, and those due for ordination were ordained.[80]

The prevailing opinion among the ministers of the Movement was against a Christian engaging in military service. It was not universal, and it differed with regard to the degree of participation. Of the founders, Ravenhill held the most pronounced pacifist view. Ford believed that a Christian should not undertake combatant service, but that he could, and should, serve in the R.A.M.C. James was clear that a Christian minister, and, perhaps a Christian layman, should refuse to fight, but he believed that there was a national duty to restrain an aggressor even to the point of military action, and that through wars nations were humbled and chastened in the will of God.

Believing that guidance should be given to its readers, Ford wrote an editorial for the September-October issue of the *Flame* stating the case for Christian pacifism. As the threat of war became more imminent, James, fearing lest the *Flame* might be officially suppressed and anxious that young Christians of the contrary opinion might not feel condemned for enlisting, arranged for a footnote to be added emphasising that the views expressed were purely personal and not an official statement on behalf of the Movement and that every true follower of Christ was free to follow the leadings of conscience.

This incident gives a fair insight into the general attitude of the Movement to war. It was mainly non-combatant but tolerant of the opposite view. Some of the young men, especially in the early days of the war, registered as conscientious objectors, but others, in increasing numbers as the war proceeded, responded to the call of military service.

Very few connected with the Movement were killed during the war, although the homes of some were destroyed in the air raids. The building in which the church at Cardiff met was destroyed by bombing, but another was obtained.[81]

Campaigns and Conventions

At the outbreak of war there was considerable uncertainty in the British churches regarding what would be the scope for Christian service. But under the bold leadership of James,[82] the Calvary Holiness Church did not hesitate for long. It was decided to proceed with the autumn convention, although on a somewhat smaller scale than hitherto, and the Houldsworth Hall, Manchester, was filled for the first wartime convention.[83] Throughout the war, conventions were held

154 • *In the Steps of John Wesley*

as previously at Easter and in the autumn, with additional seasonal conventions at Whitsuntide and Christmas.

Campaign work also continued. In 1940, tent campaigns were held in Stalybridge and Hazel Grove during the summer, and in the spring and autumn churches were raised up as a result of indoor campaigns in Sale and Llay.[84] Wales was the scene of campaign work in 1941, with campaigns at Cardiff, Bargoed[85] and Ebbw Vale. There was, however, little to show for the effort.[86] In 1942, a tent campaign resulted in a new church being established in the Roath district of Cardiff.[87] A church was established in Bath by a tent campaign in 1943.[88] The following year campaigns were conducted in Holmcroft Hall, Bromley, which joined the Movement, and in the Wesleyan Reform Church, Channing Street, Sheffield, which was rented with a view to establishing a Calvary Holiness Church centre there. In the same year, the ministers of the Lancashire Circuit established a small church in Mossley, near Ashton-under-Lyne.[89] In the final year of the war, a tent campaign was held in Walthamstow to strengthen the work at Bethany Hall, which had joined the Movement in 1944.[90]

The Admittance of Previously Established Churches

Originally it was the intention of the founders to extend the Calvary Holiness Church by raising up churches by the campaign method. They considered that churches raised up in this way had the advantage of an initial enthusiasm and would readily accept the discipline of the Movement. When the church at Bradford was received into fellowship, it was on the understanding that a campaign would be held in connection with it and that a virtual new beginning would be made. This became the pattern for established churches which applied to join the Movement in later years, though existing conditions did not always permit a complete adherence to it.

During the war, churches at Cardiff, Grimsby, Ashton-under-Lyne, Walthamstow and Bromley applied for admittance and were accepted. Both the Cardiff church and Trinity Hall, Grimsby, were formerly affiliated with the International Holiness Mission. Trinity Hall withdrew from its affiliation in 1938 and was accepted by the Calvary Holiness

The Calvary Holiness Church • 155

Church in 1939,[91] and the Cardiff church transferred its allegiance in 1940.[92]

Typical of the previously established churches was the Old Cross Mission, Ashton-under-Lyne, begun in 1874 as an evangelistic work among the unchurched poor. On September 15th, 1912, it affiliated with Star Hall, Manchester, and continued under its supervision until Star Hall was handed over to the Salvation Army in 1918. At one time a flourishing centre of evangelism and Holiness teaching, by 1939 it was at a low ebb and the leaders applied for union with the Calvary Holiness Church. After sending two successive pastors to supervise the mission, the Calvary Holiness Church received it as a church within the Movement in April, 1942.[93]

Of these five churches which joined the Movement in the war years, Trinity Hall, as well as Holmcroft Hall, reverted to its former independent existence.[94]

The Ministry

The conscription of men for national service made candidates for the ministry a major problem during the war. Nevertheless, during the six years no less than twenty-three were added to the ministerial staff of the Calvary Holiness Church. But fifteen resignations largely offset the additions. Early in the war, James and Ford interviewed representatives of the Government to define the nature of the Calvary Holiness Church's ministry, and the probationary as well as the ordained ministers were given exemption from national service.[95] Partly to maintain this status and partly to emphasise that the ministry should demand a man's full time and energies, the Executive Council declared that they were not in favour of ministers engaging in part-time secular work.[96]

Some attempt was made to remedy the frequent changes in the personnel of the ministry, and in 1940 and 1945 ministers were asked to sign an agreement of service in which they stated that they believed that they were divinely called to serve in the Calvary Holiness Church.[97]

James showed an increasing sensitivity to the opinion of the ministers and in the autumn Delegates Conference in 1944 he asked them to indicate whether they wished him to remain as president. A unanimous ballot vote in favour was recorded.[98]

Administration

The Executive Council continued to exercise decisive authority in the Movement, though the Delegates Conference increased in numbers and importance. Ravenhill, who had resigned from the Executive Council in 1938, was re-elected to it at Easter, 1940.[99] Two other ministers, who had shown administrative ability, George Deakin, assistant missionary secretary from 1938, and Cyril J. Pass, were also promoted to the Executive Council: the former at Easter, 1943,[100] and the latter in the autumn, 1944, on the withdrawal of Randolph Murray.[101]

While the lay members were able to play an important part in the bi-annual meetings at Easter and in the autumn, there was a tendency for meetings to be called at short notice to deal with emergencies, which laymen, owing to their secular occupations, had little opportunity of attending. This led to the passing of legislation concerning the constitution of a quorum. For matters other than routine measures the quorum was fixed at four Executive Council members, including at least one layman. In matters of grave emergency it was ruled that the whole Executive Council should be called.[102]

This insistence on the place of the laity in the government of the Movement was reflected also in the resolution of the Executive Council concerning the minister's power of excommunication:

> Where there are deacons, they should be consulted by the Minister; but where there are no deacons, the Pastor must bring offending members before the members previous to excommunicating them. In the event of the Minister and deacons, or the Minister and members disagreeing in their verdict, the matter should then be referred to a committee of the Executive Council, consisting of not less than three members, with at least one layman, which will give the final decision.[103]

It was further laid down that

> before new members are received into any Calvary Holiness Church membership they should be brought before the Deacons (or if no Deacons, before a Church Members' meeting) for approval.[104]

It would, however, be false to read into the above items of legislation anything approaching a sharp conflict between the ministry and the laity. No legislation could have been passed without the consent of the ministerial members of the Executive Council. But there was a genuine desire to govern the Movement on biblical lines and, since it was believed that the New Testament gave the laity an important say in church affairs, demands and needs in these areas were given sympathetic attention by the whole Executive Council.

As a witness to the corporate consciousness of the Movement, there came into being in 1941 the Central Building Fund Committee "for the acquirement of Church and Manse Property."[105] Some attention was given to the drawing up of a Model Trust Deed on which property could be held and it was decided that when it took definite shape all the churches of the Movement should use it when purchasing buildings.[106]

A further evidence of the unity of the Movement, as well as its desire to propagate, was the formation of the Pilgrim Publishing House to provide and publish literature for the Movement.[107]

Other Developments

The war years saw the development of several other important trends which had their origin in the first five years of the Movement's history.

Missionary Work. The work in Colombia was not only maintained but extended. At the outbreak of war there were five missionaries there: the Filers, the Thomases, Miss Moore and Miss Noble. Two others, Samuel E. Heap and Gwladys Jones, sailed for Magdalena at the close of 1940.[108] By Easter, 1942, there were "eight groups of believers".[109]

In spite of opposition, there were frequent reports of conversions and baptisms.[110]

War conditions imposed restrictions on the amount of money which could be sent to the missionaries and complicated the matter of furloughs.

Filer's leadership came in for favourable comment,[111] and at the home end George Deakin established himself as an able assistant missionary secretary under Grubb.[112] In

158 • *In the Steps of John Wesley*

1945, the highest income for missionary work was reported: £1,251.[113]

Youth Work. The work among the young was likewise maintained. At Easter, 1941, the terms of Junior Membership were drawn up at last,[114] though by June, 1945, no more than a dozen junior members were seported. The Calvary Holiness Church Sunday School Union reported 109 teachers and 701 scholars at Easter, 1941,[115] and several helpful teachers' conferences were convened under its auspices. Under the stimulus of the Government's scheme to direct young people into youth organisations a special Delegates Conference was called on May 29th, 1943. After considering affiliation with an existing youth organisation, it was decided to form a new one with the name of the "Calvary Holiness Church Covenanters". Maslen, and later Briggs,[116] endeavoured to draw up a scheme similar to that of the Campaigners, but only a minority of the churches participated in it.[117]

The Flame. The *Flame* continued on its course during this period in spite of the vicissitudes of war and the paper shortage. It changed shape and texture several times and at the beginning of 1942 its price was raised from a penny to twopence, but it fought a creditable battle with adverse conditions and in September, 1941, it actually reached the highest circulation of its history, 25,000 copies.[118]

The pattern set by the first issue persisted. The editorial, by James or Ford, dealt with devotional, prophetic, moral and social matters, while reports of campaigns and church activities, articles on salvation, Holiness and prophetic themes, testimonies and missionary news occupied a prominent place in its pages. It maintained an interdenominational character in its contributors and a number of articles were written by members of the Church of the Nazarene, the International Holiness Mission and the Emmanuel Bible College. The interchange of writers in the official organs of the Holiness groups undoubtedly assisted in promoting unity among them.

The Trend to Unity. In closing this section on the war years a word should be said about the movement to closer unity between the Holiness groups which took place during the period. Mention has already been made in the history of the International Holiness Mission of the agreement reached

The Calvary Holiness Church • 159

by the leaders of that denomination and the leaders of the Calvary Holiness Church in a meeting at Bolton in October, 1939. In May, 1942, following a united prayer conference at the Emmanuel Bible College, Birkenhead, in the April, a National Holiness Association was formed in London[119] in which the Calvary Holiness Church, the International Holiness Mission and the Church of the Nazarerne participated. This was perhaps the biggest step in the direction of unity between the Holiness groups which had been taken up to that time. It is not without significance that it took place in the context of the national solidarity of the war years.

CONSOLIDATION AND FRUSTRATION, 1945-1950

As the war came to an end hopes were entertained for an extension of the work.[120] These hopes were only partially realised.

Progress

The most notable extension took place in the missionary work. During the war there were seven missionaries on the field. At the beginning of 1947 they were joined by three others.[121] In 1946 Bessie Southall went to India and was joined in 1947 by Mr. and Mrs. R. Brown[122] and by Hilda Hartley a year later.[123] Headquarters were established in Abbottabad in 1949,[124] and later the party moved to Deri Ismael Khan, in a district handed over to them by the Church Missionary Society.[125] A work was also begun in France in 1947 by Mr. and Mrs. D. Cole.[126]

The Colombian work made steady if not spectacular progress. Reference was made to conversions and in September, 1945, it was claimed that not 10% of the converts had fallen away.[127] In Pakistan nothing in the way of establishing permanent churches was done. The work at Deri Ismael Khan was in the nature of an evangelising centre for the area with a dispensary for treating the sick. In France the work developed mainly on the lines of literature evangelism, and in 1949 it was reported that 50,000 Scripture portions[128] had been distributed besides which a considerable use was made of Scripture posters.[129]

In Britain the most important innovation during this period was the inauguration in 1947 of the Beech Lawn Bible

160 • *In the Steps of John Wesley*

College at Uppermill as the ministerial training college for the Movement. At first a united college with the Church of the Nazarene at Hurlet was discussed,[130] but the project came to nothing. A gift from H. H. Hales, the most generous donor to the Calvary Holiness Church, secured college premises for the Movement[131] and with James as the principal and seven students a start was made.[132] By 1948 larger premises were needed and they were obtained in Mottram Road, Stalybridge.[133] At Easter, 1950, James reported sixteen students with the following denominational alignment: Calvary Holiness Church, 4; International Holiness Mission, 3; Undenominational Missions, 5; and one each from the Church of England, the Methodist Church, the Church of Ireland and the Presbyterian Church.[134]

Ironically, the provision of a source of supply for new churches was accompanied by a decline in the effectiveness of Forward Movement evangelism. No large church was raised up. Campaigns were held in Darlington (1946),[135] Rotherham[136] and Barrow[137] (1947), Poplar (1949),[138] and Wrexham (1950).[139] Of these, only the church raised up at Rotherham became a permanent addition to the Calvary Holiness Church. Those at Barrow and Poplar left the Movement; the former in 1949[140] and the latter in 1950.[141] That at Darlington closed in 1948.[142] At Wrexham the organising of a church did not proceed beyond the initial stages.

But if the Movement experienced difficulty in multiplying churches, it found a widening sphere of influence through its official organ, the *Flame*. In 1947, James, who for many years had borne the main burden, was appointed editor and Ford and Hawkins associate editors.[143] In 1945 the ideal *Flame* secretary was found: Miss E. Howarth, the leading member of the Rochdale church.[144] She informed the Delegates Conference in September, 1950, that the circulation of the *Flame* had reached 22,000: 13,379 copies inside the Movement, and 8,621 outside.[145]

Developments in Organisation

When in 1948 C. J. Pass laid down his duties as treasurer of the General Fund and the Central Building Fund preparatory to leaving Britain for service in South Africa, he

The Calvary Holiness Church • 161

described his six years term of office as coinciding with "years of growing Movement complexity and organisation".[146]

Pass himself was a driving force in the process. He was a man with some business experience and an indefatigable worker. His reading was almost as wide as his extensive library, and he combined ability as a Bible teacher[147] with evangelistic zeal and pastoral success. Being willing and able to do work for which others were too busy or disinclined, he multiplied offices and seats on committees and played a major part in the developing organisation of the youthful society.[148]

What Pass was to home affairs, George Deakin was to the missionary side of the Movement. His conscientious attention to administration and his liaison with the missionaries, the Executive Council, the Delegates Conference and the churches[149] kept the missionary work at the heart of the Movement as a whole.

The Delegates Conference continued to play an important part in the corporate life of the Movement. It was more than an administrative assembly. It was a place where the president could present a spiritual challenge, where the Executive Council could communicate its decisions, where the sectional leaders could invite support and inform the delegates of the state of the Movement's affairs, where the delegates could challenge the leaders and where grievances could be aired.

Six committees were appointed during the period under review. In addition to the Executive Council Sub-Committee and the Triumvirate, they were the College Committee (1945),[150] the Missionary Sub-Committee (1946),[151] the Sunday School and Youth Committee (1947),[152] and the Forward Work Committee (1947).[153]

There was little change in the life of the local church. It was decided by the Delegates Conference in 1945 that deacons should be elected annually along with all other local officials. At the same time a deacon could not be removed from office between elections without the consent of the Executive Council.[154]

The preponderance of capable women in the membership was reflected in the request of the churches at Oldham[155] and Rotherham[156] for permission to elect women deacons.

162 • *In the Steps of John Wesley*

In neither instance was the request granted, but at Skipton the church took the initiative and in 1947 appointed one of the leading women to the diaconate.[157]

The position of the ministers remained much the same as in the previous period. They were consulted regarding the proposed union with the International Holiness Mission in 1948,[158] and in 1949 they recommended to the Executive Council that a united prayer conference for the two movements be called.[159] The only revolutionary change was the decision to abandon the fixed scale of remuneration. Previously the Executive Council had recorded its acceptance of the principle "to every man according to his need not according to his mental attainments".[160] In 1948, partly because they felt that diligence and responsibility should be rewarded and partly because the meagre stipends made it difficult to invite ministers of ability to pastor the larger churches, it was decided to adopt the principle of a sliding scale.[161] The maximum stipend was fixed at £6 per week, plus rent and health stamp. A recommendation was adopted from the Ministers Meeting that the minimum stipend of a married ordained minister with no children should be £5 per week.[162]

Frustration

A child of adversity, the Calvary Holiness Church had accepted poverty and sacrifice as marks of the New Testament Church. But when the attempt is made to sustain and extend a movement on slender resources, poverty can pinch until it hurts. There are many signs that the Calvary Holiness Church reached this stage during the years under review. The giving of the members was creditable and the sacrifice of the ministers and missionaries bordered on the heroic. Generous gifts at critical times were hailed as the providence of God.[163] But year after year Pass reported deficiencies in the Movement's funds and pleaded that something be done to put them on a sound basis.[164] At one time nearly half the churches were defaulting on the quota of 1-3d in the pound of local church income towards the administrative fund of the Movement,[165] not because of lack of concern but because of the pressure of balancing the local budget. By the end of the period under review the General Fund was stabilised, but in 1948 the missionary income began to de-

The Calvary Holiness Church • 163

crease in spite of increased commitments.[166] Further to complicate matters, in 1949 the devaluation of the pound made inroads into the amount being sent to the mission fields.[167] A falling off in college income was reported in 1950[168] and financial pressure made it necessary for the Central Building Fund to think in terms of selling manses rather than helping to buy them.[169]

Nowhere was the financial strain felt more than in the missionary work. At the April meeting of the Executive Council in 1946, Filer raised the question as to whether the work in Colombia should be continued by the Calvary Holiness Church. He expressed the opinion that the Thomases and the Heaps were almost at the end of their physical resources, and he mentioned the financial complications of the steep rise in the cost of living in Colombia. After a long discussion the Executive Council decided that the Filers and Miss Noble should return to the field after their furlough, with Grainger and the Thompsons as reinforcements, and that the Heaps and the Thomases should be brought home for recuperation.[170]

Problems multiplied. The Filers' re-entry permits were held up,[171] and both the Heaps and the Thomases came home on furlough and returned before the Filers eventually went back in 1951. Thomas's health remained uncertain.[172] Bessie Southall had a major operation.[173] The Thompsons returned to give their baby the chance of needed medical treatment and tendered their resignations on doctrinal grounds.[174] Most serious of all, Deakin adopted the Pentecostalist view that the sign of the baptism of the Holy Spirit is the speaking in tongues and tendered his resignation at the end of 1949.[175] Titterington's resignation as missionary treasurer was expected after the secession of the Bromley church and it became effective at the same time.[176] With falling income, divest of capable organisers and with withdrawal from the major field still under discussion, this was the situation of the missionary work in 1950.

A similar frustration was encountered in the Forward Work. Each year expectations were raised concerning a new church being born, only to find that it died in infancy or left home in its first years. A Forward Work Committee was formed to improve planning and organise support. But, as

164 • *In the Steps of John Wesley*

already mentioned, the only new church to show for the five years was that at Rotherham.

Denominational Youth Work practically came to a standstill by the close of this period. At the beginning, Briggs was set aside for youth evangelism with a free hand to conduct campaigns in the churches.[177] But, frustrated by a succession of disappointments, Briggs resigned from the Movement in August, 1946, and although he withdrew his resignation shortly after,[178] he abandoned the leadership of the Youth Work.

No one felt the tensions of this period more than James. Extension was a part of his nature and anything approaching withdrawal or a mere maintenance of the *status quo* gave him deep concern. To add to his burden, his leadership came under criticism by some. James, like most religious leaders of the charismatic type, had a strain of mysticism. "Signs" and "seals" and inward impressions as well as providential circumstances all played a part in his attempt to discern the will of God. This caused some to question his ability as an administrator,[179] although they admired his piety and his power as an evangelist.[180] James, as has already been mentioned, was not without administrative ability, but he retained from his formative years in the International Holiness Mission some of David Thomas's fear of over-organisation.[181] He deplored what he considered the excessive time spent in Executive Council meetings,[182] and there are repeated references in the minutes of this period to his late arrival and his departure before the close.[183] For most of this period he was in charge of the college and he took his responsibilities there seriously. But previously it was expected that Executive Council meetings should be given priority over other duties. When James was absent, Ford took the chair, which was probably another reason for James's irregular attendance. He wished his friend to be given opportunities of supervising the administrative work which some thought him better fitted to do than himself. In 1948, James asked that a committee of three, called the "Triumvirate", should be elected to discharge his presidential responsibilities while he was in charge of the college,[184] and Ford was chairman of this committee during the years of its existence. But it is possible to exaggerate the frustration which James experienced. He was

The Calvary Holiness Church • 165

encouraged to see the number of the students at the college rise from seven to sixteen. Some indication of his future international ministry was given in successful evangelistic campaigns in U.S.A.[185] and Paris.[186] We h a v e already commented on his success as the editor of the *Flame*. In December, 1947, his second book[187] was published, entitled "Facing the Issue", in which he gave his convictions on doctrinal issues which had challenged his attention, and for which there was, at first, a ready sale.

During the period under review the additions to the ministry balanced the resignations. But the losses were serious. Murray resigned in 1945 to take the pastorate of the Zion Holiness Mission, Birmingham.[188] Ravenhill, feeling called to interdenominational evangelism, resigned in 1951.[189] These resignations, with those of Pass and Deakin, left large gaps in the structure of the Movement. Charles Levy took over the missionary secretaryship,[190] J. H. Liversidge became missionary treasurer,[191] C. H. Warman took Pass's place on the Central Building Fund Committee[192] and J. H. Taylor became secretary of the Delegates Conference.[193] But the sense of loss remained.

At the close of 1950, the Calvary Holiness Church stood at the cross-roads. Its future was determined in the next five years.

UNION WITH THE CHURCH OF THE NAZARENE, 1950-1955

Although the Calvary Holiness Church had experienced considerable frustration during the third quinquennium of its existence, few if any of its members had any thought of the possibility that by the close of the fourth quinquennium its existence as a separate denomination would come to an end. Though the frustration of the previous years persisted, it was repeatedly challenged by sanguine attempts to dispel it, attempts which initially met with some success.

Hope and Renewed Endeavour

In September, 1950, Ford succeeded James as the principal of the college.[194] Of the record number of students during the summer term half had completed their course and there was only one application. But Ford's introduction of tuition

166 • *In the Steps of John Wesley*

for the London University Certificate of Proficiency in Religious Knowledge[195] caused two of the students who had completed their course to return for a further year,[196] and seven new students at the beginning of the 1951 session maintained the number at eleven[197] and gave some promise for the future.

Undeterred by the sparse results of the previous years, strenuous efforts were made to raise up new churches. James left for a visit to the Colombian mission field via a preaching tour of U.S.A. in May, 1951,[198] but in his absence campaigns were held in Knutsford and Deal.[199] The following year, with James back to lead the attack a campaign was held in Rotherham and another one at Deal.[200] The effort to extend was maintained in 1953 with a campaign at Dinnington,[201] near Sheffield, and a campaign in connection with the Scotstoun Mission, Glasgow, which joined the Movement.[202] In the September R. L. Travis was released from the Sheffield pastorate to become the full time organising secretary of the Forward Work,[203] and an ambitious programme was planned for 1954.[204]

In the Youth Work there were signs of a revival of interest in the form of district conventions for leaders of youth activities,[205] and rallies[206] and holiday camps [207] were organised for the young people of the Movement. Several churches reported an encouraging response among the young.

Indeed, the reports of the churches generally in the Delegates Conferences during the period under review have an optimistic tone.

Although the circulation of the *Flame* contracted from 20,000 in 1951 to a stable 17,500, the decrease was within the Movement and its ministry to the outside public actually increased.[208] As far as the Pilgrim Publishing House was concerned the appointment of Potts as its sales manager in 1951[209] brought fresh life to a dying cause and each year he reported progress in sales and profits.[210]

The financial stability of the General Fund and the Forward Fund achieved in 1948 was maintained.[211]

In the case of James himself this period had its encouragements. Released from the responsibility of the principalship of the college, he was given the opportunity of exercising his evangelistic ministry in other lands. In 1951,

The Calvary Holiness Church • 167

he wrote concerning his visit to the Nazarene Pasadena College, "I am having one of the most wonderful times of my life."²¹² In the autumn and winter of 1953-54 in his South African tour he experienced the most sustained period of evangelistic success in existing churches which he had ever known.

Elusive Success and Multiplying Problems

However, though the period had its brighter aspects the clouds of frustration remained and problems multiplied.

This was especially true of the overseas work.

The critical condition of the work in Colombia at the close of 1950 became more acute in the period under review. At first hopes were raised that the granting of the Filers' visas in 1950²¹³ after a delay of four years would give the work the needed stimulus and stabilise the situation. But Filer had not been on the field long before he became convinced that it was impossible to maintain the work on the present income.²¹⁴ James, who left England about the same time as the Filers, made his way to Colombia via a preaching tour of U.S.A. and met the missionaries there.²¹⁵ After his return to England, the Executive Council passed the following resolution:

> We do not feel that we should withdraw as a society from the Field, but we fully understand the action of any missionary who resigns if he or she cannot continue under the present distress. We believe that the present distress will pass and we look to the Lord to sustain His work till the storm passes.²¹⁶

The financial position remained acute, in spite of the efforts of the home churches.²¹⁷ The Filers considered the situation unbearable and, feeling that their presence on the field was a financial embarrassment to the other workers, they returned at the end of 1952.²¹⁸ They were followed by the Thomases six months later.²¹⁹ This left the Heaps, Miss Noble (working as a nurse for the United Fruit Company to ease the financial situation) and Martinez as the total Calvary Holiness Church missionary force in Colombia.²²⁰

By arrangement with the Worldwide Evangelization Crusade Mr. and Mrs. Alan de Gruyter were loaned to maintain the headquarters in Santa Marta.²²¹ In 1954 the Heaps were brought home for a much needed furlough.²²²

168 • *In the Steps of John Wesley*

The missionary work on the other two fields suffered a similar attenuation. In 1952 the Coles, with the full consent of the Executive Council, transferred their poster work to the Mission to Europe, retaining their membership in the Calvary Holiness Church.[223] The Browns returned on furlough from Pakistan in 1953, reduced in health and unable to return for the time being.[224]

Thus, by the end of 1954, only four Calvary Holiness Church missionaries were on the field: Miss Noble and Martinez in Colombia, and, in Pakistan, Bessie Southall and Doris Woodward, who had returned with Miss Southall after her furlough in 1953.

Forward Work presented a similar picture. Mention has already been made of the determined attempts to recapture the former success of extension by the campaign method, but the only permanent additions to the Movement were previously existing missions at Scotstoun and Thornton which united with it after campaigns had been held in them.

The college experienced a similar decline. The number of students dropped to nine in the autumn of 1952,[225] to six in 1953 (of whom only two finished the course)[226] and to two men and three women students in the autumn of 1954.[227] Ford resigned in the summer of 1954 and James was appointed principal again, reintroducing the former course and dropping the course for C.R.K., but the situation remained the same.[228]

The financial pressures which had exerted such influence on the mission field were also felt in the home ministry. But the problem with which the ministry confronted the leaders of the Movement was doctrinal rather than financial.

In spite of the sacrifice involved, perhaps challenged by it, there were fourteen who entered the ministry of the Movement during this period. Some of these, aware of the freedom permitted by the Calvary Holiness Church for the exercise of the gifts of the Spirit, put a greater emphasis upon the gifts than the founders had done. By a strange irony the gifts of the Spirit figured as a contributory cause to the end of the Calvary Holiness Church's independent existence as they had done to its origin.

It was a matter of concern to James and Ford lest the Movement they had done so much to found should exchange

The Calvary Holiness Church • 169

its original Holiness emphasis for a Pentecostalist emphasis on the gifts of the Spirit. For the gifts to be permitted was one thing; for them to become paramount was quite another. They realised that to make the Calvary Holiness Church an integral part of a larger Holiness movement would be a safeguard against such a tendency.

In addition to the factors already stated was the fact that the International Holiness Mission appeared to be functioning smoothly as a part of the Church of the Nazarene, its missionary problems solved, its resources increased, with the enhanced prestige which belongs to a large denomination and participating in that unity with those likeminded which makes its own appeal to those who take the New Testament standard as the pattern of their church life.

Steps to Union

The union of the Holiness movements of Britain had been a recurring ideal in the minds of James and Ford throughout the history of the Calvary Holiness Church. During the negotiations between the Church of the Nazarene and the International Holiness Mission in 1952, Ford had written "We pursue our course in charity towards all God's people, and welcome every opportunity of a deeper unity with our Holiness Brethren".[229]

Investigation. When, therefore, in the summer of 1954 the trends we have been tracing became so evident, it was natural that they should consider the possibility that providential circumstances were pointing in the direction of union. James and Ford took the initiative and arranged a meeting with George Frame at the City Station Hotel, Leeds, on September 6th, to discuss the prospects of union. As a result of the discussion Frame was invited to meet the Executive Council in Ashton-under-Lyne the following day. The outcome of the meeting was favourable to further investigation of the matter and the ministers of the Movement were called together for consultation at a meeting in Salford on October 27th.[230]

At the opening session James outlined the steps which had led up to the meeting.[231]

The ministers had been made aware of the nature of the meeting and had been asked to ascertain the mind of their

170 • *In the Steps of John Wesley*

deacons concerning union. Of the thirty ministers and leaders present less than a dozen were prepared to commit themselves definitely in favour of union, and the ascertained opinions of the deacons were only slightly more favourable.

In the evening Frame and Maclagan joined the conference and answered questions on the setup of the Church of the Nazarene internationally and in Britain. Further questions were asked relative to baptism, divorce, the gifts of the Spirit and pastors' stipends.

> In giving the position of the Church of the Nazarene, Dr. Frame said that he felt a basis of union with the C.H.C. should be our unity concerning Second Blessing Full Salvation. Our job as the Church of the Nazarene is not to propagate or practise the gifts of the Spirit, but to emphasise the definite experience of Full Salvation.[232]

After Frame and Maclagan had retired the following motion prevailed: "That we view with favour union with the Church of the Nazarene, and set in motion further investigations." It received twenty votes.[233] It was decided that the churches should be visited by members of the Executive Council, and, if possible, representatives of the Church of the Nazarene, and if, in the opinion of the Triumvirate, there was sufficient interest in the churches in union, that Frame and Maclagan should be invited to the Delegates Conference, which would decide whether representative committees of the two Movements should be set up.[234]

Hesitation and Reconsideration. Nevertheless, there was uneasiness among some of the ministers. Travis sought to give expression to the feeling of some by sending out a circular letter inviting those who preferred a reorganisation of the Calvary Holiness Church to fusion with the Church of the Nazarene to make their desire known by November 20th so that the Executive Council could be informed of the position. He suggested reorganisation on the following lines:

The doctrinal statement of the Calvary Holiness Church to be maintained with its doctrine of the gifts of the Spirit and believers baptism by immersion.[235] The property of the local church to be under the complete control of the local church with liberty to develop or dispose of it without reference to any outside persons.[236] The existing system of a

The Calvary Holiness Church • 171

central authority to be discontinued and some kind of Coordinating Board to be formed to consider pastoral applications and to act as an advisory council at the request of any church.[237]

There was nothing in the nature of a conspiracy about the letter. Both the president and vice-president received a copy with the other ministers. But James was quick to see that it could virtually split the Movement down the middle. He made an immediate response. On the same day[238] as he received Travis's letter he drew up a circular letter in reply. In it he assured the ministers that Travis's had no authority from the Executive Council and urged them to do nothing hasty. He reminded them that he had made it clear in a meeting on October 27th that the Calvary Holiness Church would join the Church of the Nazarene as a *society* or would remain as an independent movement, when reorganisation would be in order and necessary. He invited those who did not favour fusion to ask for a meeting of all Calvary Holiness Church ministers as soon as possible to face up to the alternative.[239]

Although only three requests for such a meeting were received by James,[240] the ministers were called together again at Oldham on December 16th.

In the meantime James had addressed a letter to Frame[241] setting out the position of the Calvary Holiness Church with regard to the baptism of the Spirit and the gifts of the Spirit. It became one of the vital documents relating to union. The following are extracts:

> We affirm as the Calvary Holiness Church that we are one with the Church of the Nazarene in the glorious doctrine of entire sanctification, wrought by the Baptism with the Holy Ghost and fire and receivable by faith....
>
> (1) We do *not* believe that speaking in other tongues is the initial evidence of the Baptism of the Holy Spirit.
>
> (2) We do not deny that there may be a genuine gift of 'tongues' in operation today, and so we dare not adopt the unscriptural attitude of forbidding to speak in another tongue *provided* we are *sure* it is really of the Holy Spirit....
>
> (3) We believe that 'speaking in tongues' is the least of the nine gifts.... Time and again it has been found that its unwise use in the Church assemblies has led to strife, spiritual pride and division....

Therefore . . . we feel, after painful experience, that we cannot encourage our people to speak in other tongues in Church gatherings. . . .

(4) We believe that the infallible proofs of a Spirit-filled life are:
- (a) purity of heart (Acts 15, 8-9).
- (b) the fruits of the Spirit (Galatians 5, 22-23).
- (c) perfect love to God and men (Romans 5:5; I Timothy 1:5).
- (d) power for effective service for Christ (Acts 1, 8).

(5) If freedom of conscience be given to us on the aforementioned matters, and confidence be reposed in us as ministers of Christ to do all in our power to further the interests of Scriptural Holiness through the agency of the Church of the Nazarene, then we would gladly welcome the fusion of the C.H.C. into the Church of the Nazarene and would count it a privilege to serve as ministers in its ranks.

It is essentially the position adopted by James, Filer, Ravenhill and Ford at the founding of the Calvary Holiness Church, though it is more cautious. There is still the refusal "to forbid to speak in another tongue", but, "after painful experience", the conclusion is reached that "we cannot encourage our people to speak in other tongues in Church gatherings".

James read his statement to the ministers assembled at Oldham on December 16th and declared that "if the Church of the Nazarene were prepared to accept the same, there was no reason which he could give to the Lord for staying outside of fusion".

But the meeting had been called to consider alternatives to fusion and suggestions were invited. There was considerable discussion. A request was made for information about the voting of the churches on the issue. James reported sixteen out of nineteen churches visited in favour of fusion with a total vote of approximately two hundred for fusion, ninety against and fifty-five doubtful.[242]

Towards the close of the afternoon a proposal was put to the meeting "that we go ahead with fusion, providing the question raised by Bro. James's statement be agreed to by the Church of the Nazarene H.Q.", on which the voting was seventeen for, three against and four abstentions. There was general agreement that if the Calvary Holiness Church was to continue reorganisation should be given priority and a proposal to this effect was carried almost unanimously.

The Final Stage

In America, the approach of the Calvary Holiness Church concerning union was brought by the general superintendents before the General Board of the Church of the Nazarene at its meeting in Kansas City in January, 1955, and authority was given by it to the British Advisory Council to negotiate the basis of union with the Executive Council of the Calvary Holiness Church.[243] The two bodies met at Beech Lawn Bible College on February 8th and 9th. Agreement was reached on both home and missionary affairs. It was agreed that the final decision concerning the missionary work of the Calvary Holiness Church should be negotiated with the general superintendent having the oversight of the British Districts and presented for approval to the General Board, and that those missionaries not favouring union should be brought home at the Movement's expense. It was also agreed that the *Flame* should be maintained as a means of conveying the Holiness message to the wider public. The Nazarene representatives indicated that they would be prepared to sponsor a revival party with James as leader. The final decision as to the location of the College was to be made in two years' time. It was agreed that the two present districts should continue for the time being, but that the question of further division should be considered at the District Assembly[244] of 1956.[245]

The item which became the major point of discussion was whether the members of the Calvary Holiness Church were to be given freedom to hold their belief concerning the gifts of the Spirit in the context of the Church of the Nazarene. This was of special concern to James and it seemed as if at this advanced stage the negotiations for union might break down. At this point Ford put forward the following resolution which overcame James's misgivings and carried the consent of all present:

> That the statement drawn up by our President, Rev. Maynard G. James, which has been laid before the General Superintendents of the Church of the Nazarene expresses the convictions of those of the Calvary Holiness Church concerning the Gifts of the Spirit.
>
> We understand that, in welcoming us into the Church of the Nazarene, the authorities give us freedom to hold these convictions although they may not express the official Nazarene attitude.

We join the Church of the Nazarene loyally accepting the Manual and desiring to serve with freedom of conscience as loyal Nazarenes.

It was agreed that this should be accepted as the preamble to a statement to be formulated as the Basis of Union.[246]

The next step was for the churches to be visited again and given the opportunity of registering their decision concerning union. All voted to participate with the exception of Hebden Bridge and Bradford, though it became evident that about half a dozen of the ministers would not take part in the union. By Easter, only the decision of the Delegates Conference was required. After it had considered the minutes of the Joint Meeting of the Calvary Holiness Church Executive Council and the Church of the Nazarene Advisory Council, Frame and Maclagan were invited into the Conference to answer questions of the delegates. A period of full discussion ensued. At the close of it, James put the motion that "We fuse with the Church of the Nazarene". Ford seconded the motion, which received thirty-five votes to one against.[247]

The official consummation of the union took place in the Houldsworth Hall, Manchester, on June 11th, under the gavel of General Superintendent Samuel Young and in the presence of a large congregation of Calvary Holiness Church members and Nazarenes.[248]

To Frame and Maclagan, and James and Ford, and others like them who had always enjoyed unity of spirit and seen the vision of ultimate union, the coming together of the Church of the Nazarene, the International Holiness Mission and the Calvary Holiness Church into one denomination seemed nothing less than an act of God. Frame said as much in an article in the *Flame* celebrating the union, and he closed it with a prayer reflecting the aspiration of the hour:

"O God, who in Thy Mercy and Goodness art making us one people, make us worthy of this great privilege and blessing. Keep alive in our minds the vision of Thy purpose in this unity, that all men might get to know Thee in the blessedness of Perfect Love. Grant unto us a purging and reviving anointing of the Holy Spirit, and make us as a Church a Channel of Revival. For Jesus Christ's sake. Amen."[249]

NOTES ON CHAPTER 4

[1] Above, pp. 119-20.
[2] April 17th, 1902.
[3] He attended the same school as Morgan Phillips, who later became the General Secretary of the Labour Party.
[4] Conversation with M. G. James at 27 College Road, Oldham, 31-10-57.
[5] Born October 21st, 1908.
[6] Miss Hasluck. She was an Anglican but she found the evangelistic services of the Holiness Church of value in her attempts at winning converts.
[7] He joined the Trekkers at Ellesmere Port in July.
[8] Several attempts were made to fit Ravenhill into an administrative office but his gifts and interest lay in other directions.
[9] The sources for this paragraph are a questionnaire filled in by Ravenhill's sister, Mrs. Pickles; the personal knowledge of the writer; relevant copies of *HMJ* and the *Flame* and the Minutes of the Executive Council (Cited hereafter as CHCECM) and the Delegates Conference (cited hereafter as CHCDCM).
[10] Interview with C. Filer, 186 Shaw Road, Royton, Lancs., undated. Personal knowledge of the writer. Relevant copies of *HMJ* and the *Flame*. CHCECM and CHCDCM.
[11] CHCECM, 8-11-34 (4).
[12] *Ibid.*, 8-11-34 (7), *Flame*, April-May, 1935, p. 8.
[13] CHCECM, 8-11-34 (3).
[14] *Ibid.* (4).
[15] *Ibid.* (11).
[16] *Ibid.*, 15-1-35 (2).
[17] *Ibid.* (12).
[18] *Ibid.* (14).
[19] Ford and Filer drew up the Calvary Holiness Church's Articles of Faith in the summer or autumn of 1936, and they were published in the *Flame*, Nov.-Dec., 1936, p. 19.
[20] *Flame*, Aug.-Sept., 1935, p. 8.
[21] *Ibid.*, Oct.-Nov., 1935, p. 5.
[22] *Ibid.*, Oct.-Nov., 1935, p. 4.
[23] CHCDCM, 26-10-36 (1). *Flame*, May-June, 1936, p. 5. Congregations, unless otherwise stated, are Sunday evening congregations.
[24] *Flame*, 1936, May-June, p. 16, July-Aug., p. 11.
[25] *Ibid.*, Sept.-Oct., p. 7.
[26] *Ibid.*, p. 15.
[27] Reduced to about 100 by CHCDCM, 27-3-37 (6).
[28] *Ibid.*, 26-10-36 (1).
[29] *Flame*, Nov.-Dec., 1936, p. 14.
[30] CHCDCM 16-4-38, p. 7: Sunday evening congregation given as 70-90.
[31] *Flame*, Sept.-Oct., 1938, p. 7.
[32] CHCDCM, 1-11-38 (5[l]).
[33] Commenced September 10th. *Flame* Nov.-Dec., 1938, p. 7.
[34] It was given as 75 in CHCDCM, 11-4-39 (11[m]).

176 • In the Steps of John Wesley

[35]*Flame*, 1939, Jan.-Feb., p. 8 and pp. 10 and 11, May-June, p. 9.
[36]CHCDCM, 31-10-39 (5[e]).
[37]*Ibid.*, (5[f]).
[38]About twenty-five.
[39]Cliff College: eight; Emmanuel Bible College, Birkenhead: seven; the Bible Training Institute, Glasgow: one.
[40]CHCECM, 12 and 13-4-39 (26).
[41]CHCDCM, 26-3-40 (4).
[42]*Ibid.*, 16-4-38 (11).
[43]*Ibid.*, 26-10-36 (6).
[44]CHCECM, 22-24-10-35 (11).
[45]CHCDCM, 26-10-36 (2).
[46]Even after churches were established a period of probation was specified for applicants for membership. *Ibid.*, 1-11-38 (16).
[47]*Ibid.*, 16-4-38 (12).
[48]*Ibid.*, 26-3-40 (11).
[49]*Ibid.*, 19-10-37 (13).
[50]*Ibid.*, 16-4-38 (12).
[51]*Ibid.*, 27-4-43 (23).
[52]*Ibid.*, 16-4-38 (10).
[53]CHCECM, 15-1-35 (13).
[54]Notably Rev. Buckhurst Pinch.
[55]This seems a combination of *Conge d'Elire* and one party government. Actually it was intended to give guidance to the delegates of the Movement during its formative years.
[56]CHCECM, 22-24-10-35 (14). See also CHCDCM, 21-10-35 (2).
[57]See CHCDCM, 23-4-46 (3).
[58]CHCDCM, 20-4-35. The precedent for this and the Delegates Conference was the meeting of Ministers, Leaders and Workers on the Saturday morning of the Easter Convention of the International Holiness Mission.
[59]CHCDCM, 21-10-35.
[60]The last reference to the endorsement of the Minutes of the Delegates Conference is in CHCECM, 7-4-42 (19), referring to the Delegates Conference of September, 1941.
[61]A list of resolutions by the Executive Council and the Delegates Conference governing church life was drawn up and distributed at the Delegates Conference on 31-10-39 under the title of "Rules and Regulations of the Calvary Holiness Church, October 23rd, 1939." Additional rules were published under the title of "Rules and Regulations. Addition No. 1", October 2nd, 1940. A printed booklet was published in December, 1943, and revised in 1947.
[62]CHCDCM, 21-10-35 (5).
[63]CHCECM, 27 and 28-10-36 (16-19).
[64]*Flame*, March-April, 1938, p. 17.
[65]CHCECM, 12-4-39 (4).
[66]The change was made in 1951. *Ibid.*, 12-14-3-51 (13).
[67]So described from Jan.-Feb. issue, 1936.
[68]Churches were expected to sell as many as possible in the neighbourhood, especially in the public houses. The circulation of the

Flame expanded with the church, rising from the initial 5,000 to 18,000 by the May-June issue of 1940 (see p. 9).

⁶⁹CHCDCM, 27-3-37 (11).

⁷⁰*Ibid.*, 19-10-37 (4), 16-4-38 (7), 11-4-39 (14).

⁷¹CHCECM, 2-11-38 (10).

⁷²*Ibid.*, 8-11-34 (11 and 12).

⁷³*Ibid.*, 15-1-35 (3).

⁷⁴*Ibid.*, 31-3-37 (21). Ordained ministers of other denominations who were received into the Movement generally had their ordination recognised, though sometimes a course of reading in Holiness literature was specified.

⁷⁵*Ibid.*, 27-3-40 (25).

⁷⁶A Sinking Fund was commenced in 1937, later renamed "The Emergency Fund", for the purpose of assisting those who were not receiving the stipulated allowance.

⁷⁷CHCECM, 27-10-38 (2 and 3), also Articles of Doctrine and Government of the Calvary Holiness Church enrolled in the Central Office of the supreme Court of Judicature, January 6th, 1939.

⁷⁸*Flame*, Jan.-Feb., 1938, pp. 3 and 4; July-Aug., 1939, p. 2.

⁷⁹Action was contemplated in this direction in the first Executive Council Meeting, (8-11-34 [5]) but the process was hastened as war became imminent.

⁸⁰CHCECM, 14-9-39 (2-6).

⁸¹*Flame*, July-Aug., 1942, p. 24.

⁸²*Ibid.*, Nov.-Dec., 1939, p. 2.

⁸³*Ibid.*, Jan.-Feb., 1940, p. 9.

⁸⁴*Ibid.*, 1940, Sept.-Oct., p. 13, Nov.-Dec., p. 11. CHCECM, 14-12-40 (2).

⁸⁵CHCECM, 15 and 16-4-41 (Home 3).

⁸⁶CHCDCM, 27-9-41 (9).

⁸⁷*Flame*, Nov.-Dec., 1942, p. 19.

⁸⁸*Ibid.*, Sept.-Oct., 1943, pp. 22 and 23.

⁸⁹*Ibid.*, 1944, May-June, p. 27, Sept.-Oct., pp. 26 and 27.

⁹⁰*Ibid.*, Nov.-Dec., 1945, p. 27.

⁹¹CHCECM, 1 and 2-11-39 (13).

⁹²*Ibid.*, 20-4-40 (2b).

⁹³The above paragraph is based on an unpublished thesis by the writer entitled, "The Old Cross Mission, Ashton-under-Lyne."

⁹⁴CHCECM, 5-10-44 (7).

⁹⁵*Ibid.*, 25-1-41 (6). The date of the interview was 7-2-41 (writer's diary).

⁹⁶CHCECM, 24 and 25-9-42 (Home 14) and CHCDCM 26-9-42 (4).

⁹⁷CHCECM, 16 and 17-10-40 (11) and 19-21-9-45 (Home 13).

⁹⁸CHCDCM, 7-10-44 (13).

⁹⁹*Ibid.*, 26-3-40 (8).

¹⁰⁰*Ibid.*, 27-4-43 (18).

¹⁰¹*Ibid.*, 7-10-44 (4).

¹⁰²CHCECM, 8-5-42 (1-4).

¹⁰³*Ibid.*, 3-12-43 (8).

¹⁰⁴*Ibid.*, 4 and 5-4-45 (Home 15).

178 • *In the Steps of John Wesley*

[105]CHCDCM, 12-4-41 (5). First called *Central* Building Fund in *Ibid.*, 25-9-43 (9).

[106]CHCECM, 23 and 24-9-43 (Home 18).

[107]Commenced as a Publishing Committee (CHCDCM, 27-9-41 [3]) and later given the name of Pilgrim Publishing House (*Ibid.*, 7-10-44 [20]).

[108]*Flame*, Nov.-Dec., 1940, p. 11.

[109]CHCECM, 7-4-42 (2).

[110]*Ibid.*, 15-4-41 (2), 7-4-42 (2), 28-4-43 (2), 23-9-43 (2); *Flame*, March-April, 1943, pp. 30-31.

[111]CHCECM, 24-9-41 (3), 24-9-42 (2), 12-4-42 (2).

[112]*Ibid.*, 15-4-41 (2). Appointed *Ibid.*, 2 and 3-11-38 (12).

[113]*Flame*, May-June, 1945, p. 22.

[114]CHCECM, 15 and 16-4-41 (Home 15).

[115]CHCDCM, 12-4-41 (3).

[116]*Ibid.*, 7-10-44 (11).

[117]*Ibid.*, 11-4-44 (9).

[118]*Ibid.*, 27-9-41 (8). By the beginning of 1945 it had fallen to 16,200 (*Flame*, Jan.-Feb., 1945, p. 24) which was the average over the years.

[119]Minute Book of the United Holiness Association.

[120]"We face the future with faith and high expectation". *Flame*, Nov.-Dec., 1944, Editorial.

[121]CHCDCM, 30-3-48 (18).

[122]*Ibid.*

[123]*Ibid.*, 19-4-49 (11).

[124]*Ibid.*, 8-10-49 (6).

[125]*Ibid.*, 11-4-50 (9).

[126]CHCECM, 26-29-3-47 (36).

[127]*Ibid.*, 20-9-45 (M.S. [16]).

[128]CHCDCM, 19-4-49 (11).

[129]CHCECM, 2-4-10-50 (23 [5]).

[130]*Ibid.*, 21-9-45 (9 and 10).

[131]*Ibid.*, 27-8-46 (4).

[132]*Flame*, March-April, 1947, p. 37.

[133]*Ibid.*, Nov.-Dec., 1948, p. 31.

[134]CHCDCM, 11-4-50 (7).

[135]*Flame*, Nov.-Dec., 1946, p. 36.

[136]CHCDCM, 4-10-47 (14).

[137]*Flame*, Nov.-Dec., 1947, p. 33.

[138]*Ibid.*, Sept.-Oct., 1949, p. 25.

[139]CHCDCM, 30-9-50 (9).

[140]*Ibid.*, 8-10-49 (10).

[141]CHCECM, 13-7-51 (1).

[142]*Ibid.*, 11-13-10-48 (8).

[143]*Ibid.*, 6-8-10-47 (11).

[144]*Flame*, Sept.-Oct., 1945, p. 23.

[145]CHCDCM, 30-9-50 (17) gives 27,000, but this was incorrect. Miss E. Howarth's letter to writer, 6-4-64.

The Calvary Holiness Church • 179

¹⁴⁶CHCDCM, 31-12-48, General Fund Report.

¹⁴⁷He lectured on the Bible at the Beech Lawn Bible College, 1947-49.

¹⁴⁸He edited the Rule Book, December 1943, and drew up the first draft of the Model Trust Deed. He was appointed assistant general secretary in October, 1947.

¹⁴⁹By conferences and the *War Cry*, an occasional pamphlet giving missionary information.

¹⁵⁰CHCDCM, 22-9-45 (6).

¹⁵¹CHCECM, 24-4-46 (19).

¹⁵²CHCDCM, 4-10-47 (18).

¹⁵³CHCECM, 6-8-10-47 (56).

¹⁵⁴CHCDCM, 22-9-45 (4). In 1942 the deacon's term of office had been fixed at 3 years (*ibid.*, 26-9-42 [6]).

¹⁵⁵CHCECM, 9-4-47 (21).

¹⁵⁶*Ibid.*, 17-2-49 (11).

¹⁵⁷CHCECM, 26-29-3-47 (5).

¹⁵⁸Ministers Meeting Minutes, 31-3-48 (1).

¹⁵⁹CHCECM, 4-6-4-49 (28).

¹⁶⁰*Ibid.*, 4-4-45 (28) and 22-24-10-46 (Home 11).

¹⁶¹*Ibid.*, 11-13-10-48 (58, cf. 59).

¹⁶²Ministers Meeting Minutes, 7-10-49 and CHCECM, 10-12-10-49 (14).

¹⁶³CHCDCM, 25-9-43 (5); CHCECM, 4-5-4-45 (Home 24).

¹⁶⁴See Pass's statements in CHCDCM, 8-4-47 (5) and 30-3-48 (6 and 9).

¹⁶⁵*Ibid.*, 9-10-48 (10).

¹⁶⁶*Ibid.*, 19-4-49 (11).

¹⁶⁷CHCECM, 10-12-10-49 (Missionary 3 [4]).

¹⁶⁸CHCDCM, 30-9-50 (14).

¹⁶⁹CHCECM, 5-7-50 (11).

¹⁷⁰*Ibid.*, (Missy. 3).

¹⁷¹*Ibid.*, 11-6-47 (1).

¹⁷²*Ibid.*, 4-6-49 (11) and CHCDCM, 30-9-50 (11).

¹⁷³CHCDCM, 9-10-48 (12).

¹⁷⁴CHCECM, 20-22-3-50 (Missy. 10) and 2-4-10-50 (Missy. 23 [1]).

¹⁷⁵*Ibid.*, 12-11-49 (pp. 1 and 2).

¹⁷⁶*Ibid.*, p. 3.

¹⁷⁷*Flame*, July-Aug., 1946, p. 33.

¹⁷⁸CHCECM, 27-8-46 (10) and 22-24-10-46 (30).

¹⁷⁹His letter to writer, 22-4-47.

¹⁸⁰He asked the ministers at a prayer conference in November, 1945, whether they wished him to continue as president and again received a unanimous affirmative vote.

¹⁸¹*Flame*, May-June, 1945, Editorial.

¹⁸²Letter to writer, 29-8-51, urging that Executive Council meetings be limited to two days.

¹⁸³E.g. CHCECM, 9-3-48 (p. 2).

¹⁸⁴CHCECM, 11-13-10-48 (80).

¹⁸⁵*Flame*, Nov.-Dec., 1947, pp. 34-37.

[186]*Ibid.*, Jan.-Feb., 1950, p. 33.

[187]His first, entitled "Evangelize", was published in 1945 (*Flame*, Nov.-Dec., 1945, cover ii and iii and p. 21).

[188]CHCECM, 7-8-45 (2) and 19-21-9-45 (Home, Thurs. [5]).

[189]*Ibid.*, 12-14-3-51 (2).

[190]*Ibid.*, 12-11-49 (p. 3).

[191]*Ibid.*, 12-11-49 (p. 3) and 28-1-50 (4).

[192]*Ibid.*, T.16-12-48 (2).

[193]CHCDCM, 30-3-48 (4).

[194]*Flame*, Sept.-Oct., 1950, p. 28.

[195]CHCDCM, 27-3-51 (13).

[196]*Ibid.*, 30-9-50 (15).

[197]*Ibid.*, 29-9-51 (15).

[198]*Flame*, May-June, 1951, p. 26.

[199]CHCECM, 17-8-51 (2 and 3), *Flame*, Sept.-Oct., 1951, p. 30.

[200]*Flame*, Sept.-Oct., 1952, p. 22.

[201]*Ibid.*, Sept.-Oct., 1953, pp. 28-29.

[202]*Ibid.*, Nov.-Dec., 1953, p. 29.

[203]CHCECM, 9-4-53 (3).

[204]*Ibid.*, 13-15-4-54 (Home 6) and *Flame*, March-April, 1954, p. 30.

[205]*Flame*, July-Aug., 1950, p. 30.

[206]*Ibid.*, July-Aug., 1951, p. 20; July-Aug., 1954, p. 30; CHCDCM, 7-4-53 (6).

[207]*Flame*, Nov.-Dec., 1952, p. 28.

[208]Cf. CHCDCM, 27-3-51 (6) and 12-4-55 (16).

[209]*Flame*, March-April, 1951, p. 27.

[210]See the Reports of the Pilgrim Publishing House in CHCDCM for this period.

[211]See reports of these two funds in CHCDCM for this period.

[212]*Flame*, Nov.-Dec., 1952, p. 29.

[213]CHCECM, 9-9-50 (1).

[214]*Ibid.*, 5-11-51 (3) and 4-1-52 (8).

[215]*Flame*, Jan.-Feb., 1952, p. 17.

[216]CHCECM, 4-1-52 (13).

[217]The amount raised was about the same. It was the devaluation of the pound and the rising cost of living which complicated matters, especially in Colombia.

[218]CHCDCM, 7-4-53 (7).

[219]CHCECM, 3-7-53 (1).

[220]CHCDCM, 20-4-54 (Add. [2]) and CHCECM, 13-4-54 (5).

[221]CHCECM, 3-2-53 (2).

[222]CHCDCM, 12-4-55 (13).

[223]CHCECM, 4-6-52 (2).

[224]CHCDCM, 20-4-54 (20) and CHCECM, 13-4-54 (3).

[225]CHCDCM, 7-4-53 (10).

[226]CHCECM, 7-9-54 (4).

[227]*Flame*, Nov.-Dec., 1954, p. 24.

[228]CHCECM, 7-9-9-54 (4).

[229]*Flame*, Sept.-Oct., 1953, p. 29.

[230]CHCECM, 7-9-9-54 (11).

The Calvary Holiness Church • 181

²³¹Minutes of the Special Ministers' Meeting held in Salford Tabernacle, October 27th, 1954. Item 1.
²³²*Ibid.*, Evening Session.
²³³*Ibid.*, Proposition 1.
²³⁴*Ibid.*, Proposition 2.
²³⁵The Church of the Nazarene makes provision for baptism by sprinkling and pouring as well as by immersion, and for the baptism of infants as well as believers baptism, according to the choice of the applicant. *Manual*, 1952, par. 18.
²³⁶In the Church of the Nazarene the approval of the district superintendent is required for the purchase and sale of real estate and the erection of church buildings. *Manual*, 1952, pars. 117 and 118.
²³⁷A copy of Travis's letter is in the writer's possession. It is undated.
²³⁸James's letter is dated 5th November, 1954.
²³⁹James's letter, 5-11-54.
²⁴⁰Minutes of the Special Ministers' Meeting, held in the Tabernacle, Oldham, on Thursday, December 16th, 1954, at 10.30 a.m. Page 1.
²⁴¹Dated 30-11-54.
²⁴²James stated the figures for the individual churches. I have assessed the total vote on the basis of his figures.
²⁴³*Proceedings of the General Board of the Church of the Nazarene, Kansas City, Jan. 7-10, 1955.* Meeting No. 5, January 10, pp. 21-22.
²⁴⁴I.e. The South District Assembly.
²⁴⁵The source of this account of the meeting is "Minutes of Joint Meeting of Calvary Holiness Church Executive Council and the Church of the Nazarene British Isles Advisory Council, 8th-9th February, 1955."
²⁴⁶*Ibid.* and notes of the writer made at the meeting. The official minutes make this motion the first item as a Basis of Union, but actually the motion was made and carried towards the end of the meeting.
²⁴⁷CHCDCM, 12-4-55 (5).
²⁴⁸*Flame*, July-Aug., 1955, p. 28.
²⁴⁹*Ibid.*, p. 27.

PART II
ANALYTICAL AND COMPARATIVE

CHAPTER 5

Their Faith and Church Order

THEIR FAITH

Their Basic Theological Position

The Holiness Movement makes no pretensions to originality. Its concern is to go back to the foundations of Christianity. In its proclamation of Holiness it believes that it is simply drawing attention to Apostolic truth. It has no quarrel with the historic doctrines of the Christian Church. In the Nazarene *Manual* the Baptismal Ritual embodies the Apostles' Creed in the questions addressed to the candidate.[1]

In its early years the Church of the Nazarene was content to use textbooks by Methodist theologians for the training of its ministers: Binney (1907-1936), Field (1907-1911), Miley "or any other standard Theology of equal merit" (1911-1919), Miley or Ralston (1919-1932). Not till 1923 was a minor theological work by a Nazarene introduced, Ellyson's Compendium; and in 1932 students were given the choice between Ralston and the work of the Nazarene scholar, A. M. Hills. In 1940, H. Orton Wiley produced his *magnum opus* for which the Nazarenes had been waiting, and it has been their recognised theological textbook ever since.

The International Holiness Mission and the Calvary Holiness Church, with much slenderer resources than the Church of the Nazarene, were also dependent on the theologies of other denominations. At one time the International Holiness Mission used Torrey's *What the Bible Teaches*, eventually adopting Wiley's *Theology*, and the Calvary Holiness Church used Benjamin Field's *Handbook of Christian Theology*, supplemented later by T. C. Hammond's *In Understanding Be Men*.

All three movements were trinitarian and orthodox according to the Wesleyan-Arminian pattern.

Their Articles of Faith included the depravity of man through the Fall, the Incarnation of the Son of God, His full Atonement, His Resurrection and Ascension, His Second Advent and His Judgment of the world, the eternal blessedness of the righteous and the eternal punishment of the finally impenitent.

All taught the simultaneous work of regeneration, justification and adoption, the Nazarene *Manual*[2] defining the first as spiritually quickening the moral nature of the repentant believer. All taught that faith is the condition on which the experience is received, and the Nazarene and Calvary Holiness Church mentioned repentance as a condition also. Besides an article on Repentance, the Nazarene *Manual* includes thoroughly Wesleyan articles on Depravity and Free Agency.

As might be expected, all included an article on Entire Sanctification, which is dealt with in chapter vii below.

The intention throughout was to be orthodox. The 1907 Nazarene *Manual* had the following article on Christ.

> The eternally existant (sic) Son, the second Personality[3] of the Adorable Trinity, is essentially divine. As the divine Son, He became incarnate by the Holy Spirit, being born of the Virgin Mary, thus *joining to Himself inseparably the divinely begotten Son of Man, called Jesus*. So that two whole and perfect natures, that is to say, the God-head and manhood, are thus joined in one person, very God and very man.[4]

The words I have italicised smack Nestorianism, though Chalcedonian orthodoxy is restored in the next sentence. The 1928 *Manual* removed the ambiguity by substituting the following article:

We believe in Jesus Christ, the second person of the Triune Godhead; that He was eternally one with the Father; that He became incarnate by the Holy Spirit and was born of the Virgin Mary, so that two whole and perfect natures, that is to say the Godhead and manhood, are thus united in one person very God and very man, the God-man.[5]

The Inspiration of the Scriptures

As might be expected, all three movements lay emphasis on the inspiration of the Scriptures in their Articles of Faith.

The International Holiness Mission: "The Divine inspiration, authority and sufficiency of the Holy Scriptures."

The Calvary Holiness Church: "That the Scriptures of the Old and New Testaments are fully inspired of God, and are the only and sufficient rule of faith and conduct."

The Nazarene statement reached its present form in the 1928 *Manual:*

> We believe in the plenary inspiration of the Holy Scriptures by which we understand the sixty-six books of the Old and New Testaments, given by divine inspiration, inerrantly revealing the will of God concerning us in all things necessary to our salvation; so that whatever is not contained therein is not to be enjoined as an article of faith.[6]

Maynard James has stated his belief in the following words:

> We believe in the plenary inspiration of the original Scriptures. By that we do not mean a stiff mechanical dictation from God to man in which the human personality is suppressed . . . Plenary inspiration contends that the original Scriptures were the result of the inbreathing of God's Holy Spirit into men, qualifying them to receive and communicate divine truth without error. . . .

He admits "that God has suffered the introduction of certain faults in the copying of the sacred text" but he does not consider that this affects belief in plenary inspiration.[7]

Orton Wiley also dissociates plenary from mechanical inspiration. Outlining the theories of inspiration, mechanical, intuition, illumination, dynamical, he favours the last.[8] He defines plenary inspiration in the following terms: "By **plenary inspiration**, we mean that the whole and every part is divinely inspired. This does not necessarily presuppose the mechanical theory of inspiration, as some contend, or any particular method, only that the results of that inspira-

188 • *In the Steps of John Wesley*

tion give us the Holy Scriptures as the final and authoritative rule of faith in the Church."⁹

It will be noted that in the Nazarene quotations the inspiration and inerrancy of the Scriptures are related to its religious message. In connection with this, in an article on "The Arminian View of Inspiration" in the *Preacher's Magazine*, Ralph Earle, professor of New Testament in the Nazarene Theological Seminary, quotes A. M. Hills: "What is the infallibility we claim for the Bible? It is infallible as regards the purpose for which it was written. . . . It infallibly guides all honest, and willing and seeking souls to Christ, to holiness, and to heaven."¹⁰

And commenting on a quotation from Wiley he adds: "It should be noted that it is 'religious truth' that is received and communicated without error."¹¹

This is a scholarly exposition of the Nazarene position. A more inclusive view of infallibility and inerrancy was held by many in the three movements under review.

The Second Coming

In a list of eight characteristics of Perfectionist or Subjectivists Sects, Clark states "Practically all the perfectionist sects are premillenarian".¹²

This was true of the International Holiness Mission and the Calvary Holiness Church, both of which included the premillennial second coming of Christ and His earthly millennial reign in their Articles of Faith. But it was not true of the Church of the Nazarene. Its pronouncement in the 1907 *Manual* is as follows:

> We believe that the Lord Jesus Christ will return to judge the quick and the dead; that we that are alive at His coming shall **not precede** them that are asleep in Christ Jesus, but that, if we are abiding in Him, we shall be caught up with the resurrected saints to meet the Lord in the air, so that we shall ever be with the Lord; and that we are to comfort one another with these words.
>
> **We do not, however,** regard the numerous theories that gather round this Bible Doctrine as essential to salvation, and so we concede full liberty of belief among the members of the Pentecostal Church of the Nazarene.¹³

The second paragraph was put in small print from 1915 and omitted in 1928. The rest is a combination of a portion of the Apostles' Creed and I Thessalonians 4:15, 17 and 18,

Their Faith and Church Order • 189

and is ambiguous enough to accommodate both pre-millennialists and post-millennialists.

Phineas Bresee was a post-millennialist and so was A. M. Hills. Most if not all the theological textbooks for ministerial studies favoured the same view. Wiley seeks to steer a middle course but seems to favour the post-millennial view. However, during the period under review the premillennial view predominated in Britain and was probably the prevailing view among the Nazarenes in America.

THEIR CHURCH ORDER

Conception of the Church

When David Thomas left the Pentecostal League to propagate Holiness outside of the churches he had a clear plan of action but probably no carefully thought out conception of the Church. In those days he wrote some harsh things about the churches which he swiftly modified. He certainly never had the notion that the Holiness Mission was the only true Church. In 1919, under the title "Beware of Narrowness", he printed Ruskin's censure of

> a little squeaking idiot (who) was preaching to an audience of seventeen old women and three louts that they were the only children of God in Turin; and that all the people outside of the chapel, and that all the people out of sight of Mount Viso would be damned.[14]

In May, 1914, he wrote

> the Holiness Mission's object is that the truth of Scriptural Holiness shall be proclaimed . . . and to support any minister in any Church all we can who is preaching the truth . . . not to establish an organisation or a sect, but simply to let the Holy Ghost unite together in a fellowship the bride of the Lamb.[15]

We have noted Jessop's reference to the Manchester Tabernacle being made a blessing to other churches. He did not regard the International Holiness Mission strictly as a denomination and maintained his credentials as a Nazarene minister for some years after he joined it. As such he would hold the Nazarene view of the Church.

The three movements under review shared with other evangelicals the view that the Church is made up of those regenerate by faith in Christ, and these are to be found in all

190 • *In the Steps of John Wesley*

denominations. They also believed that denominations had a place in the plan of God. In an editorial James refers to the rise of the Calvary Holiness Church:

> In the year 1934, amid the clash of controversy and misunderstanding, the Lord raised up a company of witnessing Christians who labelled themselves 'The Calvary Holiness Church'. Maybe it would have been better if they had been called 'The Calvary Holiness Fellowship'. For there is only one real Church of Jesus Christ; it is composed of men and women everywhere, both in heaven and on earth, who have been cleansed in the precious blood of Christ and 'born again' of the Holy Spirit. In the very nature of things there are bound to be multiplied thousands of Christian believers in the world; but each one is part of the one true Church of which our Lord Himself is the glorious Head.[16]

George Sharpe's views were no doubt summed up[17] by the statement in the 1908 Nazarene *Manual*:

The General Church
The Church of God is composed of and includes all spiritually regenerate persons, whose names are written in heaven.

The Churches Severally
The churches severally are to be composed of such regenerate persons as by providential permission, and by the leadings of the Spirit, become associated together for holy fellowship and ministries.

The Pentecostal Church of the Nazarene
We seek holy Christian fellowship, the conversion of sinners, the entire sanctification of believers and their upbuilding in holiness, together with the preaching of the Gospel to every creature. We also seek the simplicity and power manifest in the Primitive New Testament Church.[18]

In the 1928 *Manual* the third paragraph was prefaced with the words: "The Church of the Nazarene is composed of those persons who have voluntarily associated themselves together according to the doctrines and polity of the said church, and who seek holy Christian fellowship."[19]

The Church of the Nazarene has made no further addition and this remains its official conception of the Church. Obviously its founding fathers were not satisfied with the churches of their day or they would not have founded another. But they did not unchristian the denominations they left, however severe were some of their strictures on them. They had not the Anabaptist ideal of "reconstituting the Church".[20] On the contrary they acknowledged their debt

Their Faith and Church Order • 191

to the heritage of the past and saw themselves as part of a historic process from New Testament times.

In the 1964 *Manual*, the general superintendents include in their foreword this sentence: "The doctrines of our church are based upon the Bible, and have been brought to us out of the experience of the historic Christian Church."

Ministry

The International Holiness Mission began as a layman's movement in which lay leaders performed the rites of the ministry. In 1916 Rev. W. J. Willis was received as an ordained minister from the Baptist Church. Jessop and Bolt were also ordained before joining the Mission. In J. E. Griffiths the International Holiness Mission first took upon itself the right to ordain.[21] In the case of Phillips and Food it instituted a probationary ministry which later was defined as consisting of three years in which examinations had to be passed before ordination. The Executive Council, predominantly lay but with some ministers on it by this time, made the decision concerning the ordination and the dismissal of ministers, but the actual ordination service was conducted by ordained ministers.[22] However the privileges of the ordained minister were not exclusive for not only the probationary minister but the lay leader could perform the rites of the ministry.

The Calvary Holiness Church took over the International Holiness Mission order of ministry as it stood in 1934. In this case, however, the Movement was inaugurated by ministers and from the beginning the emphasis was on an ordained ministry. But the priesthood of all believers was strongly held in the Movement and in churches where a lay leader was in charge he was permitted to conduct communion, marriages and funerals, and to dedicate infants. The Executive Council, composed of ministers and laymen in almost equal numbers, made the decision concerning the ordination and dismissal of ministers, though, as in the International Holiness Mission, the ordination service was conducted by ordained ministers.[23]

The Pentecostal Church of Scotland followed the Nazarene Church in giving a minister's license as the first step to the eldership. The licensed minister was not permitted to administer communion until the necessary examinations had been passed and ordination been granted. The annual Assembly, consisting of delegates from local churches with a preponderance of lay delegates, had the authority to elect suitable candidates to elder's orders and the ordination was performed by the elders of the church.

As the ministry of the Pentecostal Church of Scotland was based on that of the Nazarene Church so the latter was based on the ministry of the Methodist Episcopal Church. At first a minister's licence was issued by the local church, giving the right to preach. From 1915, the local church made the recommendation for a licence to the District Assembly, which from the beginning had the power to elect to elder's orders licensed ministers who had successfully completed four years study with two years pastoral service.[24] The office of the local preacher was created in 1919 and later (1923) became the first step to a minister's licence. A licensed minister in charge of a church was permitted to baptise from 1915, and to administer communion in 1923 in his own pastorate, provided he passed annually the course of study. But the church recognised only one order, the eldership, the minister's licence being in the nature of an apprenticeship to it. Its "permanency" is stressed from the 1907 *Manual*,[25] but elders have always been required to report to the annual District Assembly at which their "characters are passed". Therefore, at any time the orders can be withdrawn. The district and general superintendencies are regarded as offices, not higher orders. It is customary for the general superintendent having jurisdiction over the electing District Assembly to conduct the ordination service and issue the certificates of ordination, but all that is constitutionally required is that "the candidate shall be ordained by the laying on of the hands of the elders . . . under the direction of the presiding general superintendent" and this is done by the district superintendent and the elders if, as in wartime in Britain, it is not possible for the general superintendent to be present.

All four churches were prepared to recognise the orders of suitable ordained ministers from other denominations, provided that they were satisfied that equivalent conditions of education and spiritual experience had been fulfilled.

Their Faith and Church Order • 193

There was a charismatic element in all four ministries. In the Calvary Holiness Church a minority of ministers could exercise the *glossolalia* and gave prominence to "divine healing". But in all four churches only those professing to be filled with the Holy Spirit were accepted into the ministry. They were expected to be able to lead their members into an assurance of salvation and a conscious experience of the fulness of the Spirit.

Baptism

Each of the movements under review subscribed to the Protestant belief in two sacraments: Baptism and the Lord's Supper.

The International Holiness Mission retained many of the characteristics of the interdenominational movement from which its founder came, the Pentecostal League. It made no pronouncement on baptism, though, if anything, the Baptist practice of baptising believers was favoured for infants were usually dedicated and not baptised. If individuals desired to confess Christ in baptism, there was freedom to do so, and George Walker, the secretary of the International Holiness Mission and a Baptist minister, baptised some members of the movement at their own request, including James and Ford. Nevertheless, there were some who held the view that the one baptism is the baptism with the Holy Spirit and to submit to water baptism after receiving this was to decline from the spiritual to the material.[26] The missions at Leeds and Hull adopted triune baptism in 1901 as a result of two of the members reading Thomas Aquinas in their investigations in the public library![27]

Wain was opposed to the preaching and practice of baptism in the Mission, preferring to leave it to the individual conscience. In 1948 the Executive Council gave permission for infants to be sprinkled when dedicated, and in the Easter Delegates Conference before union with the Church of the Nazarene in 1952 a resolution almost identical with the item on Baptism in the Nazarene *Manual* was recommended to the Executive Council.

In the Calvary Holiness Church baptism by immersion was included in the Articles of Faith as one of the two sacraments. It was regarded mainly as a testimony to faith in Christ as Saviour, a seal on salvation already received. It was not regarded as essential to salvation, nor was it made a condition of membership. Infants were dedicated, and in rare instances water was sprinkled on the child to meet the susceptibilities of the parents.

George Sharpe, with his Church of Scotland, Methodist Episcopal and Congregational background retained the practice of infant baptism. He baptised his mother after her conversion, probably by sprinkling, no doubt because she had not been baptised in infancy. He had little sympathy with the immersion of adults.

The eclectic nature of the church polity of the Church of the Nazarene is reflected in its article on baptism in the 1907 *Manual*:

> Christian Baptism is a sacrament, or ordinance, signifying one's acceptance of the benefits of the Atonement of Jesus Christ.
> It is to be administered by ordained ministers of the Gospel to believers as declarative of their faith in Him as their Saviour, and full purpose of obedience in holiness and righteousness.
> Baptism, being the seal of the New Testament, young children may be baptized upon request of parents or guardians who shall give assurance for them of necessary Christian teaching.
> Baptism may be administered by sprinkling, pouring or immersion, according to the choice of the applicant.
> In case a preacher, when requested to administer baptism in a mode which he deems unscriptural, has conscientious scruples against so administering the ordinance, he shall not be required to do so, but shall see to it that the candidate for baptism shall be baptized in the mode desired by the applicant.[28]

After various modifications the article attained its present form in 1928, in which no mention is made of a minister administering baptism, nor of his not being required to administer it in a form against which he has conscientious scruples and in which baptism is described as "the symbol" not "the seal" of the New Testament.

Five traditions are merged in the article: paedo-baptism, believer's baptism, sprinkling, pouring and immersion.

It was not that baptism was thought to be unimportant, but rather that every man should be allowed to choose the time and mode in the light of conscience, illuminated by the reading of the Scriptures. It has meant that some Nazarenes have been baptised as infants, according to the choice of their parents, and later baptised as believers according to their own choice. Inconsistent as this will appear to some theologians,[29] the alternative of denying believer's baptism to a member because his parents chose that he should be baptised as an infant is considered by Nazarenes to be even more inconsistent and unfair. Baptism as the admittance into the Church Visible is probably most prominent in the minds of Christian parents in the baptism of their child. Baptism as a confession of personal faith in Christ is probably most prominent in the mind of that child come of age who desires believer's baptism. Thus two prominent aspects of baptism are represented in the two acts. The Roman Catholic, Greek Orthodox and Anglican Churches make provision for the desire of parents and child in infant baptism and the rite of confirmation.

The Lord's Supper

Like baptism, no reference was made to the Lord's Supper in the Articles of Faith of the International Holiness Mission. Nevertheless, it was generally observed throughout the Movement, the frequency being left to the choice of the local missions. Being a layman's movement, the lay leader normally conducted the service, influenced by the example of Reader Harris and the "Plymouth" Brethren.[30]

The Calvary Holiness C h u r c h included the Lord's Supper as a sacrament in its Articles of Faith, but gave no official definition of its significance. In both the International Holiness Mission and the Calvary Holiness Church it was regarded as mainly a memorial feast, recalling the atoning sacrifice of Christ and His resurrection, and looking forward to His second advent. The partaking of the bread and wine, symbols of Christ's body and blood, was regarded as symbolic of the communion between Christ and His disciples and of the dependence of the latter on the former for spiritual sustenance. Some probably gave no greater significance to it than this, adopting, for the most part unconsciously, the position of Zwingli. But the majority probably believed that grace was ministered in some undefined way to the worthy participant in the act of participating.

In the Calvary Holiness Church the pastor of the local church was normally a minister, probationary if not ordained, and it was his right to conduct the sacrament. But the lay

196 • *In the Steps of John Wesley*

leader or a deacon was also permitted the same privilege if a minister was not available.

The frequency was left to the choice of the local church. Some churches followed the example of the "Plymouth" Brethren and some Pentecostal churches in observing it every Sunday morning. Others were content with twice or once a month. It was celebrated at the first service on Good Friday morning at the Easter Convention at Oldham.

The communion service was a regular feature at the annual Assemblies of the Pentecostal Church of Scotland. Only ordained ministers were permitted to conduct it. This would mean that in the first few years of its existence the churches near Parkhead would be dependent on Sharpe for the sacrament. There is nothing to indicate Sharpe's teaching concerning it, but it may be assumed to be very similar to if not identical with that of the Church of the Nazarene.

The Church of the Nazarene interpretation of the Lord's Supper is given in the *Manual*, Article XIV. It has not materially altered since 1907 and reached its present form, which is here given, in 1928:

> We believe that the Memorial and Communion Supper instituted by our Lord and Saviour Jesus Christ is essentially a New Testament sacrament, declarative of His sacrificial death, through the merits of which believers have life and salvation and promise of all spiritual blessings in Christ. It is distinctively for those who are prepared for reverent appreciation of its significance and by it they show forth the Lord's death till he come again. It being the Communion feast, only those who have faith in Christ and love for the saints should be called upon to participate therein.[31]

This statement and the Ritual for the Sacrament of the Lord's Supper[32] give the substance of the Nazarene teaching on the subject.

1. It is a Memorial Supper calling the minds of the participants back to a historical event.

2. It is a Proclamation (declarative) in symbol of faith in Christ's sacrificial death, through the merits of which believers have life and salvation and promise of all spiritual blessings in Christ,[33] and "a token of His coming again."[34]

3. It is a Communion Supper in two senses.

   a. In it "those who have with true repentance forsaken their sins, and have believed in Christ unto salvation, draw near and take these emblems, and, by faith partake of the life of Jesus Christ, to (their) soul's comfort and joy." The elements remain "Thy (God's) creatures of bread and wine" but in the prayer of consecration petition is made that as they are received "according to the holy institution of Thy Son, our Saviour Jesus Christ, in remembrance of His death and passion, we may be made partakers of the benefits of His sacrificial death."[35] Here is the classic Reformed doctrine as expressed in Article XXIII of the First Helvetic Confession (1536): "The bread and wine are holy, true symbols, through which the Lord offers and presents the true communion of the body, and the blood of Christ for the feeding and nourishing of the spiritual and eternal life."

The instrumentalism of Calvin and the receptionism of Hooker are both present in the Nazarene interpretation of the Lord's Supper.

b. It is also a Communion Supper in the sense that the participants "are one, at one table with the Lord".[36] It is for "those who have faith in Christ and love for the saints".[37]

4. It is to be administered by elders in any church or by licensed ministers only in the church of which they have charge.

5. It is for "Christ's disciples", "who have with true repentance forsaken their sins and have believed in Christ unto salvation",[38] who have "love for the saints" and "who are prepared for reverent appreciation of its significance."[39]

6. It is both a privilege and obligation. In the earliest *Manual,* 1907, the following paragraph was added to the statement: "Of the obligation to partake of the privileges of this sacrament, as often as we may be providentially permitted, there can be no doubt."

From 1915, the following item was included in the duties of the pastor: "The Pastor shall administer (or, if not an Elder, arrange for the administration of) the Sacrament of the Lord's Supper at least once a quarter."[40]

7. Unfermented wine is to be used, in the Temperance tradition, and unleavened bread was specified from 1928, though there is nothing like universal observance of the latter specification in Britain.

(The basis of both the Baptism and Communion Ritual is the Methodist Episcopal Church Ritual which owes its origin to the Anglican Prayer Book.)

Government

As indicated in the historical section, the governing body in both the International Holiness Mission and the Calvary Holiness Church was the Executive Council.

One of the clearest facts which emerges from a study of the three movements is the formative effect of the original environment. David Thomas commenced the Holiness Mission as an autocracy with four colleagues, similar to Reader Harris and the Pentecostal League. In 1915 with the creation of the self-perpetuating Executive Council (and even more so in its incorporation in 1920) it became an oligarchy. The ministers ultimately were given a place on it, but never on completely equal terms with the laity. Attempts were made to consult representatives from the missions as a General Council, as a Ministers, Leaders and Workers Conference and as a Delegates Conference, but only towards the close of the Movement's separate history did the Delegates Conference seem to have a decisive say in the government.

In the Calvary Holiness Church, while the four founders were given permanent seats on the Executive Council, only James and Ford retained theirs through the twenty-one years of its existence. There were full legal voting rights for ministers and laity, with a majority of one for the ministers. The Delegates Conference grew steadily in authority and had the power to elect the members of the Executive Council.

In both these movements, the minister or the lay leader had the main authority in the local church, though local officials—secretary, treasurer, deacons, local committee—were given a part in the government of the local church, in some churches a considerable one.

Sharpe embodied three ecclesiastical traditions: the Church of Scotland, the Methodist Episcopal, and the Congregational. His statement of the rights of the local church: "Even when other churches came into our fellowship I never could accept the idea that a 'mother Church' should lord it over another church,"[41] has the ring of a Congregational classic: "Although churches be distinct, and therfore (sic)

Their Faith and Church Order • 199

may not be confounded one with another; and *equall*, (sic) and *therfore* (sic) *have not dominion one over another;*[42] yet all the churches ought to preserve church-communion one with another."[43]

Whether there is a genetic relationship is doubtful, but Sharpe had evidently not been a congregationalist for five years without imbibing some of its principles. As previously mentioned, Sharpe carried over the Congregationalist system of deacons and managers into his organisation of the Parkhead Pentecostal Church. His fifteen years in the Methodist Episcopal Church also made a deep impression and the combination of the two systems fitted him ideally for the Methodist-Congregationalist synthesis of the Church of the Nazarene, on the church order of which he modelled his Pentecostal Church of Scotland before it became a part of it.

In the Church of the Nazarene the quadrennial General Assembly "is the supreme doctrine-formulating and lawmaking and elective authority".[44] It is composed of ministerial and lay delegates in equal numbers, elected by the District Assemblies, of executive officers, leading officials and representatives from the mission fields.[45] The church is divided into District Assemblies (at present seventy-nine, in 1915 thirty-five and in 1955 seventy-two) composed of all the elders, licensed ministers and other eligible workers in the district, those holding district office and certain offices in the local church,[46] and lay delegates, two for fifty members or less and an additional one for every successive fifty.[47] The District Assembly's work is mainly the election of officers and boards, but it is expected to "consider and care for the entire work of the Church of the Nazarene within its bounds".[48] Its senior officer is the district superintendent, whom it can decide to elect for one, two, three or four years. He presides over the District Advisory Board, the senior district board.[49] His office is to some extent what he makes it for his powers over a self-supporting, self-governing local church are severely limited. Thus far has the Congregationalist element within the Church of the Nazarene prevailed. But a district superintendent of ability and personal powers can exercise great authority and give drive and direction to the district. The pastor of the local church is the head of all departments of the local church.[50] He is assisted by the Church Board made up of the Sunday

School superintendent, the presidents of the Missionary Society and the Young People's Society, and stewards and trustees elected by the members.[51] He is called to the pastorate by a two-thirds vote of the members for one year, after which his call must be renewed by the same majority for one, two, three or four years.[52]

Worship

The Pentecostal League pattern, as in so many other ways, was reflected in the worship of the International Holiness Mission. As might be expected in a layman's movement there was opportunity in the early days for everyone to participate in its worship. This was especially true of the prayer meetings and the testimony meetings but even in the Sunday worship services anyone regarded as being in a good experience might be called upon by the leader to contribute a prayer or testimony or even a brief exhortation or exposition of Scripture. Ejaculations such as "Hallelujah" and "Praise the Lord" on the Salvation Army pattern were frequent and it was considered desirable that the meetings should be "lively" and not "dead". Hearty hymn singing was often supplemented by the singing of choruses, which were learnt by heart, and repeated several times. Use was also made of solos and, to a lesser degree, of group singing.

Those desirous of seeking salvation or entire sanctification were invited to kneel at the "penitent form" at the foot of the platform, where they would be dealt with by an experienced worker. Sometimes they were asked to raise the hand as a preliminary step, confessing their sense of need and asking for prayer. As time went on, from the mid-thirties, seekers were sometimes invited into an "enquiry room" in which they were prayed with and counselled, but many of the veterans deprecated any attempt to "by-pass" the penitent form. This development took place also in the Calvary Holiness Church and in the Church of the Nazarene.

The Sunday morning service was especially for the edification of believers and the evening service for the conversion of the uncommitted. Prayer meetings at which anyone was free to lead in extempore prayer were often held several times a week, and there was usually a weekly testimony meeting at which believers were invited to testify to conversion and entire sanctification and to share any up to date experience of Divine help or guidance. The weekly Holiness meeting was, as the name signifies, for the propagation of the Holiness message.

With the introduction and development of a full-time ministry some of the spontaneity of the early meetings was lost but by no means eliminated. For the meetings to be considered dull or lifeless would have reflected on the ability of the minister. But with competent preachers like Willis and Jessop and Bolt there was obviously less need of spontaneous expositions and the services conformed more to the pattern of other Free Churches.

The worship in the Calvary Holiness Church conformed basically to the pattern of the International Mission of 1934, especially as it existed in the churches raised up by the campaign party from 1931 to 1934. Although it enshrined its belief in the gifts of the Spirit in its Articles of Faith, for the most part little scope was given for the exercise of the *glossolalia*. What ecstatic *charismata* were exercised, such as *glossolalia* and prophecy, were usually exercised in prayer meetings. They were deprecated in evangelistic services where unbelievers were present, on the basis of I Corinthians 14: 23-25, and even in other meetings *glossolalia* was considered to be out of order if no interpreter was present.[53]

The Calvary Holiness Church found, as the International Holiness Mission had done, that when enthusiasm waned the testimony and the prayer meetings were the first casualties. By 1955, in most churches these were a shadow of what they had been shortly after the revival campaign in which the local church began.

The Pentecostal Church of Scotland was probably the most demonstrative of the three movements in its earliest days. At times when emotion was high in the services at the Parkhead church George Sharpe would lead the congregation round the hall in a "glory march". But with his pastoral training and preaching ability he had a greater place for an ordered service in his scheme of things. Indeed, the Pentecostal Church of Scotland was an interesting synthesis of American revivalism and Scottish ecclesiasticism. Paraphrases of the Psalms were sung in the Sunday morning service of the Parkhead church and a catechism was favourably considered if not actually used in the Sunday School![54] As mentioned above, the sacrament was celebrated in the annual Assemblies. A place was found for a choir in the Parkhead church at least as early as 1920, and the Sunday School choir was a prominent feature from the inception of the church. When it became a part of the Nazarene Church the pattern of worship remained the same.

Divine Healing

All three movements believed in "divine healing". The Calvary Holiness Church included it in its Articles of Faith[55] and so did the Church of the Nazarene.[56] The International Holiness Mission made no pronouncement on it but it was generally believed in the Movement that God could and from time to time did miraculously heal. Some of the missions which affiliated with the Movement put a strong emphasis on it. Alfred Place of the House of Prayer, Leeds, was a firm believer in divine healing, and under his influence the *Doctrine and Rules of the Holiness Church* for the Leeds, Hull and Dewsbury Holiness Churches contained a two-page article on the subject. But even this permitted a person to "trust the Lord with his body or not, and yet be a member". Pastor Gaskill also placed the same strong emphasis on divine healing in the two Bolton missions of which he was the pastor. But G. D. Holmes (one of the early members of the Holiness Church in Hull) and other leaders in the International Holiness Mission sounded the note of caution lest belief in miraculous healing should deteriorate into fanaticism.

The revival and healing campaigns conducted by James and his colleagues were modelled on the pattern of those conducted by Stephen and George Jeffreys of the Pentecostal Movement. After an evangelistic service with chorus and hymn singing led by a song leader and an appeal for decisions to accept Christ as Saviour, the sick were invited forward and anointed and prayed over by the revivalists. Sometimes there was an immediate improvement in their physical condition, in other cases it came later and in other cases there was no improvement at all. In some instances the improvement was remarkable, as in the case of George Johnson of Oldham,[57] said to be suffering from spastic paraplegia, and Charlotte Middleton of Salford,[58] with inflammation of the spine. Both were wheeled to the healing service in bath chairs which they were able to discard completely after being anointed and prayed over. However, "divine healing" is a subject in itself and there is scope for careful and impartial research by someone with medical qualifications into its place in the three movements under review. It certainly was an important factor in the inauguration of some of the largest churches in the International Holiness Mission and the Calvary Holiness Church.

NOTES ON CHAPTER 5

[1] 1964, par. 582 III. Virtually unchanged since 1907.
[2] 1964. Where it is not materially different from the early *Manuals* this is quoted as the maturest expression of faith.
[3] Altered to "Person" in the 1911 *Manual*.
[4] P. 21.
[5] Par. 17.
[6] Par. 19.
[7] *I Believe in the Holy Ghost* (Nelson: Coulton & Co., 1964), pp. 11-13. This represents James's maturest thought on the subject, but his views have not materially altered over the years.
[8] *Christian Theology* (Kansas City: Beacon Hill Press, 1959), vol. I, pp. 173-77.
[9] *Ibid.*, p. 184.
[10] *Fundamental Christian Theology* (Pasadena: C. J. Kinne, 1931), vol. I, p. 134.
[11] July, 1959, pp. 20-23.
[12] *The Small Sects in America*, p. 60.
[13] P. 22.
[14] *HMJ*, July, p. 54.
[15] *Ibid.*, May, 1914, p. 55.
[16] *Flame*, May-June, 1945.
[17] See above, p. 48.
[18] P. 18.
[19] Par. 3.
[20] F. H. Littell, *Anabaptist View of the Church* (Boston: Starr King Press, 1958), pp. 46-111.
[21] *HMJ*, Jan., 1925, p. 3.
[22] *Ibid.*
[23] In the two movements there would have been no objection to lay members of the Executive Council taking part and sometimes they probably did.

In the Steps of John Wesley

[24] In actual practice it adopts the recommendation of the Board of Orders and Relations composed of elders.
[25] P. 39.
[26] A view similar to the Spiritualists' like Schwenkfeld in the days of the Reformation and to that of the Quakers and the Salvation Army.
[27] Holiness Church Conference Minute Book, 6-4-01. Cf. *Summa Theologica*, Part III Q Lxvi (8). Interview with H. Saville, Leeds, 7-10-57.
[28] P. 26.
[29] Sacrilege to Roman Catholics.
[30] Although the Brethren generally opposed the Arminian emphasis of the Holiness Movement, their very opposition established contact, and they exercised an influence, often unconscious, on the International Holiness Mission and the Calvary Holiness Church, who admired their knowledge of and respect for the Scriptures.
[31] Par. 19.
[32] Par. 584.
[33] Par. 19.
[34] Par. 584.
[35] *Ibid.*
[36] *Ibid.*
[37] Par. 19.
[38] Par. 584.
[39] Par. 19.
[40] Par. 69, sec. 10.
[41] Above, p. 46.
[42] Italics mine.
[43] Cambridge Platform, ch. xv ("Congregationalism", ERE, vol. IV, p. 20).
[44] *Manual* (1964), par. 323.
[45] *Ibid.*, par. 326.
[46] *Ibid.*, par. 176.
[47] *Ibid.*, par. 177 (1). This is in districts under 5,000. For those over, one for fifty or fewer and an additional one for every successive fifty. 177 (2).
[48] *Ibid.*, par. 180, sec. 28.
[49] *Ibid.*, pars. 190-201.
[50] *Ibid.*, par. 73.
[51] *Ibid.*, pars. 121-130.
[52] *Ibid.*, pars. 80 and 88.
[53] I Cor. 14:28.
[54] Walker's letter to Reynolds, 13-4-14.
[55] "We believe in the Bible doctrine of divine healing."
[56] *Manual* (1964), virtually unchanged since 1908.
[57] *HMJ*, July, 1933, p. 5.
[58] *Ibid.*, Oct., 1933, p. 3.

CHAPTER 6

Their Attitude to the World

The years in which the three movements under review arose are probably the most momentous in the history of Britain. By the beginning of the twentieth century Britain had reached her zenith as a world power. By the middle of the century, though she was a member of the "Big Three", it was becoming increasingly apparent that she was a junior partner and that economic pressures were levering her from a central position in world affairs. The Empire was becoming the Commonwealth, which could have a leading role in a new world in which racial relationships were to be a prominent issue or be simply an intermediary phase to dissolution. The winds of change were blowing in the world. The megaton bomb dwarfed the two greatest wars in history, but the wars created chain reactions in more fields than the physical. The half century which is the main scope of our study saw a decline in religion, a flux in morals, the eclipse of the Liberal Party by the Socialists and the liberalising of the Conservative Party, a vast increase of educational facilities, a great advance in the standard of living and an extension of entertainment and sport, the enfranchisement of women with a much fuller participation by them in industry, the professions and public life, the accomplishment of the Welfare State, the establishment of the "mass media of communication", widespread facilities for travel and the inauguration of the space age.

It is the purpose of this chapter to consider how the movements under review reacted to the environment in which they originated and developed.

Citizens and Prophets

Consciously, as all Christian movements they adopted a world-renouncing and world-embracing attitude. Unconsciously, as all human beings and institutions, they imbibed the ethos of their environment.

Holding the biblical doctrine of the Fall, it was the belief of those in all three movements that they were called as those regenerated to witness in a largely unregenerate society by separating themselves from its evil and proclaiming the truth of God as they saw it. They were to live as pilgrims in this "present evil age". Drawn mainly from the Free Churches, and in any case adopting if not in every case inheriting the Free Church attitude concerning the independence of the Church, they could well have re-echoed the Donatist question, "What has Caesar to do with the Church?" But they believed that the same Bible which taught them to "render to God the things that are God's" admonished them to "render to Caesar the things that are Caesar's" and that "the powers that be are ordained of God". The Head of the State was accordingly given due respect and at times of death and coronation l o y a l tributes appeared in the official journals. They inherited the freedom won for religious minorities by the struggles of the previous centuries and the State to which they gave their loyalty gave them toleration and protection.[1] They exercised the prophetic responsibility to rebuke evil, even in high places, in the context of the British privilege of free speech. The emphasis of their protests was on such matters as Sabbath desecration, immorality and divorce, national excesses in drinking, smoking and gambling, "unsavoury remarks" on the radio, but occasionally the movements registered their disapproval of Black Market activities, war, "the evils engendered by such an Economic System viz. unemployment, means test, oppression of the poor, and slums"[2] and other social evils.[3] Both the Church of the

Their Attitude to the World • 207

Nazarene[4] and the Calvary Holiness Church[5] appointed committees on public morals and though neither of them functioned vigorously or lasted very long, they were some indication of a sense of responsibility to the community.

Politics

Some in these movements adopted a pietistic attitude, and even those who expressed their minds on current events did so as those witnessing to Christian principles which ought to be applied in society rather than as those who had a Christian programme for the redemption of society. The International Holiness Mission and the Calvary Holiness Church included in their Articles of Faith their belief in the pre-millennial Second Coming of Christ and although the Church of the Nazarene was not similarly committed to this belief it was the predominant one among its ministers and members. This meant that it was generally believed that the ideal kingdom was postponed until the Second Advent. The witness to society was a kind of by-product of the preaching of the Gospel of individual redemption. Politics were regarded with suspicion, especially in the early days and especially in the International Holiness Mission. In 1913, David Thomas wrote,

> Avoid giving your time to second-rate things; consecration means yielding your life for-ever. So when politics and other meetings come along, which are not directly open for souls to be saved and sanctified, good-bye.[6]

The official organs of all three movements quote Keir Hardie as saying:

> I often feel sick at heart with politics, and all that pertains thereto . . . If I were thirty years a younger man . . . I would . . . go forth among the people to proclaim afresh and anew the full message of the Gospel of Jesus of Nazareth. We are, all of us, somehow or other, off the mark.[7]

Some members of the movements held the other-worldly attitude so strongly that they refused to exercise their vote. After the supersession of the Liberal Party by the Labour Party, most of those who did vote in the twenties and thirties probably voted Conservative. Although the first Labour Member of Parliament, Keir Hardie, was a pronounced

Christian, there was some misgiving as time went on concerning how far the secular elements were dictating the policy of the party. Holding political meetings on a Sunday seemed to have little to do with Christianity as the Holiness movements saw it and appeared symptomatic of the way that Christianity had to take a back seat when a choice had to be made between it and socialism.[8] Reader Harris dealt critically with socialism in the October issue of *Tongues of Fire*, 1907, and Sharpe was likewise opposed to it.[9] For a Holiness minister to be a supporter of the Labour Party in the first three or four decades was unusual but not unique. George Frame was fearlessly Labour, even in America, in days when socialists were often confused with communists. So was another Nazarene minister, R. G. Deasley, who was a personal friend of Edwin Scrymgeour. It was their belief that social justice was more likely to be done and social ills remedied under a Labour Government. Probably the laity who joined these movements retained the same political alignments as they did before. Many of the working class who formed the bulk of the converts in the International Holiness Mission and the Calvary Holiness Church campaigns from 1931 probably voted Labour. Normally members of the three movements came under no political pressure from the pulpit, a member's political opinions being regarded as his personal affair.

Social Work

The concentration of the movements under review on the spiritual and eternal salvation of the individual made them inclined to regard any organised attempts to better the material and mental condition of men as less than the supreme task which God has assigned to them. What David Thomas would class as "second-rate things". Moreover, engaging in such activities could divert the Holiness worker from the supreme task. The Salvation Army was sometimes quoted as an illustration of how a great evangelising agency could be diverted from concentrating on salvation and Holiness to the lesser work of ministering to physical and social needs. It was recognised that some in it were allies in the proclamation of the message of Holiness, but with many the vision had become blurred by concentration on material things and the raising of the money which social work involved. This outlook was not shared by all. Both Reader Harris and Frank Crossley, recognised Holiness leaders, had found a place for a measure of social work. The American Holiness Movement never saw the antithesis between the spiritual and the social so sharply as did some in the British counterpart, and the Church of the Nazarene included in its Church Membership and General Rules: "Seeking to do good to the bodies and souls of men; feeding the hungry, clothing the naked, visiting the sick and imprisoned, and ministering to the needy, as opportunity and ability are given."

In line with this, the first four Nazarene missionaries from Britain were Dr. and Mrs. D. Hynd, Dr. M. Tanner and Miss M. K. Latta, a school teacher. Dr. Hynd has received the C.B.E. and Miss Latta the M.B.E. for medical and educational services to the Swazis. In the Second World War, the British Nazarenes, assisted with gifts from Canadian and American Nazarenes, put mobile canteens in service to visit the bombed areas in Scotland, England and Northern Ireland.[10] The International Holiness Mission, too, built a hospital and instituted educational work in its South African mission field, and Good Samaritan Bands which made clothes for the natives became an institution in the home missions. The Calvary Holiness Church operated a dispensary in connection with its work in Pakistan and at one time had two trained nurses ready for work among the lepers in Colombia, but an opening did not occur.[11] Besides these denominational programmes, a good deal of social work was done by churches and individual members. For instance, at the close of the war, the Calvary Holiness Church in Sheffield not only entertained a party of German prisoners of war to tea but sent a hundredweight and a half of rationed goods from its members to German families for the Christmas of 1946.

The Christian and War

The question of the Christian attitude to war was thrust upon all three movements. As was to be expected, each movement declared its abhorrence of war itself, but none took the official attitude that its members must not join the armed forces. Few, if any, were conscientious objectors in the First World War and many were influenced by the Allied propaganda, if a letter from William Turnbull, the secretary of

210 • *In the Steps of John Wesley*

the British Isles District of the Pentecostal Church of the Nazarene, is any indication. It is addressed to General Superintendent Reynolds and dated 3rd May, 1917.[12] Here are extracts:

> I can assure you that the German race in this country, assuming we are successful in the war, will, for decades to come, be a byword for everything that is brutal, unmanful, and unholy. Our enemy's nameless abominations committed in France and Belgium, and his cruel and inhuman methods, has put him outside the pale of civilisation, and reduced him to a lower level than that of a heathen country, which knows not God.

The inter-war period gave birth to a number of pacifist organisations[13] and there was a spate of pacifist propaganda. This had its effect on the movements under review, probably the greatest on the Calvary Holiness Church, the attitude of which is described on pages 152-53 of its history.[14] In the Church of the Nazarene the outstanding pacifist was James Macleod who thoroughly enjoyed fighting in the First World War, but who subsequently after his conversion became as courageous and whole-hearted a pacifist as he had been a soldier. After he became joint-editor of the *Holiness Herald,* the official organ of the Church of the Nazarene, an article appeared in it by A. Redford strongly urging the Christian pacifist position.[15] In the *Holiness Mission Journal* the subject was dealt with in the form of question and answer:

> When the Christian is sanctified wholly how can he in time of war take up arms to kill?
> This is a question on which the best souls differ. Our business is to preach Holiness and leave each one to settle these other things between his own soul and God, We respect the honest soul whatever may be his conviction. 'Let every man be persuaded in his own mind' (Rom. xiv. 5).

These words, written in 1922,[16] sum up the attitude of the three movements during 1939 to 1945 and up to the present time.

Puritan Morality

The standards of conduct current among the movements under review were what are sometimes described as Puritan morality. The emphasis was upon sexual purity and marital fidelity, total abstinence from alcohol and tobacco and worldly amusements, honesty and diligence.[17] Thrift and simplicity of living were more thought of in former days than in the present affluent society. Debt was avoided as a contravention of Romans 12:8, and at one time buying goods on credit was regarded as tantamount to running into debt. There is not the same opposition to purchase by instalments now. A sturdy independence was fostered which caused some to view the growth of the Welfare State with some suspicion at first as likely to undermine responsibility. This attitude is by no means as prevalent as it used to be. At one time the principle of insurance was rejected by some as displaying a lack of faith in the providence of God. This view was more widely held in the Calvary Holiness Church than in the International Holiness Mission, led by business men, and the Church of the Nazarene, which had the beginnings of a ministerial retirement scheme from 1919.[18] The Calvary Holiness Church was giving favourable consideration to a retirement and benefit scheme on the eve of its union with the Church of the Nazarene but there were still some of its ministers opposed to it.[19]

The husband was regarded as the head of the house, but women played a prominent part in church life and the wife was sometimes the dominant figure in the home. Birth control with the use of contraceptives, an important social factor in the twentieth century, was treated with conservative disapproval or at least with misgivings in the first three or four decades of the century, partly because of the belief that children were a gift from God and a large family a sign of His blessing and partly because the use of the contraceptive was regarded as "unnatural". In this the movements shared the general attitude of the churches in the early part of the century. But although some Holiness preachers preached against it, birth control with the use of contraceptives was not officially proscribed and was no doubt practised by those who felt no convictions against it. It is seldom made a point at issue today.

The use of tobacco was condemned mainly as a dirty habit, injurious to health, bringing an addiction inconsistent with the freedom which should be the privilege of the children of God and causing money to be wasted which could be devoted to useful ends.[20] Alcohol was forbidden as a beverage. The Nazarene *Manual* from 1907 onwards states:

212 • *In the Steps of John Wesley*

> The Holy Scriptures and human experience alike condemn the use of intoxicating drinks as a beverage. The manufacture and sale of intoxicating liquors for such purpose is a sin against God and the human race. Total abstinence from all intoxicants is the Christian rule for the individual, and total prohibition of the traffic in intoxicants is the duty of civil government.[21]

Gambling was also frowned upon as being inconsistent with the Christian experience.[22]

Entertainment

The Nazarene *Manual* from 1907 onwards also insisted on the avoidance of "such songs, literature and entertainment as are not to the glory of God; the avoidance of the theatre, the ball room, the circus and like places . . ."[23] "Like places" was taken to include the cinema, which in 1907 was in its infancy, though remarkably enough it was never added to the list in subsequent *Manuals*. The reason for proscribing attendance at such places is apparently that they are not considered to be "to the glory of God". They are mentioned in a list with several other items headed by the following paragraph:

> It is required of all such who desire to unite with the Pentecostal Church of the Nazarene, and thus to walk in fellowship with us, that they shall show evidence of salvation from their sins by a Godly walk and vital piety, that they shall earnestly desire to be cleansed from all inbred sin, and that they will evidence this:
> First: By avoiding evil of every kind, such as:

Then follows the list.

This would indicate that attendance at the places mentioned is a "kind of evil" and is inconsistent with "evidence of salvation from sins" and "with a Godly walk and vital piety" and with evidence of an earnest "desire to be cleansed from all inbred sin". All this assumes that the inconsistency will be self-evident to one saved from his sins and earnestly desirous of being cleansed from all inbred sin without further explanation being necessary. Reasons sometimes given by members of the movements under review for not attending the theatre and cinema were the low moral tone of many of the plays and films and the immoral lives of many of the actors and actresses. When asked why discrimination should not be used and only good plays and films be patronised the answer was that this placed the Christian in the category of the theatre-goer and the cinema-goer and might well induce "weak" Christians and others to develop the habit of attending such places indiscriminately and thereby incur harm from the plays and films of low moral tone. Sometimes it was explained that the atmosphere of the places proscribed was "worldly". This and the fact that it is easier to exercise discrimination in one's own home probably explains why television has not been added to the forbidden list (though some members of these movements refuse to own a set). Television is permitted but discrimination in the choice of programmes is strongly urged. The basis laid down by the 1952 General Assembly was the standard given to John Wesley by his mother:

> "Whatsoever weakens your reason, impairs the tenderness of your conscience, obscures your sense of God, or takes off the relish of spiritual things, whatever increases the authority of your body over mind, that thing for you is sin."[24]

Members of the movements under review would be of the opinion that the dance hall with its sensuous music and the contact of the sexes in the dances of this century would come under the censure of the above standard.

But some members of these movements would claim that their abstinence from certain entertainments went deeper than logic and was rooted in a kind of spiritual instinct. Miss L. Denning (later Mrs. J. D. Drysdale) testifies in the *Holiness Mission Journal* (1914)[25] that God showed her that she must separate herself from "pleasures which were not conducive to a closer walk with God" (in her case "good classical concerts and an occasional picture palace"). Later, after receiving Holiness, she testifies that the "very desire for the things of the world, such as concerts and picture palaces, has been removed . . ." These two principles are very important for an understanding of the Holiness movements' separation from "worldly entertainments": an instinct or "revelation" that they are a hindrance to a close walk with God and a deliverance from the desire for them. This constituted an esoteric understanding among those initiated into a deep experience of the Spirit and existed as a kind of unwritten code, something of the "it isn't done" of the "Establishment."[26] The International Holiness Mission and the Calvary Holiness Church did not include such detailed proscriptions in their standards of membership, but their unwritten codes were almost identical.

Another element which certainly played a part in the avoidance of "worldly entertainments" by these movements was what Whitney R. Cross calls "Ultraism",[27] which could be sympathetically rendered, "an utter devotion to God and His service which delights in going to extremes in self-denial and self-sacrifice". And to this must be added a wholehearted concentration on worship and service which left no time for pursuits which were regarded as of a trivial nature.

Sport

The intense devotion of the Holiness pioneers left little time for sport, another of the social trends of the twentieth century. Open air work and street visitation could supply all the exercise which the zealot required. Sport was regarded with suspicion as a diversion from and a possible rival to the chief purpose of the Christian.[28] But as time went on the negative attitude became less rigid. Games were played at the Sunday School outings by adults as well as children from the earliest days of the movement,[29] and in 1925 Jessop mentions football and boating at an August Bank Holiday outing of the members of the Manchester church.[30] George Longley, a member of the Executive Council of the International Holiness Mission, used a croquet set in the spacious grounds of his home, Apsley Lodge, and during an interval in the annual convention there in 1933, Ford played a game with him and Frank Lucas, whose orthodoxy was above reproach.

In one of the early Prayer Retreats at Emmanuel Bible College in the early forties the ministers of the Calvary Holiness Church played a game of football against those of the Church of the Nazarene and members of the college staff. There was a little criticism, but the record stands. In 1914, David Thomas wrote, "Holiness kills golfing!"[31] But in the second half of the century some did not see such a mortal antipathy. "It was not done" to attend football matches, but

Their Attitude to the World • 215

Leonard Wain occasionally attended county cricket matches, where the atmosphere was considered to be better and swearing not likely.

In the Church of the Nazarene the colleges in America brought the question of sport to the forefront. Phineas Bresee frowned on "college and university athletics", though he recognised the need of "such exercise as would strengthen and train the body to be the efficient servant of a clear brain, noble heart, and pure soul".[32] However, college athletics were progressively adopted and by the thirties most of the colleges had a full athletics programme. Among the British Nazarenes there was no counterpart to this, but games were a regular feature of the Nazarene Young People's Society Institutes which began in 1946.

Dress

A prominent feature of the experience of Holiness was considered to be separation from the world. When the less sophisticated members of the Holiness movements were asked why they regarded something as wrong they would sometimes say, "It's worldly". This was one of the reasons why the pioneers in the Church of the Nazarene and the International Holiness Mission dressed plainly and usually in dark colours. The Pentecostal League bonnet was probably first introduced so that Reader Harris might know who were his lady workers, for whom he felt responsible, at open air meetings. Later a similar bonnet was introduced into the International Holiness Mission. The fact that these bonnets were worn at other times besides at open air meetings is an indication that they served also as symbols of separation. Another reason given for simplicity in dress was to avoid "the indulgence of pride in dress or behaviour".[33] From 1928 "modesty" was added to "the Christian simplicity that becometh holiness" though from 1908 the text I Timothy 2:9, 10, containing the words "that women adorn themselves in modest apparel" had been added to the solitary scripture reference, I Peter 3:3. It would be a good summary of the attitude of the British Holiness movements to say that they considered that dress should be unostentatious and modest in contradistinction to costly, gaudy and immodest, features which they associated with the world. This would mean that there would be times when they, the women more than the men, would be "out of fashion", but this should be cheerfully borne as part of the Christian testimony.[34] Like most respectable women, the women of the British Holiness movements did not use make-up in the early part of the century, and even after the use of powder became increasingly widespread in the decade after the mid-twenties it was still the custom for them to abstain from its use. However, towards the close of the period under review, when make-up became not so much the mark of a fast woman but more the sign of a well-groomed woman, increasing numbers of the younger Holiness women made use of make-up and they approximated more closely to the average woman in dress, not without censure from those who deprecated such practices as indications of spiritual decline.[35]

Secret Societies

Separation is also enjoined in the Nazarene *Manual* from "oathbound secret orders or fraternities". The reason given in the 1907 *Manual* is that "the spirit and tendency of these societies are contrary to the principles of our holy religion".[36] From 1915 the *Manual* [37] follows the prohibition by quoting in full James 4:4 (friendship of the world) and II Corinthians 6:14-17 ("Be ye not unequally yoked together with unbelievers"). This reflects the situation in America where the Ku Klux Klan, the Knights of the White Camelia and many kindred secret societies existed, sometimes openly and sometimes below the surface. It was never an important issue in Britain and apparently the rule was not rigidly enforced in the early days of the Church of the Nazarene in Britain.[38] An article in the *Holiness Herald*[39] on "Secret Orders" asserts that "secretism" destroys the principle of the golden rule, makes the "monstrous assumption" that it is better than the Gospel, leads to Christians doing in secrecy what they would not do openly e.g. drinking alcohol, and leaves Christians less time for family ties and for God and the Church. In the *Way*,[40] in reply to a query why Freemasons are excluded from membership in the Church of the Nazarene two additional reasons are given: (i) Christ's injunction, "Swear not at all", and (ii) that Freemasonry

Their Attitude to the World • 217

teaches "salvation by self-effort". Neither the International Holiness Mission nor the Calvary Holiness Church legislated against secret societies, but it would be generally assumed that the Holiness people did not join them.

Education

The twentieth century witnessed a great increase in educational facilities in Britain. With several set-backs, progress was made towards the implementation in 1944 of full-time education until fifteen years of age. In 1900 there were 30,000 university students. The figure after World War II was 80,000. The three movements under review treated education with a mixture of appreciation and caution. Three prominent trends in the world of thought in the first quarter of the century all came under the censure of the Holiness movement: the theory of Evolution, the Freudian emphasis on sex and rationalistic interpretation of religious mysteries, and modernistic theology. These and the danger of substituting intellectual attainment for spiritual power were behind the frequent warnings of David Thomas and similar admonitions in the *Flame* and the official organ of the Church of the Nazarene. But Thomas admitted that "learning is exceedingly valuable"[41] (though he did add "but valuable only as an auxiliary") and Jessop said forthrightly, "For ever drop the notion that knowledge is sinful."[42] The Church of the Nazarene, probably on account of its Scottish environment, set a greater store by learning than either of the English movements. Sharpe was glad of the services of Olive Winchester in his Bible school while she was reading for the Glasgow B.D., and both his daughter, Kanema, and David Hynd, later her husband, graduated at the Glasgow University. When Ford passed the London B.D. examination the Executive Council of the Calvary Holiness Church recorded its congratulation,[43] and James's three sons and Ford's daughter have taken degrees or the equivalent. There is an increasing emphasis in the Church of the Nazarene at present upon an educated ministry. Some indication of the seriousness with which the modern Church of the Nazarene treats education is the Education Commission Report in 1964 entitled "A Study of the Educational Structure in the Church of the

Nazarene". This was produced by leading Nazarene educationalists assisted by Dr. Walter Johnson and associates of the Michigan State University. The Lilly Endowments trustees made a grant of 25,000 dollars to the cost of the project.

Culture

The fact that the theatre and cinema are "out of bounds" for the members of these movements puts an important element of culture beyond their reach. This has been mitigated since the advent of radio and television and with an increasing number of the young people proceeding to higher education a taste may be cultivated for drama and Third Programme items. In the Nazarene colleges in America drama is given a place—indeed, the 1940 General Assembly warned, "There is danger in the excessive use of dramatic productions in our schools and colleges."[44] The Parkhead church has a proud tradition of Sunday School and church choirs, though there was little in the way of choirs in the other two movements. Formerly, as per Miss Denning's testimony, most members of these movements would regard classical concerts as outside the Holiness orbit, but towards the close of the period some, probably few in number, would feel free to attend. Contained by an ideal of plain church buildings[45] and limited resources, church art was given little scope, though the fine Presbyterian church which became the Manchester Holiness Mission Tabernacle was regarded with appreciation.[46] It is interesting to note that in all three movements some have aspired to verse, among them Farmer, Milbank, Jessop, Ravenhill and Ford, and verse is given a place in all the official organs. Douglas Simons, who served with the Calvary Holiness Church for two short spells, showed real ability and a number of his poems were published in the *Flame*. Some of the rank and file made attempts in this direction. Here is the attempt of one of the Oldham mill-girls who was converted in the tent campaign there to express her feelings when the tent had been moved:

It is gone, it is gone, and I gaze with regret,
On the place where it stood, now all muddy and wet,
Not a vestige of rope or of canvas, or wood,
Now marks out the spot where the Gospel Tent stood.

And where the Tent stood I can trace every hour,
The spot where the Saviour first showed me His
power.
And ofttimes I gaze on the now vacant plot,
And cry from my heart, "Oh sweet hallowed spot!

It was here that I gave the Saviour my heart,
No wonder I'm sad, with the Old Tent to part,
I laughed when it came, but I cried when it went,
For I found a Dear Friend in the Old Gospel Tent."[47]

And here is Leonard Ravenhill's attempt to express the spirit of utter devotion which was the ideal of the three movements under review, and without an appreciation of which their attitude to the world will be largely unintelligible:

> *I am a slave;*
> *I have no will, no claim*
> *To property, to time, nor sleep;*
> *I am a sláve and bear my owner's name;*
> *His ways are mine,*
> *With Him I joy or weep.*
> *No tears are spent for ease,*
> *Nor do I freedom crave;*
> *A willing slave am I*
> *To follow to the grave*
> *My Master—Blessed be His name!*[48]

NOTES ON CHAPTER 6

[1] For instance, their ministers were granted exemption from military service.
[2] *PBIDCN*, 1934, pp. 25-26.
[3] Such protests appear frequently in the editorials and in such items as "Current Comments" and "Spiritual Spotlight on World Affairs" in the *Flame*, "Items of Interest" in *HMJ*, "Christian Commentary" in the *Way of Holiness* and in *PBIDCN*.
[4] *PBIDCN*, 1934, p. 17.
[5] *CHCDCM*, 8-4-46 (16).
[6] *HMJ*, Oct., 1913, p. 114.

220 • *In the Steps of John Wesley*

⁷*Ibid.*, Dec., 1922, p. 133, *Flame*, Sept.-Oct., 1945, p. 3 and *Way of Holiness*, March-April, 1950, p. 13. I have abbreviated the quotation.

⁸Ramsay MacDonald in an article in 1923 traces the Christian and materialist elements in the Labour Party and frankly admits the effect of the latter in alienating Christian sympathisers. Ramsay MacDonald, "The Labour Movement and Its Implications for Christianity", *An Outline of Christianity*, ed. A. S. Peake and R. G. Parsons, (London: Waverley Book Co., n.d.), vol. V, Book II, chap. xii.

⁹See also *HMJ*, Sept., 1921, p. 99.

¹⁰*PBIDCN*, 1941, p. 7, and 1942, p. 10.

¹¹*Flame*, July-Aug., 1947, pp. 16-17.

¹²In BIDF.

¹³By 1952 the Standing Joint Pacifist Committee included the Society of Friends Peace Committee, the Anglican Pacifist Fellowship, the Fellowship of Reconciliation, the Peace Pledge Union, the Movement for a Pacifist Church and the Fellowship Party. Sybil Morrison, *I Renounce War* (London: Sheppard Press, 1962), p. 88.

¹⁴For a frank dialogue in wartime see *Flame*, 1943, Sept.-Oct., pp. 10-11 and Nov.-Dec., pp. 12-14.

¹⁵1939, June, p. 2.

¹⁶April, p. 40.

¹⁷Well summarised in the General Rules in Nazarene *Manuals* from 1907.

¹⁸*Manual*, 1919, pp. 76-77. Though Sharpe himself did not favour insurance.

¹⁹But the insurance of missionary equipment was favourably considered in 1950. CHCECM, 20-22-3-50 (Missy. 15).

²⁰*Holiness Herald*, March, 1933, p. 1, *HMJ*, March, 1929, p. 5, *Flame*, Jan.-Feb., 1947, pp. 30-32.

²¹1964 *Manual*, par. 35. The other two movements simply make the prohibition without giving reasons.

²²Nazarene *Manual*, 1964, par. 25, sec. 7. Not specifically proscribed by the other two movements, but certainly considered covered by "abstinence from all appearance of evil", item 2 on Member's Card.

²³1907, pp. 27-30.

²⁴*Manual*, 1964, par. 603, sec. 6.

²⁵June, pp. 67-68 and July, pp. 79-80.

²⁶See for instance Brian Inglis, *Private Conscience and Public Morality* (London: Andre Deutsch, 1964), chap. v "Done and Not Done."

²⁷Whitney R. Cross, *The Burned-over District* (New York: Cornell University Press, 1950).

²⁸E.g. *HMJ*, 1909, Feb., pp. 9-10 and March, p. 26.

²⁹E.g. *Ibid.*, July, 1921, p. 81.

³⁰*Ibid.*, Sept., 1925, p. 5.

³¹*Ibid.*, July, 1914, p. 78. See also George Sharpe, *This Is My Story*, p. 118.

³²E. A. Girvin, *Phineas F. Bresee: A Prince in Israel*, p. 440.

³³Nazarene *Manual*, 1907, pp. 28-29.

³⁴See George Sharpe, *This Is My Story*, pp. 125-26. Though apparently David Thomas, who was a draper, felt no compulsion to adhere

to this standard in his business. In *Tongues of Fire*, Jan., 1892, the following advertisement appears on the back page: "David Thomas is now showing in every department a large assortment of all the LATEST FASHIONS and NOVELTIES prepared expressly for the present Season".

[35]E.g. *PBIDCN*, 1946, p. 19.

[36]P. 34.

[37]From 1915 this prohibition is included in "Church Membership and General Rules".

[38]Sharpe permitted members of the Parkhead church who were members of the Orange Order to remain such after the union with the Pentecostal Church of the Nazarene in 1915. (Conversation with Rev. J. B. Maclagan, 13-3-58.)

[39]Aug., 1922, p. 2.

[40]Feb., 1953, p. 12.

[41]*HMJ*, Nov., 1914, p. 127.

[42]*Ibid.*, April, 1928, p. 5.

[43]*CHCECM*, 7-8-48, p. 1.

[44]*Manual*, 1964, par. 601, sec. 6.

[45]*HMJ*, April, 1908, p. 4. See also Nazarene *Manual*, 1907, p. 10.

[46]See above p. 112.

[47]*HMJ*, March, 1933, p. 5.

[48]*Flame*, March-April, 1945, p. 31.

CHAPTER 7

Their Special Emphasis: Holiness

It has already been stated in chapter five that those of the Holiness Movement believe that the doctrine which they hold and teach is one of the essential truths of the Bible. They appeal to the testimony of the early church and the witness of various individuals and groups in church history to demonstrate the authenticity and antiquity of their message. Among these they give a special place to John Wesley, whose contribution to the doctrine of entire sanctification by faith they consider to be similar to Martin Luther's rediscovery of justification by faith. They claim a place among his spiritual children who have taken up the torch which he bore.

The idea of perfection has been traced in the Bible by scholars such as W. B. Pope, H. W. Perkins, R. Newton Flew, W. E. Sangster, George Allen Turner and John L. Peters. F. Platt, R. H. Coates, Perkins, Flew and others have indicated its recurrence in the Church, and E. G. Rupp and Jean Orcibal, in enumerating the sources of Wesley's doctrine of perfection, have given a further insight into the range of its devotees.[1] The relationship of the three movements under review to other Holiness movements in Christian history is dealt with in chapter eight. But in view of their claim to be in the Wesleyan doctrinal succession, after setting out the

Their Special Emphasis: Holiness • 223

Holiness teaching of these three movements a comparison will be drawn between it and the teaching of Wesley on this subject.

Their Exposition of Holiness

In arriving at the doctrine of Holiness held by these movements there are four main sources of data. The primary sources are the definitions of entire sanctification in their official declarations of doctrine; secondly, the exposition of Holiness in their official journals and the writings of the founders and others holding positions of authority; thirdly, the exposition of Holiness in the Holiness literature stipulated in their ministerial courses of study and recommended in their official journals and generally approved by the Holiness Movement (a selected list is given in the bibliography); and fourthly, the testimonies to the experience of Holiness by members of these movements or those quoted in their literature.[2]

The fullest definition of entire sanctification is in the Nazarene *Manual*.

In the 1908 *Manual*, the one from which the Pentecostal Church of Scotland derived its faith and order, it is as follows:

> Entire Sanctification is that act of God, subsequent to justification, by which regenerate believers are made free from inbred sin, and brought into the state of entire devotement to God, and the holy obedience of love made perfect. It is provided through the meritorious blood of Jesus, and wrought upon the full and final consecration of the believer, and a definite act of appropriating faith, by the gracious agency of the Holy Spirit; and to this work and state of grace the Holy Spirit bears witness.
>
> This experience is also known by various terms representing different phases of the experience, such as 'Christian Perfection', 'Perfect Love', 'Heart Purity', 'The Baptism with the Holy Spirit', 'The fullness of the blessing', 'Christian Holiness', etc.

In the 1911 *Manual*, some of the phrases were re-arranged, without altering the sense, and the word "immediately" was inserted after "wrought". Also the following paragraph was added:

> There is a marked distinction between a perfect heart and a perfect character. The former is obtained in an instant, but the latter is the result of growth in grace. It is one thing to have the heart all yielded to God and occupied by Him; it is quite another thing to have the entire character, in every detail, harmonize with His Spirit, and the life become conformable to His image.

224 • *In the Steps of John Wesley*

This remained in the *Manual* until 1928 when it was omitted[3] and the definition was given the form which has continued up to the present time:

> We believe that entire sanctification is that act of God, subsequent to regeneration, by which believers are made free from original sin, or depravity, and brought into a state of entire devotement to God, and the holy obedience of love made perfect.
>
> It is wrought by the baptism with the Holy Spirit, and comprehends in one experience the cleansing of the heart from sin and the abiding, indwelling presence of the Holy Spirit, empowering the believer for life and service.
>
> Entire sanctification is provided by the blood of Jesus, is wrought instantaneously by faith, preceded by entire consecration; and to this work and state of grace the Holy Spirit bears witness.
>
> This experience is also known by various terms representing its different phases, such as 'Christian Perfection', 'Perfect Love', 'Heart Purity', 'The Baptism with the Holy Spirit', 'The Fullness of the Blessing', and 'Christian Holiness'.

In the Articles of Faith of the International Holiness Mission is this item on Entire Sanctification:

> The privilege and obligation of every believer to receive the blessing of entire sanctification through the Baptism with the Holy Ghost and Fire, purifying the heart through faith and filling with the Holy Spirit. Acts xv 8, 9.

On the application for membership form the applicant is expected to declare that he (or she) is "a possessor of or seeker after that Holiness without which no man shall see the Lord."

From 1927 to 1932, "Definitions of Sanctification" appeared from time to time in the *Holiness Mission Journal*. It contained quotations from five dictionaries, one from Wesley and one from Pope's *Theology*. The "Webster Dictionary" is quoted as follows:

> 1. To make sacred or holy, to set apart to a holy or religious use, to consecrate by appropriate rites, to hallow.
>
> 2. To make free from sin, to cleanse from moral corruption and pollution, to purify. Esp. (Theol.). The act of God by which the affections of men are purified or alienated from sin and the world and exalted to a supreme love to God.

Quotations from the other four dictionaries are on the same lines. Below are given any additional ideas:

Imperial Dictionary: To purify in order to prepare for divine service and for partaking of holy things.

Standard Universal Dictionary: The gracious work of the Spirit whereby the believer is freed from sin and exalted to holiness of heart and life.

Century Dictionary: The act of God's grace by which the affections of man are purified and the soul is cleansed from sin and consecrated to God.

The quotation from the *Worcester Dictionary* adds nothing to the foregoing.[4]

Wesley is quoted as follows, "Sanctification in proper sense is an instantaneous deliverance from all sin and includes an instantaneous power then always to cleave to God."[5]

Pope is quoted: "Sanctification in its beginnings, process and final issues is the full eradication of the sin itself, which reigning in the unregenerate co-exists with the new life in the regenerate, is abolished in the wholly sanctified."[6]

The Articles of Faith of the Calvary Holiness Church contain the following article on Entire Sanctification:

It is the privilege and duty of every Christian to receive the blessing of entire sanctification wrought by the baptism with the Holy Ghost and Fire, and received instantaneously by faith. It comprehends in one experience, the cleansing of the heart from original sin, and the infilling of the Holy Spirit, empowering the believer for Christian life and service.

It is an interesting synthesis of the Nazarene and International Holiness Mission article, and an indication of how close the Holiness movements sought to keep to each other in Holiness doctrine and how little they sought originality. The Standard of Membership on the Member's Card of the Calvary Holiness Church was exactly the same as that of the International Holiness Mission, and it contained the item: "The possession or pursuit of that Holiness without which no man shall see the Lord."

From the foregoing it is possible to draw up a list of the main features of the Holiness doctrine of the three Holiness movements:

1. There are two main works of grace, justification and entire sanctification.

2. The second work of grace, entire sanctification, cleanses the believer from original or inbred sin.

3. It is received instantaneously on the conditions of (a) consecration[7] and (b) faith.

226 • *In the Steps of John Wesley*

4. It is wrought by the Holy Spirit.

5. The Holy Spirit bears witness to it.

6. It brings the believer into a higher category of Christian experience, namely, Christian perfection, with the following features: (a) purity of heart; (b) the fulness of the Spirit, producing the fruit of the Spirit; (c) perfect love for God and man; (d) complete dedication to God; (e) power for Christian living and service (a victorious experience); (f) separation from the world.[8]

7. Christian perfection is a definite stage in Christian progress from which further, continuous progress should be made.

8. It is an obligation as well as a privilege to receive this experience, which is essential for heaven and the beatific vision.

To these should be added three other features, not mentioned in the doctrinal statements, but prominent in the presentation of Holiness by these groups:

9. Testimony should be borne to entire sanctification. It is remarkable that this does not figure more prominently in the official statements. It is not insisted on in George Sharpe's *This Is My Story*, or Maynard James's *Facing the Issue*, or H. E. Jessop's *Foundations of Doctrine*, though each of them testified to the experience and encouraged others to do the same. But it was a feature of the presentation of Holiness by all three groups.[9]

10. Christian Perfection is consistent with infirmities, mistakes and temptation.[10]

11. It can be lost, and, if lost, regained.[11]

A Comparison of Their Exposition of Holiness and Wesley's

In comparing the teaching of these groups with what Wesley taught it is important rightly to understand the founder of Methodism. There has been some discussion among Methodist scholars whether Wesley altered his views concerning Christian perfection as he grew older. The prevalent opinion today is that he did not. A recent statement of Wesley's doctrine by a Methodist scholar is the article by Rupert Davies in *A History of the Methodist Church in Great Britain*, Vol. I, entitled "Our Doctrines". The following excerpts indicate the relationship between the teaching of the movements under review and what Wesley taught: [12]

(i) "Justification and Sanctification are two distinct things and must not be confused; but the latter invariably follows the former."[13]

(ii) Entire Sanctification is "an instantaneous change which eradicates all sin".[14]

(iii) "Sanctification, of course, is the gift of God; it is received, like justification, by faith alone."[15]

(iv) " 'The one (justification) implies what God does for us through His Son; the other what He works in us by His Spirit'; and when God has done the one thing, His Spirit is at once at work to do the other."[16]

(v) "It is accompanied by the witness of the Spirit to itself. 'But how do you know that you are sanctified, saved from inbred corruption? . . . We know it by the witness and the fruit of the Spirit'."[17]

(vi) "Of the perfect Christian Wesley says: . . . he is 'pure in heart'. 'Love has purified his heart from envy, malice, wrath, and every unkind temper;' . . ."[18]

(vii) "The fruit of the Spirit is the necessary mark of sanctification."[19]

(viii) "Christian Perfection is, above all, loving God with all our heart and mind and soul and strength, and our neighbour as ourselves; . . . The best possible description of it, therefore, is Perfect Love."[20]

(ix) " 'In one view (perfection) is purity of intention, dedicating all the life to God. It is giving God all the heart: it is one design ruling our tempers. It is devoting, not a part, but all, our soul, body, and substance to God.' "[21] cf. 6 (d).

(x) ". . . It is clear that Wesley here and always teaches a 'relative' perfection. The perfect, he says, grow in grace to all eternity."[22] cf. 7.

(xi) "The 'perfect' man is not free from errors. . . . He is not exempt from infirmities. . . . Nor is he free from temptation."[23] cf. 10.

(xii) "They who are sanctified, yet may fall and perish."[24] cf. 11.

This list covers most of the items in that of the Holiness movements under review.

John Lawson, in the chapter entitled "Our Discipline"

228 • *In the Steps of John Wesley*

(vi), speaking of the essence of Wesley's doctrine, states, "This is that the Holy Spirit should eventually lift the believer to entire victory over all wilful sin"[25] which is very near 6 (e). The whole chapter reveals Wesley's aim to develop societies with a clear line of demarcation from worldly standards and worldly conduct (cf. 6 [f]).[26]

Item 8 is Wesleyan enough, but it needs qualification. Wesley believed, in common with all Christian theologians, Catholic and Protestant, that the believer must be entirely sanctified before admission into heaven. But he deprecated fear being used to persuade the justified to receive entire sanctification.[27] There is more than a hint of warning in the "obligation" to receive it in the International Holiness Mission and Calvary Holiness Church Articles of Faith. In all three movements the alternative of "Holiness or hell" was sometimes vigorously put,[28] but there was generally a marked reluctance to state that an unsanctified but justified believer would be lost. The warning was usually in the form that wilful rejection of Holiness could result in the loss of the experience of justification.[29] In so far as these movements made fear a motive for seeking entire sanctification they departed from the counsel of Wesley.[30]

The Nazarene *Manual* lists "entire devotement" as one of the features of entire sanctification and "full and final consecration" as one of the conditions. The former is derived from Wesley, but there is little in his writings in the way of explicit statements regarding the latter. Paget Wilkes of the Japan Evangelistic Band, recognised in other ways as a competent Holiness teacher by these three movements, was an exception to the rule in denying that consecration is a condition of the experience and quoted Wesley as insisting on faith alone:

> Look for it every day, every hour, every moment; why not this hour, this moment? Certainly you may look for it now, if you believe it is by faith: and by this token you may safely know whether you seek it by faith or by works. If by works, you want something to be done first, before you will believe; you think, I must first obey or do thus and thus; then you are seeking it by works unto this day.[31]

At the same time, it is inconceivable that Wesley would have taught that anyone unwilling to consecrate his life completely to God could have been a candidate for Christian

Their Special Emphasis: Holiness • 229

perfection. He was well aware that it was possible to dedicate the life to God without receiving the experience. Early in his search for the experience, after reading Law's *Christian Perfection* and *Serious Call,* he "determined to be all devoted to God, to give Him all his soul, his body, and his substance",[32] but for many years he still remained in the "wilderness" until he learned to enter the "promised land" by faith. This may account for the slight emphasis he gives to consecration as a condition for entire sanctification. It appears in some of the hymns of his brother in the section "For Believers Groaning for Full Redemption":

> *Is there a thing beneath the sun,*
> *That strives with Thee my heart to share?*
> *Ah! tear it thence, and reign alone,*
> *The Lord of every motion there!*[33]
>
> *Lord over all sent to fulfil,*
> *Thy gracious Father's sovereign will,*
> *To thy dread sceptre will I bow!*[34]
>
> *Let earth no more my heart divide,*
> *With Christ may I be crucified,*
> *To thee with my whole soul aspire;*[35]
> (See the whole of Hymn 352.)

It is, however, significant that the spirit of dedication is more prominent in a subsequent section, "For Believers Saved". Here is Wesley's emphasis. Consecration is not a reluctant "paying of the price of the Blessing". It is *a desideratum,* a precious part of the goal of perfection. It is assumed rather than stated to be one of the qualities of those who engage in the quest.

It will be noticed that while a definite place is given by the Holiness groups to spiritual development *after* the crisis of entire sanctification, they have not given the place that Wesley did to the progressive work leading up to the crisis. Wesley taught that a believer usually made gradual progress up to the crisis and it was actually possible for him to pass it without being aware of the exact moment. Very little place is given to this side of Wesley's teaching by the movements under review.[36] Out of over two hundred testimonies scrutinised in their literature only two speak of enjoying the experience without being aware of the time it was received. It was recognised, therefore, that the crisis could be so much a part of the process that it could occur unobserved. But this was rare. The movements under review have been so taken up with obeying Wesley's exhortation to "press the instantaneous blessing" that they have omitted to a large extent his emphasis on the process leading up to it.

Wesley taught that the entirely sanctified should testify to the experience.[37] Nevertheless he qualified the circumstances in which the witness should be given.[38] Fletcher believed (according to Hester Ann Rogers, whose evidence is accepted by most scholars) that he lost the experience four or five times because he did not confess it.[39] The Holiness movements have stressed the importance of testimony to the experience as necessary to maintain it and as a duty to God and man. This has been one of the main causes of separation from the larger denominations by the Holiness groups. In some cases those who have testified have been put out of their churches, in other cases, when opportunity to testify has been withdrawn, they have formed churches of their own.[40] Where their witness has caused offence should they have kept silent? Wesley, probably because a witness to Christian perfection by him would have obscured the issue and drawn the fire of his opponents from the logic of his doctrine to what they considered to be the fallibility of his life,[41] has left historians in doubt as to whether he bore an indisputable witness to the experience. But although tempted in a moment of depression "Quietly to drop it",[42] he overcame the temptation and to the end of his life, in spite of opposition and misunderstanding, he preached the offending doctrine and urged his preachers to do the same. It is difficult to believe that he would have advised those holding a doctrine which he believed to be an essential part of the Christian Gospel to maintain a complete silence about it, however much he may have cautioned them about the terms and circumstances in which they should bear their witness.

Whatever perils there are in testifying to the experience which Wesley preached, and Flew and Sangster among others have rightly drawn attention to them, it may be questioned whether the doctrine can survive as a living credo as opposed

Their Special Emphasis: Holiness • 231

to a subject of theological discussion without witnesses. Wesley, though profoundly convinced of its scriptural foundation, was unwilling to preach it if no witnesses to it could be found.[43] Conscious of this, the Holiness movements have urged their members not only to seek to possess but also fearlessly to profess the experience.

In Wesley's time a minority of the Methodists professed entire sanctification, and they were carefully examined by Wesley and his officers. In the Holiness movements under review it was considered normal for the regenerate to press on into the second blessing. The Nazarene *Manual* insists that all local church officers must be "clearly in the experience of entire sanctification".[44] This may be criticised as turning rare ventures by the spiritual elite to the Himalayas of Holiness into excursions for all and sundry to the foothills of an everyday experience within the reach of all. Nevertheless, it does not seem out of character with the atmosphere of the New Testament where even the δουλοι and the δουλαι were promised the outpouring of the Holy Spirit, and where all who repented were assured not only of the remission of sins but also of the gift of the Holy Spirit.[45] Moreover, it offers some antidote to the peril of spiritual pride. If it is normal to press on into entire sanctification, there is not the same temptation to feel lifted up above one's fellows.[46] And it makes the cleansing from sin and the fulness of the Spirit the clearing of the ground for steady progress to spiritual maturity, of which Wesley would approve. The chief danger is formality, the changing of a rare and rapturous experience into a matter of course. But the rite of confirmation, ideally the reception of the Holy Spirit, is beset with the same danger and yet is practised in the major part of the Christian Church. Moreover, the context in which the reference to "perfect love" occurs in the First Epistle of John suggests that the lack of a "love made perfect" is more a deficiency belonging to the early stages of Christian experience rather than the perfecting of love being the rare possession of a spiritual elite.[47]

Among the movements under review an expression very frequently used to describe the crisis of entire sanctification was "the baptism with the Holy Ghost and with fire". This appears very frequently in the testimonies in their official journals. This emphasis is also reflected in the name given to the united church of 1907: "The Pentecostal Church of the Nazarene". Sharpe likewise named the church he founded "The Pentecostal Church of Scotland.[48] The idea is present in Wesley but not prominent,[49] but some of his followers made use of it, and Wesley certainly taught that entire sanctification was accomplished by the Holy Spirit.[50] Perhaps a factor in its popularity in the Holiness movements is that it carries the twofold idea of fulness and cleansing, the "fire" being considered a symbol of the latter. This expression is given even greater prominence in the Pentecostal Movement which arose at the beginning of this century, but the Pentecostal emphasis is on the Spirit's enduement of power and the accompaniment of *glossolalia* as the indispensable proof of its authenticity, whereas the Holiness Movement emphasises purity of heart and life and the fruit of the Spirit as being of even greater importance than the power and gifts of the Spirit.[51] The insistence of the Pentecostal Movement on the *glossolalia* as the sign of the Spirit's baptism has been the main factor in creating the Holiness Movement's attitude of reserve and, to a large extent, of opposition towards it.[52] The *glossolalia* was not permitted in the churches of either the Church of the Nazarene or the International Holiness Mission.[53] The Calvary Holiness Church included belief in "the Bible doctrine of divine healing and the gifts of the Holy Spirit" in their Articles of Faith, but they insisted as strongly as anyone else in the Holiness Movement that the *glossolalia* was not the sign of the baptism with the Holy Spirit, and insisted on the resignation of any minister who attempted to propagate such teaching.

A number of expressions are employed to describe the experience of entire sanctification, such as "Holiness" or "Heart Holiness", "The Blessing of a Clean Heart", "The Second Blessing", "Perfect Love", "The Promised Land", "Christian Perfection", etc. The most frequent description was "Entire Sanctification" or simply "Sanctification". "Christian Perfection" was used in articles and addresses defining the doctrine, but it was seldom used in testimony. J. A. Wood in *Perfect Love,* a book regarded as an authority by all three movements, sums up the general attitude to the spirit and terms for testimony:

Their Special Emphasis: Holiness • 233

There are some who profess holiness carelessly, and use objectional and unguarded terms. These, in most cases, are those whose life and spirit present but a sorry idea of Christian holiness. Such persons sometimes say 'I am perfect,' 'I am pure,' 'I have not committed a sin for so long'.[54] These things ought to be true, and may be true; but their careless utterance by some of the professed friends of holiness has done much to injure this precious doctrine, and bring its profession into disrepute. It was so in Mr. Wesley's day, and it is so in our day.[55]

The defence of the word "Perfection" involved Wesley in sustained and serious conflict with those who denied the possibility of perfection in this life. The Holiness Movement, adopting the same position as Wesley, is similarly involved. Like Wesley they assert that they did not invent the word but found it in the canon of Scripture. Admittedly, a "limited perfection" is open to censure as a contradiction of terms, but it is an attempt to explain how Paul could apparently consider himself to be one of the "perfect" in one sense (Philippians 3:15) and yet disclaim the ultimate resurrection perfection (v. 12). Samuel Chadwick's contribution to the problem (quoted with approval in Jessop's *Foundations of Doctrine*, pp. 171-72) by fastening on the Greek word καταρτιζω as representing a limited perfection for this life and the word τελειος as standing for the ultimate consummation of grace and perfect development is no real solution,[56] for τελειος is used in Philippians 3:15, in the limited sense, and in I Corinthians 2:6, where Paul contrasts the τελειοι of the Corinthian church (who are also apparently the πνευματικοι [v. 15]) with the σαρκινοι, the νηπιοι ἐν Χριστῳ (i) (3:1). From this, and other passages in the New Testament, it is clear that there were those in a deeper spiritual experience than the "babes in Christ". This experience was not automatically entered into by the mere passage of time, for Paul chides the "babes" with still being in an elementary, carnal experience when they should be πνευματικοι. In Philippians 3:15, the Revised Standard Version and the New English Bible translate τελειοι as "mature". J. B. Phillips translates it "spiritually adult", which has much to commend it. It suggests a stage of maturity and responsibility has been reached and yet leaves room for the conception of further development. Most people would appreciate the significance of the expression "adult Christianity". It is not too pretentious and

234 • *In the Steps of John Wesley*

challenges with a sense of desirability and availability. Admittedly, it does not include all the ideas present in τελειος and its cognates, and it would be out of place in some of its contexts in the New Testament. But it might be more significant to the modern mind than "Christian Perfection", and lead to a better understanding of the message of the Holiness Movement.

Wesley taught that the justified did not sin in the sense of committing voluntary transgressions.[57] In the experience of entire sanctification he taught that inbred sin was eliminated from the believer.[58] In one or two places in his writings he seems to suggest that it was a point on which room was left for a difference of opinion,[59] but there can be no question that he firmly believed in the extinction of sin.[60] The Holiness movements have made this the criterion of Scriptural Holiness. They can overlook differences of opinion on other matters. Reader Harris taught a fourfold salvation: conversion, regeneration, entire sanctification and a progressive spiritual maturity. Frank Lucas, a vice-president of the International Holiness Mission, testified to receiving negative cleansing from sin before the positive fulness of the Spirit,[61] and J. G. Govan testified on similar lines.[62] Paget Wilkes of the Japan Evangelistic Band denied that consecration is a condition of entire sanctification but taught that it followed the appropriation of faith. But all these believed that entire sanctification eliminated inbred sin and were regarded as orthodox. Anything which stopped short of this seemed to the Holiness Movement to be in the nature of compromise. They strove to give an adequate definition of sin, though often the less educated used expressions which were unimaginative and materialistic. Some idea of the thoughtful exposition they sought for is given in a recent statement in the official organ of the Church of the Nazarene, the *Herald of Holiness*. It is by a present day Nazarene scholar, W. T. Purkiser, and it includes an exposition by J. B. Chapman, a former general superintendent. It is in reply to the question, "How does the sin nature re-enter the heart when a man goes back on God?"

> I don't think it was ever better explained than by Dr. J. B. Chapman in his book 'Let the Winds Blow': 'Negative holiness is a concept of thinkers, but it does not exist in fact. Sin is dethroned only when

Their Special Emphasis: Holiness • 235

Christ is enthroned, and the heart continues pure only while Christ remains . . . Just now I have the electric light on and the whole room is full of light. But the darkness is gone conditionally, rather than absolutely. It is gone on the condition that the light remains. Likewise, only a Spirit-filled heart is a pure heart—no theory can invalidate this fact.'

Purkiser continues:

If I might suggest some other analogies, I would say that sin re-enters the heart of a man who goes back on God just as poverty re-enters the life of a man who had been given a fortune which he has lost; or as disease invades the body of a man who had been healed; or as the twist, bent, or warp comes back into the steel that had been straightened.

None of these analogies should be taken to deny that carnality is a positive evil, with dynamic force inherent in it. It is this. But it is not a "thing", a bit of "stuff", something which could exist apart from the soul and therefore could go "in" or "out" of the soul. It is rather a positive corruption of the moral nature which comes because that nature is cut off from the Source of spiritual purity. It consists of tendencies, propensities, and attitudes which are changed and kept changed by the sanctifying fulness of the Holy Spirit in the soul. 'But if we walk in the light, as he is in the light, we have fellowship one with another, and the blood of Jesus Christ his Son cleanseth (Greek, present tense, *is cleansing*) us from all sin' (I John 1:7).[63]

This statement makes clear that the Holiness movements, in common with Wesley,[64] teach an experience of Holiness which is completely dependent on the presence and merits of Christ.

Their Relationship to the Keswick Movement

It is of interest that one of the pioneers of the Keswick movement, Evan H. Hopkins, uses the identical illustration of the light dispelling the darkness and keeping it dispelled.[65] It is an indication of how narrow was the line which separated the Holiness Movement from the Keswick Movement in its early days. Indeed in its first few years the Keswick Convention was attended and sometimes addressed by those who believed in cleansing from sin. Methodists like John Brash and Charles Inwood were invited to the platform. But as the Keswick leaders stressed their denial of the possibility of a believer being cleansed from sin in this life the Keswick Movement and the Holiness Movement were inclined to form different camps.[66]

236 • *In the Steps of John Wesley*

At times they openly joined issue as in 1895 when Reader Harris responded to the statement by Prebendary Webb-Peploe that no man could "be free from sin experimentally while in the mortal body" by publicly offering £100 (for the benefit of the Keswick Mission Fund) to the first Keswick speaker who forwarded to him a passage of Scripture which, read with the context, positively affirms the necessity of sin in the Spirit-filled believer.

The controversy raged for some months in both the religious and secular press with eminent Christians taking opposite sides.[67]

But in 1908, in an earnest appeal for unity and to forget differences he wrote:

> We say the *supposed* differences of doctrine, because in reality the difference as far as regeneration is concerned is, we believe, nil, but for sanctification Keswick teaches suppression of sin, and the Pentecostal League proclaims deliverance from it. There may be other differences, but we wish to forget the differences and remember only the truths upon which we both agree.[68]

There was the same awareness of differences and similarities in the Holiness Mission.

In 1912, indignant at the refusal of the *Life of Faith* to publish replies from men of the Mission to what they considered to be a misrepresentation of their teaching,[69] David Thomas and two others visited the Keswick Convention and conducted open air meetings and distributed 3,000 *Journals*.[70] Keswick was called "the greatest hindrance" because "it proclaims what we must call a spurious Holiness."[71]

But in 1913, in "A Plea for Unity", with special reference to "the counteractionists" (Keswick), Milbank wrote:

> Can no ground be found on which God's people can unite? Surely forbearance and patience from those who are ahead with those who are behind, agreeing with what they have in common, and refusing to dispute with what they disagree, will tend towards this end.[72]

The Church of the Nazarene also could draw the line sharply between their Holiness teaching and that of Keswick,[73] but they could also, with others, "lovingly express . . . their joy at any manifestation of the quickening of the Holy Ghost evidenced in the deepening of Christian experience as represented by the Keswick movement . . ."[74]

Their Special Emphasis: Holiness • 237

Therefore the kinship between the two movements should not be overlooked. Keswick stems from the visit of Mr. and Mrs. Pearsall Smith, and Mrs. Pearsall Smith's *The Christian's Secret of a Happy Life* is read with approval by many in the Holiness Movement. A. T. Pierson, writing on Keswick's message in *Forward Movements of the Last Half Century* (1905) gives Wesley's definition of sins as voluntary transgressions and declares that in this sense Keswick teaches the privilege of the Spirit-filled believer not to commit sin.[75] Although Keswick has invited speakers from time to time who have taught doctrine which has not resembled the original emphasis of a second crisis and a life of victory, recently two prominent members of the Holiness movement have been invited to the Keswick platform: Major Allister Smith of the Salvation Army and Dr. Paul Rees, a frequent speaker in Nazarene and other Holiness circles in America.

Attempts at Psychological Interpretation

Little work has been done by the Holiness movements in the presentation of the experience of Holiness in psychological terms. The pioneers were not interested in such a presentation, and the leaders of the International Holiness Mission particularly treated psychology with suspicion. There was not quite the same reserve in the Calvary Holiness Church for in 1939 D. A. Simons sympathetically outlined Professor Starbuck's psychological interpretation of entire sanctification in the *Flame*.[76] In his summary of Starbuck's theory he states:

> From a psychological point of view, the whole struggle after conversion and the consequent necessity which people feel of passing on to a second work of grace grows out of the conflict between the old habitual life and the new set of functionings which have not yet become well-established in the nervous mechanism....
>
> Sanctification is the step, usually after much striving and discontent, by which the personality is finally identified with the spiritual life which at conversion existed as a possibility. In other words, the state aimed after and attained at entire sanctification is that in which a person is no longer a mere participant in the divine life, but is a medium through which it expresses itself.

Simons expresses the opinion that this psychological interpretation "tallies with Wesley's statements in the main". But probably others in the Holiness Movement would consider that it did not take sufficient account of the problem of sin.

The Nazarenes included a textbook on psychology in their ministers' course of study as early as 1911. For several years from 1932 Woodworth's *Psychology* was prescribed. But it appears that few attempts have been made to state entire sanctification in psychological terms.

L. T. Corlett, president of the Nazarene Theological Seminary,[77] describes man's sinful condition in terms of self-centredness. At the Fall, man centred himself in himself as the object of his choices instead of centering himself in God, and thereby deprived himself of the sustaining Personality who made finite beings holy. He thus became depraved and plunged the race into the quagmire of inherited sin. Part of his fallen condition is the presence of antagonistic motives which counteract his purpose to live on the highest of his levels. These are sometimes called the "false ego"; the biblical term is the "carnal mind". Entire sanctification involves the severance of all claims to the self-life and the centering of the self in God. When this is done under the leadership of the Holy Spirit complete faith in the promise of God enables God to cleanse from sin (the false ego), perfect in love and sanctify man through and through. This leads to an integration of the personality.[78]

At the same time Corlett makes it clear that entire sanctification does not automatically cure nervous disorders or deliver from moods.[79] W. Curry Mavis, one of the contributors to a symposium of Holiness teaching sponsored by the American National Holiness Association, declares that it does not necessarily resolve complexes. They may be resolved by the Spirit in the instantaneous work but usually they are part of the continuing process. "Before the complete resolution of repressed complexes, the Holy Spirit gives spiritual strength to annul repressed urges that move in the wrong direction."[80]

There is much common ground between Mavis's interpretation and Sangster's treatment of the Holy Spirit and the unconscious,[81] and Stanley Jones covers some of the same ground in *The Way to Power and Poise*.[82] In connection with the progressive work after the crisis of entire sanctifica-

Their Special Emphasis: Holiness • 239

tion, J. G. Morrison, a former Nazarene general superintendent, in *Our Lost Estate*[83] insists on the importance of self-discipline. "The fruit of the Spirit is . . . self-control."[84]

NOTES ON CHAPTER 7

[1]*A History of the Methodist Church in Great Britain*, ed. Davies and Rupp (London: Epworth Press, 1965), vol. I, pp. ix-xxxvi, 81-111.
[2]We shall concentrate on the official declarations of doctrine and draw on the other sources as necessary.
[3]The first two sentences "There is a marked distinction . . . growth in grace" were transferred to par. 40 under "Special Rules".
[4]The quotation from *Webster's Dictionary* appears to be from the 1927 edition. I have not been able to trace the exact definitions in the terms given in *HMJ* in any edition of the other dictionaries but the variations are very slight and unimportant. There are the same slight inaccuracies in the quotations from Wesley and Pope.
[5]*Letters* (Standard Edition), Vol. IV 188.
[6]W. B. Pope, *A Compendium of Christian Theology* (London: Wesleyan Conference Office, 1877), vol. II, p. 64.
[7]From Nov., 1908, issue of *HMJ* in "How to Lead Believers to the Experience of Entire Sanctification", "Man's side" was given as "Consecration", Rom. xii 1, 2.
[8]See chap. 6 above, "Their Attitude to the World", esp. pp. 212-17.
[9]E.g. *HMJ*, Sept., 1908, p. 44. A testimony to Holiness appeared on the front page of every issue for the first three years. See also *Flame*, Aug.-Sept., 1935, p. 4.
[10]H. E. Jessop, *Foundations of Doctrine* (Chicago: Chicago Evangelistic Institute, 1949), p. 168; Maynard G. James, *Facing the Issue* (Burnley: Pilgrim Publishing House, 1948), chap. vii.
[11]J. B. Chapman, *Holiness the Heart of the Christian Experience* (Kansas City: Beacon Hill Press, 1963), pp. 62-64.
[12]Lest it should be thought that a biassed selection has been made of those of Wesley's statements which are in line with the emphasis of the Holiness movements, this summary of an independent Methodist scholar is given.
[13]P. 167.
[14]P. 172.
[15]P. 167.
[16]P. 167.
[17]Pp. 171-72.
[18]P. 171.
[19]P. 168.
[20]P. 171.

[21]*Ibid.*

[22]P. 170.

[23]P. 169.

[24]P. 170; see "Plain Account of Christian Perfection", *Works* (1841), Vol. XI 410 for restoration.

[25]P. 186.

[26]"So we find insistent warnings in Wesley's later writings of the danger that increase in wealth will lead to worldliness, and the decay of single-minded zeal for Holiness," p. 207.

[27]"Plain Account . . .", *Ibid.*, Vol. XI 352.

[28]*HMJ*, April, 1913, p. 42.

[29]*Ibid.*, July, 1925, p. 2.

[30]For the development of this emphasis in Methodism after Wesley's death see Raymond Brown, "Evangelical Ideas of Perfection" (unpublished Ph.D. dissertation, University of Cambridge, 1964), pp. 45-50.

[31]A. Paget Wilkes, *Sanctification* (London: Japan Evangelistic Band, 1949), p. 66. Sermons, *Works*, Vol. VI 50.

[32]"Plain Account . . .", *Ibid.*, Vol. XI 352.

[33]*A Collection of Hymns for the Use of the People Called Methodists*, comp. John Wesley (London: J. Paramore, 1780), No. 335, v. 4.

[34]*Ibid.*, No. 343, v. 4.

[35]*Ibid.*, No. 341, v. 3.

[36]J. Ford, *What the Holiness People Believe* (Birkenhead: Emmanuel Bible College, n.d., c. 1955), pp. 32-33.

[37]"Q. But would it not be better to be entirely silent, not to speak of it at all? A. . . . But this could not be done with a clear conscience; for undoubtedly he ought to speak." "Plain Account . . ." *Works*, Vol. XI 381-82.

[38]*Ibid.*, 381.

[39]See Sangster, *Path to Perfection*, p. 163.

[40]See e.g. *HMJ*, Sept., 1913, p. 102.

[41]See Peters, *Christian Perfection*, etc., pp. 214-15.

[42]*Letters*, Vol. V 93.

[43]". . . I want living witnesses . . . if I were certain there are none such, I must have done with this doctrine." "Plain Account . . .", *Works*, Vol. XI 389.

[44]1964, par. 39. Introduced in 1908.

[45]Acts 2:18, 39.

[46]Though this does not avert but probably aggravates the temptation to denominational pride.

[47]I John 4:16-18.

[48]Cf. also "The Pentecostal League".

[49]See his paraphrase of Matt. 3:11: "He shall fill you with the Holy Ghost inflaming your hearts with that fire of love which many waters cannot quench." *Notes upon the New Testament* (London: William Bowyer, 1755). Also his quotation of his brother's statement that when his day of *Pentecost* had come he would hear of persons being *sanctified* as frequently as he previously did of persons justified. *Journal*, Vol. IV 532. Also his sermon on "Scriptural Christianity", preached on Acts

Their Special Emphasis: Holiness • 241

2:4, "They were all filled with the Holy Ghost", in which he undoubtedly has in mind the disciples on the day of Pentecost as being in the experience of Christian perfection (see especially IV, par. 1.) *Works*, Vol. V 43.

[50] Raymond Brown in Part II A (5), *op. cit.*, draws attention to the attempt of the Methodist leaders of the early nineteenth century to relate the doctrine of Christian perfection more specifically to the work of the Holy Spirit.

[51]*Holiness Herald*, Nov., 1923, p. 2; *HMJ*, Aug., 1921, p. 87; *Flame*, Jan.-Feb., p. 3.

[52]See Nils Bloch-Hoell, *The Pentecostal Movement* (London: Allen and Unwin, 1964), p. 32.

[53]Mainly because the genuineness of much of the modern variety was doubted. But the possibility of a revival of the genuine gifts of the Spirit was not denied. See *HMJ*, March, 1923, p. 28.

[54]This type of testimony has been generally deprecated in the movements under review. On the other hand it featured fairly prominently in the *Holiness Advocate*, the official organ of the Holiness Church. See Jan., 1884, pp. 6-7; March, 1887, pp. 39-41.

[55]P. 89. See also J. B. Chapman, *op. cit.*, p. 21.

[56]This is not to deny the valuable contribution to the subject of his *Call to Christian Perfection*.

[57]"Plain Account . . .", *Works*, Vol. XI 359-61, 380 par. 3.

[58]*Ibid.*, 371-72: "Q. Does this imply that all inward sin is taken away? A. Undoubtedly; or how can we be said to be 'saved from all our uncleannesses?' (Ezek. xxxvi.29)". See also pp. 373-74.

[59]*Letters*, Vol. IV 213.

[60]Sangster, *Path to Perfection*, p. 82.

[61]*HMJ*, June, 1908, p. 23.

[62]*In the Train of His Triumph* (Edinburgh: The Faith Mission, 1946), pp. 14, 17, 18.

[63]11-9-63, p. 17.

[64]"Plain Account . . .", *Works*, Vol. XI, 379-80.

[65]*The Law of Liberty in the Spiritual Life* (London: Marshall, Morgan and Scott, 1957), pp. 25-26.

[66]Pollock, *The Keswick Story*, chap. viii; Brown, *op. cit.*, pp. 417-20.

[67]For Harris's version see Reader Harris, *Is Sin a Necessity?* (London: Partridge and Co., 1896). Hugh Price Hughes asserted that Harris's doctrine was "precisely the doctrine which John Wesley taught". P. 38.

[68]*Tongues of Fire*, April, 1908, p. 6.

[69]*HMJ*, Aug., 1912, pp. 90-92.

[70]*Ibid.*, Sept., 1912, p. 102.

[71]*Ibid.*

[72]*Ibid.*, Feb., 1913, pp. 14-15.

[73]A. M. Hills, who became a Nazarene, wrote *Scriptural Holiness and Keswick Teaching Compared* (Manchester: Star Hall, n.d., c. 1912).

[74]*Holiness Herald*, Feb., 1924, p. 3.

[75](London: Funk and Wagnalls), pp. 21-23.

[76]May-June, p. 5.
[77]Retired in 1966.
[78]*Holiness the Harmonizing Experience* (Kansas City: Beacon Hill Press, 1955), chap. iii.
[79]*Ibid.*, chap. iv.
[80]"Repressed Complexes and Christian Maturity", *The Word and the Doctrine*, comp. Kenneth E. Geiger (Kansas City: Beacon Hill Press, 1965), pp. 307-15.
[81]*Path to Perfection,* chap. xv.
[82](New York: Abingdon Press, 1949), pp. 71-106.
[83](Kansas City: Nazarene Publishing House, 1929), pp. 168-73.
[84]Gal. 5:22-23 (N.E.B.).

CHAPTER 8

Their Relationship to Holiness Movements in Christian History

Holiness in the New Testament

Ideally the whole Christian Church is a holiness movement. The New Testament name for disciples is ἅγιοι, "saints" or "holy ones". They are the ἐκκλησια, the "called out" congregation, "called out of darkness into God's marvellous light".[1] To them all things are given that pertain unto life and godliness,[2] and they are called not to ἀκαθαρσια but to ἁγιασμος.[3] They are bidden to be τελειοι as their heavenly Father is τελειος[4] and they are commanded to "awake up righteously, and sin not".[5] Christ loved the (whole) church, and gave Himself up for it; that He might sanctify it, having cleansed it by the washing of water with the word, that He might present the church to Himself a glorious church, ... holy and without blemish.[6] No one reading the New Testament is left in doubt that union with Christ involves death to sin,[7] and a pilgrimage to the holy city[8] on the highway of holiness.[9]

There has, however, been a considerable difference of opinion among Christians concerning the depth of deliverance from sin which is possible in this life. Indeed, in the New Testament there is indubitable evidence that in spite of their high calling some Christians remained "babes" and σαρκινοι.[10] It seemed to be taken for granted that in every church there were the ἀτακτοι, the ὀλιγοψυχοι and the ἀσθενεις.[11]

Even if it be asserted, and with good reason, that these were subnormal Christians and that in contradistinction some of their brethren are described as τελειοι[12] and πνευματικοι,[13] who are fathers in maturity,[14] whose love has been made perfect,[15] disciples who are perfected as their Master,[16] the question is still raised as to whether they had found full deliverance from sin.

What was the perfection which Paul disclaimed in the same breath as apparently classing himself with the τελειοι?[17] Is Romans chapter 7 Paul's testimony as a mature Christian or a memoir in the historical present of a past conflict or even of his legal bondage as as Jewish rabbi? Is it still self delusion to say that "we have no sin" even after we have confessed our sins and trusted God to be faithful and righteous to forgive us our sins, and to cleanse us from all unrighteousness?[18]

So the New Testament, while undoubtedly holding out the promise of complete deliverance from sin and ultimate perfection, does not close the loopholes of controversy concerning the time and the extent of the deliverance.

The Early Fathers

The dichotomy[19] present in the New Testament persisted in the succeeding centuries. The *Didache* is the first of the Patristic writings to concede a low road as well as a high road to heaven,[20] but the two levels of living were discernible from the first.

Clement of Rome, dealing with the truculence of the Corinthian Church, calls them to the ideal Christian life with the assumption that however far they had fallen short it lies within their reach.[21]

Athenagoras of Athens appeals to the purity of the Christians' lives as evidence of their belief in God.[22] He claims that they so faithfully regulated their lives by reference to Him that each one of them stood before Him blameless and irreproachable, not even entertaining the thought of the slightest sin.[23] Theophilus of Antioch asserts that with Christians "temperance dwells . . . iniquity is exterminated, sin extirpated . . ."[24] Due allowance should be made, however, that they both wrote as apologists for a misrepresented and persecuted religion and perhaps overstated their case as far as Christians in general were concerned. But as Gwatkin puts it, "if many of the Christians fell far short of saintliness there were saints enough among them to overcome the world."[25]

While Irenaeus of Lyons bears witness to the consciousness of the Christians of being a community which had been liberated by the operation of divine miracle from the dominance of the devil and sin,[26] he indicates that there is a category of the "perfect" which lies beyond the initiation into the Church.[27]

Clement of Alexandria made sanctity a special study. "More fully than any before him, he drew up a doctrine of the Perfect."[28] Indeed, in the words of J. G. Davies, "while Clement sought to distinguish between the true Church and the gatherings of heretics, he also tended to set the invisible Church of the mature Christian against the visible Church consisting of sinner and saint alike."[29] Nevertheless his standard for every baptised Christian is high. Baptism implies perfection.[30] Even in the elementary experience we should "try to sin as little as possible" and "to keep clear of voluntary transgressions",[31] but ahead lies the full unification of the powers of the soul.[32] In *Stromateis,* Book VII, the pattern for John Wesley's "Character of a Methodist", he describes the steps to perfection as $\pi\iota\sigma\tau\iota\varsigma$, $\gamma\nu\omega\sigma\iota\varsigma$ and $\dot{\alpha}\gamma\alpha\pi\eta$.

Origen, his illustrious successor, taught the possibility of a relative perfection in this life, of which the Apostle Paul is an example.[33] He gives a greater place to the Cross than Clement,[34] and even speaks of those, few in number, who are pure and sin no more.[35]

These witnesses to sanctity in Rome and Athens, in Alexandria and Antioch and Lyons, bishops, apologists and scholars, in the first, second and third centuries, are typical of many others whose testimony space forbids.

A Basis of Comparison: Five Characteristics

Thus have arisen in Christian history individuals and movements who have felt it their duty not only to seek the highest Christian experience for themselves but to stir up others to join them in the quest. To these is applied in a special sense the name of "holiness movements". The three movements which are the subject of this thesis come into this category. It is a large category, and if every movement which made holiness its aim were to be given adequate notice a library would be required, not the narrow scope of one chapter of a thesis such as this. It seems best therefore in making a comparison to mention *five characteristics of the three movements under review* and to select from Christian history those movements and individuals who bear the closest resemblance.

1. *They each taught that a qualified perfection was attainable, in which the power and defilement of indwelling sin was removed and the believer was enabled by grace to live a life regulated by love, free from conscious, voluntary transgressions.*

2. *This experience was received as a second work of grace, within the context of justification and on the basis of justification, wrought by the Holy Spirit in response to consecration and faith, and concomitant, if not synonymous, with the fulness of the Spirit.*

3. *They claimed to base this teaching of Holiness on the Bible, especially the New Testament, and within the context of orthodox Christian theology, in the sense that they subscribed to such doctrines as the Trinity, the deity of Christ, the personality of the Holy Spirit, generally subscribed to by Christian churches, and made no pretensions to theological novelties.*

4. *They each established a witness to Holiness outside of the existing churches but within the context of a church order of their own creation.*

5. *They taught a Holiness which should be lived in the sphere of the common life, with a concentration on otherworldly values and at the same time a sense of mission to the world.*

Gnostics

The Gnostics' use of Pauline terms such as ψυχικοι, σαρκικοι, πνευματικοι and τελειοι, and their distinction between the initiated and the uninitiated give an appearance of similarity to the three movements under review, but the appearance is deceptive. They believed in a second work of grace and some of them believed that it was possible to live without sin. Their aim was to win the Church over to their opinions, but they were quite prepared, if need be, to commence a sect of their

Their Relationship to Holiness Movements • 247

own. Nevertheless the differences are greater than the similarities. The three movements under review have nothing in common with the speculations of Basilides and Valentinus, the antinomianism of the Ophites nor the cavalier treatment which Marcion meted out to the Old Testament nor his subjective selection of parts of the New Testament. The Gnostics majored on knowledge whereas these three movements placed their emphasis on faith and consecration, and decried "head knowledge" as opposed to "heart knowledge". And they constantly maintained in opposition to the Gnostics that the body is not essentially sinful: it has become the vehicle of sin but through entire sanctification it can become the temple of the Holy Spirit.

The Montanists

They have a much closer resemblance to the Montanists, whom Rupert Davies lists as ancestors to the Methodists[86] and John Wesley considered to be "real, scriptural Christians".[37] Montanism was an apocalyptic movement which professed to call the church back to its original ideal and protested against its tepid devotion and formal worship. Some historians regard them as innovators,[38] teaching that the dispensation of the Paraclete began with Montanus, who, with Prisca, one of his prophetesses, made exaggerated and blasphemous claims; others regard them as reformers, calling a lax church back to first principles, who in their enthusiasm took orthodoxy to excess. No doubt the movement differed in expression in different places, but it is difficult to believe that Tertullian would have been carried away by a heresy.[39] They believed in a special enduement of the Holy Spirit which placed them among the πνευματικοι as opposed to the initial state in which they were ψυχικοι. But it is not clear whether this experience excluded sin, nor what prominence was given to love. We may infer from their rigorism that consecration played an important part but we cannot be sure what emphasis was laid upon faith. They appear to have been excommunicated rather than taking the initiative in schism, but they created a church order of their own with emphasis on a charismatic ministry in which women were given a place. The laity were encouraged to live the Spirit-filled life in the daily round.

The Novatianists and Donatists

Two other protest movements in the early church had some similar features to the three movements under review. They are the Novatianists and Donatists. Their emphasis was more on the communal holiness of a pure church rather than the individual sanctity of a pure heart. Nevertheless among the Novatianists a distinction was made between the *perfecti* and the *credentes*,[40] indicating the possibility of a deeper spiritual experience beyond conversion. They were called *"Cathari"*, which gives an insight into their emphasis on purity but is not sufficient evidence for assuming that they taught cleansing from indwelling sin. Both movements were prepared to separate from a church which they believed to be corrupt in order to maintain what they believed to be Scriptural standards, but though accused of schism they were not charged with doctrinal error.[41] In their separation there were less worthy elements: personal rivalry, duplicity and intrigue, and, in the case of the Donatists an underlying nationalistic cause.[42] Although the Donatists prided themselves on setting a higher standard of devotion than the Catholic Church, exalting a full abandonment to God manifested in the fearless embracing of martyrdom, carried to fanatical extremes in the case of the Circumcellions, they were rigorists rather than perfectionists.[43] In a lesser degree the same is true of the Novatianists, but they were closer to the movements under review in teaching a perfection which was made possible by a plenary outpouring of the Holy Spirit, though what part consecration and faith played in the obtaining of it is uncertain. Both the Donatists and the Novatianists sought to propagate their beliefs and in this way showed a sense of mission, even though their sphere of activity was more among the converted rather than the pagan world. The Donatists were not so absorbed with the other world as to be indifferent to political manoeuvring. Both churches taught a rigorist sanctity which could nevertheless be lived in the context of the common life by those who were willing to endure the sacrifices involved.

Augustine

The great Augustine, becoming involved in the controversy over communal purity with the Donatists and personal sanctity with Pelagius, insisted on the holiness of origin and institution of the Catholic Church as against an attempted holiness of individual membership on the part of the former, and a sanctity of grace, mourning the continuing presence of sin, in opposition to a sincere but superficial morality on the part of the latter. Thus one of the church's greatest saints became a bulwark against those who left the mixed crop of the Catholic Church to sow a new patch of pure wheat, and a rallying point for all those who shudder at the term of "sinless perfection".[44]

The Roman Catholic Church

But if Augustine set bounds to the extent of the deliverance from sin in this life (bounds prescribed by the wisdom of God, not by the possibility of His grace), he was foremost in the quest of holiness. He has a place in the *monastic movement*, in some ways the most serious and sustained search for sanctity which has stirred in the bosom of the Church. Beginning in the third century, it is with us today. How far its methods are consistent with the New Testament is a matter of debate. To mention its abuses is to emphasise its human content. But of the presence of a single-minded passion for holiness in its origin and its history there can be no doubt. Its withdrawal from common life and its emphasis on mortification stand in sharp contrast with the attitude of the three groups under review but there are elements in Catholic theology which both movements share.

It is a matter of some interest that modern Holiness movements like the Church of the Nazarene, which place a high value on their Protestant heritage, have no hesitation in quoting the pronouncements of *popes* in support of the Holiness message. M. E. Redford, a Nazarene historian, quotes Leo the Great, Innocent III and Urban I as witnesses to the work of the Holy Spirit in sanctification subsequent to baptism in the rite of confirmation. More to the point is his reference to the great Catholic theologian, *Thomas Aquinas*.[45] His teaching concerning Christian perfection has much in common with what John Wesley taught five centuries later, and to which the three movements under review subscribe. Especially impressive is his maintenance that it is possible to live free from mortal sins and all that hinders the soul from turning wholly to God.⁴⁶ A comparison between the Catholic teaching and Wesley's concerning the possibility of deliverance from indwelling sin is complicated by the Catholic belief that original sin is washed away in the sacrament of baptism, but that *concupiscentia* still remains. *Concupiscentia* is not evil in itself, but it can become evil and lead to evil.⁴⁷ It therefore does not correspond with the Wesleyan view of indwelling sin, which *inter alia* is a corruption of the human instincts, which still remain and must be controlled after the corruption has been removed. If, in Christian perfection, the soul is set free from all that hinders it turning wholly to God, it is set free from indwelling sin in the Wesleyan sense.⁴⁸

Aquinas taught a qualified perfection of love. Those thus perfect fulfilled the law so modified as to be accommodated to the fallen state of man. Here again there is a striking resemblance to what Wesley taught.⁴⁹ But he taught that this state was reached by spiritual growth rather than a crisis of faith.⁵⁰ Redford sees a connection between the rite of confirmation and the Nazarene teaching concerning the fulness of the Spirit.⁵¹ But confirmation is not identical with Aquinas's doctrine of Christian perfection, though the latter was achieved by an infusion of love by the Holy Spirit.⁵²

The Roman Catholic Church has always had within it those who have made perfection their aim and urged others to join them in the quest. To a large extent, however, it has involved the withdrawal from the common life and a formal commitment to the "counsels of perfection". Nevertheless, concerned as he was to maintain the *status quo* and limit the "state of perfection" to the "religious", Aquinas clearly taught that "seculars" could attain Christian perfection and that those in the formal "state of perfection" might be far from truly perfect and might ultimately be damned.⁵³

Similar in many respects in their teaching to the perfection taught in the Catholic Church, the three movements under review differed from it in at least two important respects. According to the Catholic conception of justification as a free infusion of Divine grace producing inward righteousness, perfection is a development of justification. According to the Protestant conception of justification, held by the three movements under review, perfection is the development of sanctification within the context of justification, the reconciled relationship with God. And, of course, to a Roman Catholic it is unthinkable to separate from the church. To him the action of the Holiness groups in forming separate churches for the promotion of Holiness involves the basic inconsistency of committing the sin of schism for the sake of sanctity!

The Mystics

In the many successions in the Catholic Church, besides its claimed apostolic succession of its bishops, the mystical succession was especially prominent in the Middle Ages. It helped to off-set the externalising of religion by elaborate ceremonies and the *ex opere operato* doctrine of the sacraments. Prominent and influential in this succesion was Bernard of Clairvaux who with Johannine and Pauline insight saw love as the secret of union with God. Love has four stages: natural love, grateful love, the love of God for His own sake and, fourthly, and Bernard was doubtful whether this stage could be reached on earth, ecstatic love, in which one only loves oneself for the sake of God.[54]

Other honourable names in this spiritual succession are Hugo and Richard of St. Victor, Bonaventura, Albertus Magnus, and Gerson, notable for their attempt to combine scholasticism and mysticism. The greatest of all speculative mystics, Eckhart, owed much to Thomas Aquinas and in turn influenced Ruysbroek, Suso, and Tauler, who with the writer of the *Theologia Germanica* helped to shape Luther's thoughts on inward religion.[55] Tauler was attacked by Eck for teaching some kind of perfectionism.

Catharism

The emphasis on the inner life as opposed to externals and the exaltation of spirit above matter took unorthodox forms, the most prominent and widespread in the Middle Ages being Catharism. It conceived all being as governed by a dualism of good and evil: everything spiritual was good, everything material, creation in all its visible forms, was evil. Hence man was seen as a soul—or spirit—imprisoned in a body, which it must be his end to escape: if he did not he went from body to body. The only way to achieve this was by renunciation of all material sustenance other than that needed to sustain life which already existed, but not to propagate it. Hence marriage, meat eating, sexual intercourse, wealth, worldly goods were all condemned.

The Cathars were divided into the *perfecti* (to whom the name "Cathars" properly belonged), who practised these deprivations, and the *credentes*, who followed the authority of the *perfecti*. The category of the *perfecti* was entered by a rite called the consolamentum which was supposed to bring about the baptism of the Holy Spirit by the laying on of hands by a Cathar minister or one of the *perfecti*. Many of the *credentes* postponed this rite until the approach of death because of the strict standard which it involved, but it was the only way of admittance into the Cathar church, outside of which it was believed there was no salvation.

These ideas, which reached Western Europe probably after 1140, were of non-Christian origin, coming through the Bogomils in Bulgaria. The Cathars had some points in common with the three movements under review but their theology was basically different.[56]

Quietism

In the latter part of the sixteenth and seventeenth centuries Quietism, which has been described as the exaggeration and perversion of the mystical doctrine of the interior quest, swept over Europe and took deep root within both Catholicism and Protestantism. John Wesley had a qualified admiration for some of the Quietists, especially Madam Guyon and Archbishop Fenelon, and in this he has been followed by some in the three movements under review. He published *An Extract of the Life of Madam Guion*[57] and an edition of her autobiography figures in the book-lists of the *Tongues of Fire*.[58] H. E. Jessop,[59] Maynard James[60] and M. E. Redford[61] all give her a qualified place in the Holiness succession.

In her autobiography Madam Guyon relates an experience on Magdalen's Day, 1680, in which her soul was "perfectly delivered from all her troubles" and attained a state in which she enjoyed purity of heart and committed no voluntary fault, in which she was lost in the infinite abyss of God's love, but in which there was still room for progression.[62] It was undoubtedly a second spiritual crisis in which surrender

Their Relationship to Holiness Movements • 253

to the will of God figures prominently, but little reference is made to faith and she does not explicitly refer to the Holy Spirit. The impression is given that the steadfast endurance of suffering was the tunnel which led to the sunlit landscape. She was possessed of a strong sense of mission to lead others along the path by which she believed God had led her, a path which she believed lay within the confines of Catholic orthodoxy and for some within the context of the common life, though she herself took the vow of chastity after the death of her husband,[63] later entering into the experience described above.

Antoinette Bourignon is sometimes classed with the Quietists, though Knox insists that she was a Jansenist who was also a Pelagian. Wesley found a place for an extract from her "Treatise of Solid Virtue", suitably abbreviated, in his *Christian Library,* approving of her emphasis on the love of God as the essence of all virtue, but critical of the "peculiar" strain in her teaching, and placing her below the level of a good Methodist.[64]

There is a mystic element in the Holiness movement, as there is in all vital religion. Quietism stressed the importance of pure love, utter dependence on Divine grace and the possibility and supremacy of union with God. But it tended to empty love of its ethical content, magnify the one act of surrender to the exclusion of the daily covenant and reduce a vital communion with God to a passive absorption, leaving no place for the means of grace. Wesley gave only a qualified approval to the mystics and sharply condemned their belittling of the means of grace.[65]

The Greek Orthodox Church

One of the disadvantages of a divided Christendom is that western Christians have but slight connections with the Greek Orthodox Church. Wesley, being a student of the Fathers, had contacts with it which the three movements under review lacked. High in his esteem were Ephrem Syrus, the apostle of the broken and contrite heart,[66] and Macarius,[67] who drew deeply of the wells of Gregory of Nyssa.[68] He sat at the feet of Clement of Alexandria, Chrysostom and Basil, and found a place in his *Christian Library* for Polycarp, Ignatius, Irenaeus, Origen and Dionysius of Alexandria.

The teaching of Eastern Orthodoxy concerning perfection is grounded in the Trinity. It centres in the doctrine of θέωσις, which originates from the Father, is communicated by the Son and is perfected by the Spirit. The partaking of the eucharist plays an important part in this process. Christ's death and resurrection wrested man from the demonic power of evil and the Holy Spirit perfects the will of the Father and the work of Christ. Perfection is envisaged as perpetual progress, but it is possible to achieve sainthood in the communion of the Holy Spirit in a personal relationship of holiness between the believer and his Lord.[69]

The Reformers

The Reformers treated the word "perfection" with suspicion, partly because of its association by the Roman Catholics with the monastic orders and their (from the Protestant viewpoint) confusion of sanctification with justification and partly because of fanatical interpretations of it by some of the Anabaptists. In several places in his writings Luther defines a perfection which is possible to all devout believers as opposed to the perfection sought by the religious,[70] but he strongly denied the possibility of being cleansed from the *"fomes peccati"* in this life.[71] Following Augustine's interpretation of the parable of the Good Samaritan he regarded the church as a hospital in which the cure of souls made progress but was not completed in this life.[72]

Zwingli's closest affinity with Wesley's teaching was his definition of sin as a voluntary transgression of a known law.[73] Calvin had the same reserve as the other Reformers concerning the word "perfection" and for the same reasons. He was prepared to allow it to the saints, provided it was defined in the words of Augustine that "part of this perfection consists in the recognition of our imperfection in truth and humility".[74] But only wilful perversion could find any grounds for antinomianism in an intelligent reading of either Luther's or Calvin's works.

Pietists, Puritans and Moravians

Pietism found sufficient in Luther (if not in Lutheranism) to develop a deep personal piety and among the British Puritans were those who, in confirmation of Calvin's claim, demonstrated that the doctrine of Election bore holy fruit.[75] Both these movements exercised a strong influence on the founder of Methodism. He had Puritanism in his blood and he sought the help of the Puritans in cultivating the spirituality of the Methodists.[76] He was also deeply influenced by the Moravians, that blending of the *Unitas Fratrum* with Pietism at Herrnhut, on the estate of Spener's godson, Count Zinzendorf. Although at a later date Zinzendorf strongly repudiated Wesley's teaching of perfection, there was at the time of Wesley's visit in 1738 a strong testimony to full deliverance from sin. Several of those who testified to it declared that they received it as a second work of grace.[77] There was an emphasis on faith and peace, but love does not figure prominently in the testimonies which Wesley records in his *Journal*. In spite of possible contacts with the Euchites, the Paulicians and the Cathari in their origins,[78] the theology of the Herrnhut phase was orthodox enough, apart from an exaggerated Christo-centricity which bordered on Patripassianism and the excesses of the "Sifting Time" at Herrnhaag between 1746 and 1750. Those of the "Diaspora" bore witness to a sanctity which shone in the common life and under Zinzendorf's influence were a proto-ecumenical movement. The settlements, however, claimed to be part of an ancient church with its own faith and order. Of their sense of mission there can be no doubt. They were the harbingers of Protestant world missions.

The Anabaptists

There is a kinship between the three movements under review and certain elements in two movements of reaction[79] from Lutheranism and Calvinism. They are Anabaptism and Arminianism.

Anabaptism is a very many sided movement involving many different groups of people: at one end violent and apocalyptic elements which culminated in the disaster of Munster, and at the other end a devout and godly pietism which found its enduring form under Menno Simons. Most evangelical Anabaptists, like Menno and Marpeck, though stressing the importance of living a righteous life, were willing to admit the persistence of evil after regeneration. Melchior Hofmann, however, went so far as to declare that sin was unnecessary and, indeed, unforgivable after baptism.[80] The Spiritualist, Caspar Schwenckfeld, approached mediaeval and patristic Catholicism in his confidence in the possibility of personal sanctification.[81] Both he and Hofmann emphasised the divinisation of the believer through assimilation of the celestial flesh of Christ. More closely akin to the three movements under review, Henry Niclaes sought the destruction of sin from boyhood and, becoming a "begodded man", he taught his Familists an experiential holiness wrought by the descent of the Holy Spirit and issuing in a life of Divine love.[82] Schwenckfeld bore witness to a "second awakening" in 1526 from which he later dated his matured religious life.[83] Besides these features similar to those of the movements under review, each of the above stressed the other-worldly side of Christianity, was possessed of a deep sense of mission and, particularly Hofmann, a furrier, and Niclaes, a merchant, remained in touch with the workaday world. They each had a following rather than formed a sect. That of Niclaes, the Familists, was the most closely organised, but even they were not compelled to break with the existing churches.[84] Hofmann's views on the celestial flesh of Christ were essentially Valentinian,[85] and Schwenckfeld's, though nearer orthodoxy, were not fully Chalcedonian.[86] The Familists were accused of heresy and immorality but it is difficult to assess the validity of the accusations.

The Quakers

Before dealing with the Arminians it is pertinent here to consider the place of the Society of Friends in the perfectionist succession. Not only are there strong similarities between George Fox and Hans Denck, Sebastian Franck and Caspar Schwenckfeld but the founder of the Quakers reaped a rich harvest from the fields of the Seekers and the Familists, and to a lesser degree from the Libertines and the Ranters. George Fox and the early Quakers are regarded as spiritual ancestors by the modern Holiness Movement in their teaching of Christian perfection, heart purity and freedom from sinning, in the sense of voluntary transgressions,[87] though they did not put the same emphasis as Wesley did upon the primacy of love. Fox taught the possibility of Adamic perfection, which Wesley and the movements under review denied, and

Their Relationship to Holiness Movements • 257

claimed to have received it himself. "I found none that could bear to be told that any should come to Adam's perfection into that image of God and righteousness and holiness that Adam was in before he fell, to be so clear and pure without sin, as he was."[88] But Barclay qualified it in terms similar to Wesley's.[89] It was received subsequent to justification and in the context of justification[90] and was wrought by the Holy Spirit. Quaker perfection fitted its recipients for this life and the next, produced heavenly minded men and women with a sense of mission and a social conscience. Was George Fox orthodox? Would he have owned the term? The chief charge brought against him is that of subjectivism, the exalting of the "inner light" above the Scriptures[91] and his dispensing with the sacraments. But he states his mission in biblical terms and professes to have no slight esteem for the Holy Scriptures. They were precious to him and he claimed to be in the Spirit by which they were given so that what the Lord "opened" to him he afterwards found to be in keeping with their teaching.[92] His sense of mission made him a leader of the Radical Reformation. He considered the Friends to be the very offspring of the true Church.[93]

Arminianism

Arminius did not commit himself on whether sin could be eliminated and a believer live without sin as a practical possibility in this life.[94] But he raised the question and his Dutch followers discussed it sympathetically. In so far as they believed that perfection was possible they regarded it in the context and on the basis of justification by faith. The fact that they taught a progressive perfection of the beginners, the proficient and the truly perfect[95] indicates that they envisaged perfection being attained by a process of obedience rather than a crisis of faith. Arminius taught that sanctification was wrought through the Spirit but it was not completed in a single moment.[96] The genius of Arminianism has been a reasoning toleration but this has not been inconsistent with a sense of mission strong enough to remonstrate with opposing systems and to form a separate church to maintain its own. Arminius was scrupulously careful of his orthodoxy and presented both the temporal and eternal aspects of the Gospel in his teaching.

John Wesley

The three movements under review were Arminian because Wesley was an Arminian and the teaching of Arminius was known mainly through him. There is no positive evidence that Wesley read the works of Arminius himself, however strong the presumption. But he was in the succession of English Arminianism[97] with forbears such as Jeremy Taylor, Stillingfleet and William Law, and if he did not build directly on the stones which Arminius laid he formulated his doctrine of Christian perfection in the climate which the great Dutch theologian helped to create. In the previous chapter we have compared the Holiness teaching of the movements under review with that of Wesley.

To what extent was Wesley a Separatist? He was born of parents who were Anglicans by choice with Dissent in their blood. That he loved the Anglican Church and valued his place in it is beyond dispute. But he suffered no man, bishop or archbishop, to divert him from his convictions. The Methodist societies were intended to be religious societies in the Church of England and nothing more. But as time went on it became increasingly evident that they were moving to the ecclesiastical parting of the ways. Some of Wesley's actions, notably the consecration of Methodist *episcopi*, paved the way for separation, and before he died, reading the writing on the wall, he made provision for the separation along lines of which he approved. Thus he virtually gave his consent, albeit reluctant, to a separate denomination which named him as its father.[98]

Wesley and the early Methodists are outstanding examples of the power of the Gospel to transform ordinary men and women in the sphere of the common life, and of a sense of mission great enough to turn the world into a parish. And with all his practical concern, Wesley envisaged himself as "a spirit come from God, and returning to God: just hovering over the great gulf" about to "drop into an unchanging eternity" and wanting "to know one thing—the way to heaven".[99]

Methodism

Wesley was a man of both spiritual and intellectual stature with a rich variety of interests. Methodism has re-

Their Relationship to Holiness Movements • 259

flected many of the manifold facets of his personality. There has been a persisting strain of perfectionism in it, sometimes strong and sometimes slight. Most of the characteristics of the three movements under review have been present among the groups in Methodism which have held to Wesley's emphasis on instantaneous sanctification by faith. Their literature has been valued and their example esteemed by the three movements. William Booth retained this teaching when he left Methodism to found the movement which later became the Salvation Army.[100] In the Salvation Army in its early days (and the same is true to some extent today) holiness of heart and life was powerfully presented in the Holiness meetings and clearly expounded in the Army literature. Some of this literature has circulated freely among the movements under review. In Methodism, the witness to Holiness at Cliff College, where some of the ministers of these movements received training, and at the Southport Convention has borne most of the characteristics under consideration, except that this witness has been maintained within the Methodist Church.

The American and British Holiness Movements

In the Introduction to this thesis reference has been made to the American Holiness Movement which played a large part in the origin and formation of the British Holiness Movement. Its precursors were the Quakers, among whom there remain to this day some groups who maintain a definite witness to entire sanctification as a second work of grace, and the Methodists. As in Britain, there has always been a perfectionist strain in the American Methodist Church which has varied in strength from time to time. This has been potent in influencing members of other denominations by personal testimony and by circulating the writings of Wesley and other Holiness literature. As stated in the Introduction, the leaders of Oberlin College, Finney and Mahan, and Thomas Upham of Bowdoin College and his wife came under this influence and were led to adopt a similar position to the Wesleyan. They were typical of many.

When the great upsurge of aspiration after Holiness in the years succeeding the Civil War took definite shape in the creation of the National Camp Meeting Association for the

Promotion of Holiness at Vineland, New Jersey, in 1867, some from the Methodist Church were at the source and in the main stream. Elmer T. Clark says it "was essentially a Methodist institution".[101] Later, when many of its members became dissatisfied with an interdenominational association and began to form Holiness denominations to provide a church home for themselves and their families they enshrined the Wesleyan teaching of entire sanctification in their articles of faith.

There were already in existence denominations subscribing to this doctrine such as the Wesleyan Methodist Church and the Free Methodist Church, both secessions from the Methodist Episcopal Church.[102] Under Methodist influence also denominations had been formed among those of German extraction such as the United Brethren in Christ (1800)[103] (from which seceded the United Brethren in Christ [Old Constitution] [1889]), the Evangelical Church (originally Evangelical Association) (1803) (from which the United Evangelical Church seceded [1894]), the Apostolic Christian Church of America (1847), the Apostolic Christian Church (Nazarean) (1850) and the Mennonite Brethren in Christ (originally the Reformed Mennonites [1874]).[104] All these in their inception placed a strong emphasis on entire sanctification as a second work of grace. In the last two decades of the nineteenth century they were joined in the Holiness testimony by a number of other Holiness sects. Some of these later united with one another to form larger sects such as the Pentecostal Church of the Nazarene[105] and the Pilgrim Holiness Church (formed in 1922 as a result of the union of the International Apostolic Holiness Union [1897] and the Holiness Christian Church [1882] with the Pentecostal Rescue Mission and the Pilgrim Church [1917]). Others like the Christian Congregation (1887), the Missionary Church Association (1898), the Pillar of Fire (1901) and the Church of God (Anderson) (1880) continued as separate units. The latter denied that it was a sect but rather a movement within the Church Universal to restore Christian unity. Similarly the Christian and Missionary Alliance (1887), the Metropolitan Church Association (1894) and the Peniel Missions claim to be interdenominational in character in their proclamation of Holiness.[106]

As stated in the Introduction[107] the British Holiness Movement drew much of its inspiration from the American

Their Relationship to Holiness Movements • 261

Holiness Movement, and in both of these the Wesleyan emphasis on entire sanctification in the Methodist Church played a vital part. The three movements under review are part of the British Holiness Movement and the characteristics which they have in common which we have used as a standard of comparison in this chapter were generally present in the groups which made up the British and American Holiness Movements. There are, however, two important qualifications.

The first refers to the question of secession. As indicated above some of the groups within the modern Holiness Movement maintained a Holiness witness within the churches. Indeed, within the American National Holiness Association considerable pressure was exerted to prevent Holiness denominations from being formed. In Britain, Reader Harris was most concerned to keep the Pentecostal League an interdenominational society and it was a grief to him when David Thomas left it to form the Holiness Mission as a separate denomination. On the other hand, George Sharpe's eviction from the Parkhead Congregational Church for his emphasis on the Holiness message was responsible for a deepening conviction in him of the necessity of forming Holiness churches. Sometimes the difference of opinion as to the value of the Holiness testimony inside or outside of the churches has been sharp and the criticism of those holding the opposite view has been keen. But when the dust of controversey has settled there has been a mutual recognition by those holding opposite views that both sides are part of the Holiness Movement.[108] Nevertheless those movements within the Holiness Movement which left the existing churches to create a new church for the propagation of Holiness and for the sustenance of those who had received its message bear the greatest resemblance to the three movements under review.

The second qualification relates to the exact form of the presentation of the Holiness message. It is possible to limit the modern Holiness Movement to those groups maintaining the Wesleyan teaching of cleansing from indwelling sin. But as indicated in the Introduction the scope of it can be widened to take in the teaching of Oberlin College and the ministries of Rev. and Mrs. W. E. Boardman and Rev. and Mrs. Pearsall Smith.

262 • *In the Steps of John Wesley*

The writings of Asa Mahan such as his *Christian Perfection* and *The Baptism of the Holy Spirit* were quoted with approval by teachers in the three movements under review. In so far therefore as he represents the Oberlin School there is no material difference between it and the "Wesleyan" part of the Holiness Movement. The earlier writings of Charles G. Finney on the subject also show a close kinship to the Wesleyan teaching,[109] stressing the attainability of entire sanctification, its dependence on the indwelling Spirit of Christ, the possibility of losing it and the scope for development.[110] It differs from the usual Wesleyan presentation in being set in a modified New England Theology.

Mention has been made in the Introduction of the influence in Britain of the writings and visits of Rev. and Mrs. W. E. Boardman and Rev. and Mrs. R. Pearsall Smith, themselves products of the American Holiness Movement. The Pearsall Smiths met with even more spectacular success in Germany. As a result of a series of meetings conducted by them in 1874-75 the Fellowship Movement (*die Heiligungsbewegung*) was brought into being with a strong emphasis on entire sanctification as a second work of grace. Warfield states that Pearsall Smith worked on the material of the Pietistic Fellowships which go back ultimately to the *ecclesiolae in ecclesia* established by Spener. France also felt the effect of Pearsall Smith's influence through Theodore Monod, the Low Countries through Lion Cachet and Switzerland through Otto Stockmayer. In Germany, under the leadership of Theodor Jellinghaus and others, a doctrine of entire sanctification was taught similar to the three movements under review. Some, like Pastor Paul, were certainly as radical and perhaps rather more extreme. But in face of outbreaks of fanaticism Jellinghaus withdrew to a doctrinal position more in line with the Keswick teaching in England.[111]

Rev. W. E. Boardman's chief attraction in his presentation of the "Higher Christian Life" was its comprehensiveness. His examples of those who enjoyed the experience of Holiness include Luther,[112] D'Aubigne, Hester Ann Rogers, Mahan, Finney and Henry Havelock but he draws the line at a Shakeress.[113] He mentions the debt the "Oberlinians" owed to Wesley and explains how both of them could hold and profess entire sanctification.[114] He does not commit himself to the Wesleyan definition, though both he and his wife were indebted to the Methodist testimony.[115]

The Pearsall Smiths had a similar presentation, especially suited to an interdenominational ministry. A comparison is made between the teaching of the Keswick Convention, which stems from their visits to Britain in 1874-75, and the three movements under review in the previous chapter. Their teaching was apparently capable of being interpreted by some as a complete deliverance from sin and by others as victory over the continuing presence and power of sin. Both in Britain and in Germany there were both types in the movements which their ministry called into being, but ultimately both Keswick and *die Heiligungsbewegung* adopted the latter emphasis.

The Pentecostal Movement arose out of the Holiness Movement and many of the groups within it teach entire sanctification as a second work of grace receivable by faith. But they teach that the baptism with the Holy Spirit is a third work of grace, the sign of which is an utterance in an unknown tongue.[116] This marks them off as distinct from the Holiness Movement in general and the three groups under review in particular. The Calvary Holiness Church conceded that *glossolalia* was scriptural, but strongly resisted any attempt to make it the evidence of the baptism with the Holy Spirit.

Formative Influences

In closing this section, let us briefly consider to what extent the Holiness movements in Christian history exercised a formative influence on the three groups under review.

As shown in the history of the International Holiness Mission, this movement took its origin from the Pentecostal League, founded by Reader Harris, under whose ministry David Thomas claimed an experience of regeneration and whose influence and teaching left an indelible impression on his mind. George Sharpe was also at one time a member of the Pentecostal League, and as the four founders of the Calvary Holiness Church were formerly members of the

264 • *In the Steps of John Wesley*

International Holiness Mission, they too came under the influence, albeit indirect, of Reader Harris.

Reader Harris came into the experience of entire sanctification through the ministry of Rev. F. D. Sanford and Rev. G. D. Watson, both ministers of the Methodist Episcopal Church, U.S.A. It was as a minister of this church that George Sharpe claimed the second work of grace. The writings of G. D. Watson, Daniel Steele, Mrs. Phoebe Palmer and other ministers and members of this church moulded the thinking of members of the three movements under consideration.

The Salvation Army has also made a contribution. Milton Williams, at that time one of its officers in U.S.A., was the evangelist at the time when Sharpe claimed the experience of Holiness. Commissioner Brengle's books have exercised a powerful influence in these three movements. Through the Salvation Army Francis Crossley, the founder of Star Hall, Manchester, claimed the second blessing. At Star Hall both Sharpe and Thomas received encouragement, and the Pentecostal Church of Scotland had a share in the *Way of Holiness* magazine when it was commenced by Miss Crossley and Miss Hatch in 1909. Nor must the Quaker influence in Star Hall in the person of Dr. Rendel Harris be forgotten.[117]

The American Church of the Nazarene has influenced all three movements. The constitution of Sharpe's Pentecostal Church of Scotland was based on its *Manual* and joined it in 1915. The Calvary Holiness Church borrowed some of the phrases from its *Manual* in attempting to define the second work of grace in its Articles of Faith. Before its union with the Church of the Nazarene, the International Holiness Mission was using the Nazarene systematic theology by Orton Wiley in its ministerial curriculum.

The American Congregational Church has had some share in the moulding of the three movements through the writings of Asa Mahan and Charles G. Finney of the Oberlin School, and of Thomas Upham of Bowdoin College.

Not only were the writings of John Wesley given a special place in these three movements but the Methodist Church in Britain has made a contribution through the writings of such Holiness expositors as Thomas Cook and Samuel Chadwick, and through Cliff College, where a number of ministers of the International Holiness Mission and the

Their Relationship to Holiness Movements • 265

Calvary Holiness Church received training. Four Methodists, Principal D. W. Lambert, and Revs. J. H. Stringer, J. Baines Atkinson and J. H. J. Barker, each served as directors of ministerial studies for the latter church.

Some of the ministers of these movements received training at the Emmanuel Bible College, the principal of which, J. D. Drysdale, entered into a religious experience under the ministry of George Sharpe.

There were other American influences. Ministers of the Pilgrim Holiness Church such as Revs. Seth and Paul Rees and Arnold Hodgin ministered on visits to the International Holiness Mission, and Rev. E. E. Shelhamer of the Free Methodist Church conducted services in the International Holiness Mission and the Calvary Holiness church. In the formative years of the International Holiness Mission visits by Rev. and Mrs. C. Cowman, founders of the Oriental Missionary Society, and Rev. Charles Stalker, an American Quaker minister, made an abiding impression.

When Alfred Place began the Holiness work in Leeds at the close of the last century, which later joined the International Holiness Mission, he received inspiration and help from Mr. Huskison, of the Holiness Church in Albion Street, later the successor to Mrs. Clift, the founder of the Holiness Church denomination.[118]

And finally, the Roman Catholic Church exercised a certain influence through such writers as Thomas à Kempis, Madam Guyon and F. W. Faber. G. D. Watson openly acknowledged his debt to Faber and paid a glowing tribute to his insight into devotional truth.[119]

NOTES ON CHAPTER 8

[1] I Peter 2:9.
[2] II Peter 1:3.
[3] I Thess. 4:7.
[4] Matt. 5:48.
[5] I Cor. 15:34.
[6] Eph. 5:25-27.
[7] Rom. 6:1-11.

⁸Rev. 21:2.
⁹Heb. 12:14.
¹⁰I Cor. 3:1.
¹¹I Thess. 5:14.
¹²I Cor. 2:6.
¹³*Ibid.*, 15.
¹⁴I John 2:13 and 14.
¹⁵*Ibid.*, 4:17 and 18.
¹⁶Luke 6:40.
¹⁷Phil. 3:12 and 15.
¹⁸I John 1:8 and 9.

¹⁹This does not mean that there was a sharp division into two classes because there would always be some moving on from the elementary experience to the higher.

²⁰"If you can bear the Lord's full yoke, you will be perfect. But if you cannot, then do what you can." VI, 2.

²¹xxx-xxxv.
²²*Apology*, 12.
²³*Ibid.*, 31.
²⁴*Ad Autolycum*, III, xv.
²⁵*Early Church History to A.D. 313* (London: Macmillan and Co., 1912), Vol. I, p. 201.

²⁶Hans Lietzmann, *The Founding of the Church Universal* (London: Lutterworth Press, 1950), p. 282.

²⁷Flew, *Idea of Perfection*, p. 137.

²⁸H. W. Perkins, *Doctrine of Christian Perfection* (London: Epworth Press, 1927), p. 142.

²⁹*The Early Christian Church* (London: Weidenfeld and Nicolson, 1965), p. 145.

³⁰*Paedagogus*, I, vi.
³¹*Ibid.*, I, i.
³²Flew, *op. cit.*, p. 141.
³³*Ibid.*, p. 155.
³⁴*Ibid.*, p. 152.
³⁵*Contra Celsum*, III, 69.
³⁶*Methodism* (Penguin, 1963), pp. 13-16.

³⁷*Journal*, Vol. III, 490. But he also declared in his letter to the "London Magazine" (17-2-61) the parallel between Montanism and Methodism truthfully drawn "would not fill a nutshell". *Letters*, Vol. IV, 133.

³⁸Gordon Rupp regards Montanism as a paganised form of Christianity.

³⁹For the opposite view see R. A. Knox, *Enthusiasm* (Oxford: Clarendon Press, 1950), pp. 44-49.

⁴⁰*ERE*, "Perfection (Christian)", p. 735.

⁴¹See S. L. Greenslade, *Schism in the Early Church* (London: S.C.M., 1953), pp. 17-23.

⁴²See W. H. C. Frend, *The Donatist Church* (Oxford: Clarendon Press, 1952), chaps. ii-v.

⁴³R. A. Knox, *Enthusiasm*, p. 66.

⁴⁴"But see Newton Flew's contention that there was a place for a relative perfection in Augustine's teaching. *Op. cit.*, chap. x.

⁴⁵M. E. Redford, *The Rise of the Church of the Nazarene*, pp. 23-24.

⁴⁶*Summa Theologica*, II (ii), Q. 184. A. 2.

⁴⁷Karl Rahner, *Theological Investigations* (London: Darton, Longman and Todd, 1961), Vol. I, pp. 347-82.

⁴⁸Though Wesley himself asserted that the Papists neither taught nor believed the perfection which he taught. *Letters*, Vol. IV, 158.

⁴⁹Cf. *Summa Theologica*, II (ii), Q. 184. A. 2. and J. Wesley, "Plain Account . . .", *Works*, Vol. XI, 398-99.

⁵⁰*Summa Theologica*, II (ii), Q. 184. A. 4.

⁵¹Redford, *op. cit.*, p. 24.

⁵²*Summa Theologica*, II (ii), Q. 183. A. 4.

⁵³*Summa Theologica*, II (ii), Q. 184. A. 4.

⁵⁴Flew, *op. cit.*, pp. 219-24. Perkins, *op. cit.*, pp. 181-83.

⁵⁵W. R. Inge, *Christian Mysticism* (London: Methuen, 1933), pp. 140-96.

⁵⁶I am indebted to Dr. Gordon Leff for the substance of this summary of the Cathars. See also S. Runciman, *The Medieval Manichee* (Cambridge: Cambridge University Press, 1947) and S. R. Maitland, *Facts and Documents Illustrative of the History, Doctrine and Rites of the Ancient Albigenses* . . . (London: 1838).

⁵⁷Printed by R. Hawes, London, 1776. For Wesley's strictures on her see *Letters*, Vol. V, 341-42, Vol. VI, 39, 44, 125. Ronald Knox in his *Enthusiasm* stoutly asserts that the similarity between Madam Guyon and her Protestant admirers is more fancied than real. Chap. xiv.

⁵⁸E.g. Jan. 1893.

⁵⁹*Foundations of Doctrine*, pp. 226-27.

⁶⁰*Facing the Issue*, pp. 45-46.

⁶¹*Op. cit.*, pp. 27-28.

⁶²*Autobiography*, trans. Thomas T. Allen (London: Kegan Paul, Trench, Trauber and Co., 1898), Vol. I, pp. 216 ff., 274-75, 310.

⁶³*Ibid.*, Vol. I, p. 177.

⁶⁴*Letters*, Vol. VII, 66-67.

⁶⁵Madam Guyon valued the sacraments and other means of grace so does not come into this category.

⁶⁶Mentioned frequently in Vol. I of the *Journal* and in Vol. III (284) and IV (457 ff.).

⁶⁷Devoted 60 pages to him in the *Christian Library*, Vol. I.

⁶⁸G. S. Wakefield, *Methodist Devotion* (London: Epworth Press, 1966), p. 26.

⁶⁹A. J. Phillippou, "The Mystery of Pentecost", *The Orthodox Ethos* ed. A. J. Philippou (Oxford: Holywell Press, 1964), Part I, chap. iii.

⁷⁰Flew, *op. cit.*, pp. 246, 250.

⁷¹E. G. Rupp, *The Righteousness of God* (London: Hodder and Stoughton, 1953), pp. 177 ff. See also M. Piette, *John Wesley in the Evolution of Protestantism* (London: Sheed and Ward, 1938), pp. 6 ff., re Luther and Concupiscence.

[72] Rupp, loc. cit. See also p. 180: *"Semper peccator, semper penitens, semper justus."*

[73] Art. "Zwinglianisme", *Dictionnaire de Théologie Catholique*, 1950, cols. 3796-7.

[74] *Institutes*, Bk. III, xvii, 15.

[75] *Institutes*, Bk. III, xxii, 2-3. See G. S. Wakefield, *Puritan Devotion* (London: Epworth Press, 1957). John Preston and Richard Greenham even ventured to use the word "perfection", pp. 136-38.

[76] G. S. Wakefield, *Methodist Devotion*, pp. 37-39.

[77] *Journal*, Vol. II, pp. 28-32, 35-37, 40, 48 and 49.

[78] Art. "Moravians", *ERE*, pp. 837 ff.

[79] So they are often described, but some historians are inclined to see the roots of Anabaptism in late mediaeval sectarian religion rather than in the teachings of Luther and Zwingli, and Carl Bangs claims that Arminius represented the original Dutch Reformation. (See "Arminius and the Reformation", art. in *Church History*, Vol. XXX, No. 2, June, 1961).

[80] G. H. Williams, *The Radical Reformation* (London: Weidenfeld and Nicolson, 1962), p. 263.

[81] *Ibid.*, p. 792.

[82] *Ibid.*, pp. 478-82.

[83] *Ibid.*, p. 113.

[84] *Ibid.*, pp. 480-81.

[85] *Ibid.*, p. 329.

[86] *Ibid.*, p. 332.

[87] Robert Barclay, *An Apology for the True Christian Divinity* (Glasgow: R. Barclay Murdoch, 1886). Prop. VIII, "Concerning Perfection."

[88] *The Journal of George Fox* (Cambridge: Cambridge University Press, 1952), p. 32.

[89] *Op. cit.*, pp. 172-73.

[90] *Ibid.*, p. 171. Though Wesley accuses Barclay of "confounding justification with sanctification" "as the Papists do". *Letters*, Vol. II, 118.

[91] See Barclay's exposition: *op. cit.*, Prop. III, "Concerning the Scriptures".

[92] *Fox's Journal, op. cit.*, p. 34.

[93] Rufus M. Jones, *Spiritual Reformers in the 16th and 17th Centuries* (London: Macmillan, 1928), p. 338. See whole chap.

[94] *The Works of James Arminius*, trans. James Nichols (London: Longman, Hurst, etc., 1825), Vol. II, pp. 608-27; Vol. II, pp. 55, 56, 260, 408-10.

[95] Art. "Arminianism", *ERE*, pp. 810 ff.

[96] *Op cit.*, Vol. II, pp. 408-10.

[97] Cell stresses the reaction against Arminian Anglicanism, which is also true. George C. Cell, *The Rediscovery of John Wesley* (New York: Henry Holt and Co., 1935), p. 17.

[98] For a good account of Wesley's view of the Church see C. W. Williams, *John Wesley's Theology Today* (London: Epworth Press, 1960), pp. 141-58.

[99] *Works*, Vol. V, 2.

Their Relationship to Holiness Movements • 269

[100]H. Begbie, *Life of William Booth* (London: Macmillan, 1920), pp. 86-87, 409-10.

[101]Elmer T. Clark, *The Small Sects in America* (New York: Abingdon Press, 1949), p. 73.

[102]See Introduction, p. 13.

[103]Date indicates year of origin.

[104]The official Mennonite attitude has not been sympathetic to the Wesleyan teaching of entire sanctification but the insistence on righteous living and separation from the world which is a part of the Mennonite ethos has favourably disposed individual Mennonites to it. See Art. "Holiness Movement", *Mennonite Encyclopedia* (1956), Vol. II, pp. 790-91.

[105]See Introduction, pp. 14-28.

[106]Clark, *op. cit.*, pp. 68-81.

[107]Pp. 28-30.

[108]See for instance the eulogistic obituary of Reader Harris in *HMJ*, May, 1909, p. 48, and that of David Thomas in *Spiritual Life*, August, 1930, p. 7.

[109]B. B. Warfield, *Perfectionism*, Vol. II, p. 67.

[110]Charles G. Finney, *Lectures on Systematic Theology* (London: William Tegg and Co., 1851), pp. 593-94, 598-644.

[111]Warfield, *op. cit.*, Vol. I, chap. vi.

[112]Even though he admits Luther disclaimed it.

[113]The Shakers are not given a place in this survey, though the writer visited the Shaker settlement, Pleasant Hill, Kentucky, in 1957. Ann Lee, their founder, derived her perfectionist ideas mainly from the Quakers, who are considered, but her development of their teaching bears little relationship to the Holiness Movement.

[114]W. E. Boardman, *The Higher Christian Life* (Edinburgh: Alexander Strahan and Co., 1862), p. 21. He seeks to reconcile the Lutheran view with them also, pp. 32-33.

[115]Mrs. Boardman, *Life and Labours of Rev. W. E. Boardman*, pp. 48-56.

[116]This is generally but not universally the Pentecostal position. See Nils Block-Hoell, *The Pentecostal Movement* (London: Allen and Unwin, 1964), pp. 125-41. Donald Gee, however, insists that "the Pentecostal Movement has consistently taught that speaking with tongues is the scriptural initial evidence of that baptism". *The Pentecostal Movement* (Luton: Assemblies of God Publishing House, 1949), p. 8.

[117]He wrote Crossley's biography and was a speaker at the Star Hall Holiness Conventions. See *The Life of Francis William Crossley*, ed. J. Rendel Harris (London: James Nisbet and Co., 1900), chap. viii.

[118]See Introduction, p. 29.

[119]G. D. Watson, *Soul Food* (Cincinnati: Revivalist Office, 1896), p. 77.

CHAPTER 9

Conclusion

From the beginning of this thesis I have been of the opinion that my main contribution to scholarship has been to give a factual, balanced and impartial account of the three movements which are its subject. I have access to all the available primary documents and therefore I am in a unique position to give the facts. Inevitably the selection of the facts has involved discrimination and interpretation, deciding what to include and what to exclude, and what are the major trends, but apart from this I have endeavoured to let the facts speak for themselves with the minimum of comment. Although involved in the study which I have undertaken, I have made a genuine and sustained attempt to detach myself as far as possible from the events which I have recorded and to maintain an objective attitude and give an unbiassed account. This has been particularly true of the historical section. In Part II, Analytical and Comparative, after analysing their chief characteristics, I have drawn comparisons between the movements under review and other holiness movements in Christian history which has called for a certain amount of interpretation and criticism.

In closing, I wish to make some comment on the data and to suggest some conclusions which can be drawn from it. My conclusions can be summed up under five heads.

1. The Factors in the Origin of the Three Movements

These are of a pattern familiar to the student of church history.

a. To begin with, there is the *charismatic leader*. We have seen how the Parkhead Pentecostal Church, and later the Pentecostal Church of Scotland, not only originated in George Sharpe, but was actually built round him. He was without rival as a dynamic preacher and able adminstrator and not until eighteen years after the commencement of the church, and then only because of his promotion, did anyone succeed him in the place of leadership.

The same was true, but in a different sense, of David Thomas. He had neither Sharpe's preaching nor administrative gifts, but he was looked up to as a "spiritual" man, especially gifted in leading others into the experience of entire sanctification. Moreover, he was a prosperous business man, the employer of his lay colleagues and later the main supporter of the first ministers.

And in James also we have an example of a charismatic leader, respected not only as a powerful preacher but also as a man of prayer through whose ministry the sick were healed.

b. Another factor in the origin of these movements was *the support of an inner circle of colleagues* for each of the leaders. It is doubtful whether Sharpe would have had such a substantial following without the four officials who took the side of the evicted minister: Bolton, Robertson, Gray and Barrie. Likewise Wain, Seekings, Dunning and Milbank joined with Thomas to make the Five Men of the Holiness Mission, and Filer, Ravenhill and Ford were named with James as joint founders of the Calvary Holiness Church.

One charismatic leader is probably enough to initiate a movement, but the value of colleagues should not be overlooked. They give the pneumatic leader an air of acceptance and save him from the appearance of peculiarity and fanaticism.

c. But there was more than the foregoing in the founding of the three movements. Each founder was possessed by a *message* and a *mission* and confronted with an *occasion* which called for a decision. In the case of Sharpe the occasion was thrust upon him, but his belief in Holiness and his conviction about preaching it precipitated the occasion. With Thomas it was the mission rather than the message which was the point at issue between him and Reader Harris. He felt that the message, which they both believed, should not be confined to the churches. The occasion which called for a decision was the recurrence of backsliding on the part of those professing entire sanctification, which Thomas believed was due to the unsympathetic attitude of the leaders of the churches. Much the same was true of James. He held the same views of Holiness as the leaders of the International Holiness Mission but he felt more urgently than they did the need to propagate those views through the revival and healing campaigns. The restraint of the leaders through the Constitution which made them the final authority coupled with his demonstrated success in raising up new churches made the occasion which caused James and his colleagues to begin a new movement.

d. It may seem to be stating the obvious but it was an indispensable factor that there were *those prepared to follow*. Sharpe was probably aware that if he was evicted some would leave the church with him, though he could not be sure. Thomas probably thought he could count on others who felt the same about interdenominational work as he did. James and his colleagues had reason to believe that the churches at Oldham and Salford would join them, though they had resolved to advise them against doing so. But they knew that through the revival and healing campaign people could be gathered and churches formed.

Generally speaking a sect begins with a charismatic leader, but more than this is required.

2. *Features in Their Development*

a. *Originally, all three movements bore most of the marks of a sect* as defined by Troeltsch. They were voluntary associations, emphasising doctrine and a personal relationship with God, separating themselves from the world and the existing churches and preaching a high standard of spiritual experience and conduct. The International Holiness Mission was the nearest to a sect in this sense, being a layman's movement with only a secondary place for the sacraments and no place at all for a separated ministry at first. And yet

Thomas was the one who emphasised most that the Mission was not a sect. It should also be stated that in all the three movements redemption through Christ by grace through faith was insisted on, and although they gave Christ the place of Lord and example, their main emphasis was on His redemption, which Troeltsch lists as one of the marks of a church,[1] though, admittedly, they believed the grace of redemption was received through faith and not through sacraments.

b. It is customary today to divide the Church into three categories: *churches, denominations and sects.* One of the features of a sect according to this classification is that it considers itself as the one true church and rejects all others as apostate or false.[2] None of these three movements has officially taken this view; from their inception they were more in the class of the denomination rather than the sect in this respect. Indeed, at its very commencement, Sharpe's Pentecostal Church of Scotland had some of the marks of a church, with an ordained ministry and the Lord's Supper given an honoured place.

c. *The routinization of the charisma* can be discerned, with qualifications, in each of the three movements. It is seen most clearly in the Holiness Mission. Originally Thomas was the founder-leader, a position unique and unqualified. In 1916 the Executive Council was created to govern the Mission and Thomas took the official position of president. In the Calvary Holiness Church the four founders formed themselves into the Executive Council from the first and elected James as president. In 1938 James was elected president for life by both the Executive Council and the Delegates Conference, which also elected Ford as his successor. Twice James asked for a vote of confidence from the ministers, in 1944 and 1945, but the routinization of the charisma proceeded no further than this. From the first under the influence of Sharpe the Pentecostal Church of Scotland elected its leaders, an interesting case of the charisma routinizing itself!

In the Pentecostal Church of Scotland there was a recognised and routinized ministry from the first. Again the Holiness Mission provides the clearest instance of a sect developing into a denomination in the introduction of ministers into a layman's movement. What is remarkable is that none of the leading laymen sought ordination in the Mission. The ministers were brought in from outside or rose from the ranks of the members through probationary service. The Calvary Holiness Church ministry was patterned on that of the International Holiness Mission at the stage of development which it had reached in 1934.

d. The attitude of all three movements became more *sympathetic to other churches* as time went on. This process was hastened by the growth of the ecumenical spirit in the older churches, causing them to manifest a greater friendliness to the smaller sects and denominations. Several of the ministers of the movements under review have served as presidents of local councils of the Free Church Federal Council. But the movements remained voluntary associations of "converted" individuals, building an elect society within an "unregenerate" nation, with which, however, they felt a kinship and to which they owed a responsibility both as citizens and evangelists. They became increasingly denominations, but they did not up to the time of 1955 bear all the marks of a church.

e. Each of the three movements was prepared to surrender its independence to join a larger Holiness denomination. *The basis of the union* was a common cherishing of the belief in Christ as a Saviour from all sin in *the doctrine of Holiness*. But there were other factors.

(1) There was *the basic recognition that* although they had exercised the right to divide *the ideal of the New Testament* is *the unity of all believers*. It was often said that unity of spirit can exist without organic union. But the former gives impetus to the latter.

(2) There are *contributory factors* such as Frame's statesmanlike qualities, Maclagan's superintendency in the International Holiness Mission, the needs of its mission field, the vacant presidential chair, and in the case of the Calvary Holiness Church a check in its advance and the need of safeguarding its doctrinal emphasis.

(3) *The idea of becoming a part of a large worldwide denomination* attracted some, though others would have preferred the intimacy of a small, familiar community. Undoubtedly, the setting of the belief in Holiness in an international

context is a corrective for and a safeguard against parochial conceptions of its ethics.

(4) Finally, there was *no opposition from the leaders* of the uniting denominations. They were prepared to sacrifice primacy in a small group for a place in a large one, because they believed it to be the will of God.

3. *Their Special Emphasis: Holiness*

All three movements held in common the belief in and propagation of Holiness. This has been defined and discussed in the chapter bearing the above title. Their presentation has been shown to have strong similarities to that taught by John Wesley and such as has persisted in varying degrees in Methodism and the modern Holiness Movement.

a. *Criticisms.* Some account has been taken of the abiding objection of many Christians to the word *"perfection"* and of the dangers inherent in bearing *testimony* to the experience. In my Drysdale Memorial Lecture I have mentioned the *need of confession* among those professing to have received the experience of entire sanctification and the *place of penitence* in the mature.[3] A self-righteous Pelagianism is at the antipodes of what Wesley taught and far from the Holiness for which these three movements professed to stand. Nevertheless, as in the case of the doctrine of justification by faith, so also that of Christian perfection is always open to misunderstanding and misrepresentation not only by those who oppose it but also by some of its most zealous advocates.

A criticism levelled against Wesley is that *he did not work out the social implications* of the doctrine. There is a difference of meaning with regard to the term "social work". With some it means any attempt to alleviate the distress of the sick, the poor and the deprived. In the opinion of others this is only administering "first aid"; the real social contribution of the Church to society is to assist in bringing about a just social order.

It would be difficult to bring Wesley under criticism for lack of social concern in the former sense. Timothy Smith has shown the connection between *Revivalism and Social Reform* in his thesis for Harvard University of that title, and among the reformers in mid-nineteenth century America were a notable company of those belonging to the Holiness groups. As shown in chapter six above, the three movements in Britain have not been without social concern, but it has not figured prominently in their conception of service. This they have envisaged as an emphasis on the regeneration of the individual as the Church's chief contribution to society and as meeting the deepest and eternal need of man. This certainly seems to be the emphasis of the New Testament.

It is sometimes asserted today that Christ's teaching of the Kingdom of God envisages the redemption of society and commissions the Church to this task.[4] Scholars such as Ritschl, Adams Brown, H. W. Perkins and Newton Flew have seen a social challenge to Christian perfection in the conception of the Kingdom of God. Christ was recognised by His contemporaries as being in the succession of the prophets and in Him their passion for social righteousness finds its fulfilment. But however strong the Christian's social concern should be, and however active he should be in promoting social righteousness, there is a strong case in Scripture for the belief that his chief concern is in the reconciliation of the individual to God, that regeneration of persons without which it is doubtful whether any righteous social order can be created or stand.

It has been objected against the teaching of Christian perfection that *the perfection of the individual is not possible in an imperfect environment*. As often as this objection has been raised it has been pointed out that it involves far more than the limited and qualified perfection taught by Wesley and his followers, the "imperfect perfection"to quote Warfield's thrust. For if this qualified perfection is impossible in this imperfect world, what of the sinless perfection of the Incarnate Son of God? Nevertheless a genuine sanctity involves a concern to transform one's environment, to see God's will being done on earth as it is in heaven.

b. *Holiness by faith as a vital Protestant doctrine.* Whatever the deficiencies of its advocates and the inadequacy of their presentation, does not Christian history indicate that there is value in the proclamation of an attainable experience of the fulness of the Spirit bringing deliverance from sin and power for Christian service? The very limited survey of individuals and groups under the narrow qualifications of the previous chapter is evidence for the longing of the awakened soul for some such experience. It is found by few at conversion. If the only hope of attainment is at the climax of sustained endeavour, is not the faint soul likely to lose heart?

Luther believed that the preaching of justification by faith would vitalise the church, and if not transform the State Church into the New Testament *ecclesia* at least permeate it with *ecclesiolae*. But he was disappointed, and the low level of Christian conduct in the Lutheran Church was the butt of Anabaptist criticism and the text of many a Roman Catholic sermon. Is not Wesley's "fusion of the Catholic ethic of holiness with the Protestant ethic of grace" a needed contribution to the Protestant *kerygma* and *didache*?

c. *Holiness as a Unifying Factor*. Below the connection between the teaching of Holiness and schism will be discussed. But there is another side. It has a unifying as well as a divisive effect. Only in the case of Sharpe was Holiness the cause of division. With Thomas and James the dispute was not about the doctrine but about its presentation. On the other hand the three movements were brought together because they held the same doctrine, and it a doctrine of perfect love. The same has been true of the growth of the Church of the Nazarene in America. Bresee left the Methodist Church with reluctance to work among the unchurched poor. Hillery it is true left the St. Paul's Methodist Church, Providence, on the issue of Holiness, but Hoople and BeVier raised up churches in Brooklyn where none existed that Holiness might be preached in them. Harris in Tennessee was concerned to "set in order" a New Testament Church of which Holiness was one of several features. Jernigan's aim in Texas was to provide a church home for believers in Holiness but with no definite denominational attachment. This doctrine, which all held in common, drew these groups together and made them one church.

The Holiness Movement has never claimed exclusive rights to sanctity. Its definition of Holiness is sharp and clear; perhaps in the opinion of some altogether too neat and tidy. But it has always recognised that there are saints who do not subscribe to its definition, and they can be found in all denominations. It has already been remarked that staunchly

Protestant though the Holiness Movement is, it has a place in its reading for such Roman Catholics as Thomas à Kempis, Fenelon, Madam Guyon and Faber. Might it not be that divided as they are over justification Catholics and Protestants might find common ground in the search for sanctity?

4. Their Place in Society

a. *The Value of Sect Type Christianity.* It is often too readily assumed that whatever makes a division in a community is a bad thing. It could serve a useful purpose. A nation should contain a rich variety of interests with a difference of viewpoints and emphases.

Sociologists have seen a value in sects in meeting the need of different segments of population, especially the deprived classes. Richard Niebuhr states:

> The rise of new sects to champion the uncompromising ethics of Jesus and "to preach the gospel to the poor" has again and again been the effective means of recalling Christendom to its mission. This phase of denominational history must be regarded as helpful, despite the break in unity which it brings about.[5]

In a recent study of two Holiness groups, Emmanuel and the Faith Mission, T. R. Warburton makes the following comment: "These groups provide a refuge and a positive sense of personal fulfilment which secular society and the more orthodox religious denominations have failed to give them."[6]

The fact that the three movements under review had a following is an indication that they met a need. Although some of their members and adherents were drawn from other churches, others were outside the orbit of organised religion and there were those who were redeemed from vicious and unhappy modes of life. Standards of honesty, industry and neighbourliness were inculcated into them and a clean and temperate life was taught as part of the Christian ideal. Not only were the ministers engaged in social activities such as visiting the sick, bereaved, deprived and delinquent, but members also were urged to be active in good works.

b. *Reasons for their comparative smallness.* In spite of being in existence for over sixty years, the membership of the Church of the Nazarene in Britain in 1966 was 3,646, with a Sunday School enrolment of 7,337. Allowing for adherents who are not members, a reasonable total would be fifteen thousand. The following are put forward as explanations why the total is not higher after so many years:

(1) These movements arose in *a century of church declension*. During the years since union, the membership numbers have actually shown a small increase, while most of the other denominations have reported decreases.

(2) Besides an evangelistic element in all three movements *there has been a pessimistic element* which has assumed that "Holiness will never be popular", and that small numbers are an indication of "faithfulness" in preaching "the Truth". Indeed, sometimes converts have been driven away by a premature insistence on standards of dress, habit and pastimes.

(3) *The "by-products" of Holiness have too often been given a central place.* It has been assumed that the experience of entire sanctification will so satisfy that "the things of the world" such as dancing, cinemas, theatres and sport will no longer have a place in the sanctified life, and that habits detrimental to the body, such as smoking and drinking alcohol, will drop off. This has meant that to some this renunciation of what has formerly been prized figures out of all proportion in their testimonies and their conceptions of Holiness. The result has been a negative asceticism. Only the incoming of the Holy Spirit and the positive communion with Christ finding expression in joyful service can sustain the average believer.

(4) *Many of the children of the members* have felt the standards of membership too narrow, and lacking the convictions of their parents *have refrained from becoming members.*

(5) There has been *a shortage of competent pastors.* Many of the churches are small and unable to support a full-time pastor, and all the salaries are at a low level. The college has not yet been able to supply sufficient pastors to fill the vacancies and offset the number of pastors who have from time to time left the denomination.

5. *Their Place in the Church*

The theologian looks at a sect from a different standpoint from that of a sociologist. First, is it an expression of Christian truth or a deviation from it, and, secondly, how can it justify breaking the unity of the Spirit and exposing the Church before the world to the scandal of schism?

Troeltsch maintains that a sect usually revives a truth of Primitive Christianity which has become obscured in the Church.[7] In this it is complementary to the witness of the Church, and without the contribution of the sects the presentation of Christianity would not be complete. Catholicism has succeeded in containing the sect type of Christianity within the Church in the form of the Orders or ruthlessly crushing those who refuse to conform. Lutheranism and Calvinism, in themselves containing initially some of the features of the sect, by claiming the right to divide for the sake of Christian truth have given tacit consent to sectarianism, though actually the minorities of the Radical Reformation were ruthlessly persecuted by them.

The gravity of schism depends to some extent on the context in which it occurs. The three movements under review came into existence in the context of a world in which Christianity existed in a great variety of forms. Their founders believed that the essence of Christianity was union with Christ by personal faith and commitment. This made a believer a member of the Church of Christ, the community of the redeemed. After this, the next step was to find a community of fellow believers or to create one. The association together of regenerate persons by the leading of the Spirit formed a local church which was part of the Church of Christ. To divide that church would inevitably cause grief to both sections and to Christ and should not be done lightly, but sometimes it was for the ultimate benefit of the Church of Christ.[8] The division in the Parkhead Congregational Church caused a wound which took years to heal.[9] Hearts were sore for many years after Thomas and his colleagues left the Pentecostal League. When James and his companions withdrew from the International Holiness Mission there was distress and confusion in many minds, and persistent efforts were made to heal the breach. Yet in each case it was felt right to cause these unhappy divisions for the progress of the truth and the benefit of the Church as a whole. Whether the Church would have benefitted more if agreement had been reached is an open question. But it takes two to make

Conclusion • 281

an agreement and in a schism usually both parties are convinced that they are right, however trivial their difference may seem to the observer.[10]

These may be defective views of the Church, but they were sincerely held by the leaders of the three movements and are sincerely held by many in the churches today, a fact which must be borne in mind in any attempts at securing a closer union in the modern Church.

What is the place in the Church today of such movements as these three which are now a part of the Church of the Nazarene, for, as Greenslade has shown, many schisms are not *from* the Church but *in* the Church? Have we here something in the nature of a Protestant Order? The Church of the Nazarene insists that her members not only have an experience of Christ but also that they abstain from such things as smoking and alcohol. Many Nazarenes recognise that a person may well be a Christian even though he does not abstain in these particulars. If then the standard of membership is higher than that of regeneration, does it not suggest that to be a Nazarene is a special calling? The Nazirite[11] of the Old Testament took vows beyond the standard expected of his brother Israelite, just as those in the Orders of the Catholic Church take vows not obligatory on the ordinary Catholic. But if this is the case, can the Church of the Nazarene minister to the community in which she is the only church? There is no reason why she should not, because she does not confine her pastoral care, or even the administration of the sacraments to her own members.

The Church of the Nazarene, in which these three movements which are the subject of this thesis are now united, does not "pass over the garnered experience of the centuries" but openly acknowledges her debt to the historic Christian Church for her doctrines and her government. In spite of her tender years, "a little sister" among the ancient communions, can the Church in these days when union is in the air learn anything from her? She is formed of movements which have arisen in the east, west, south and north of North America, and in other parts of the world. These diverse elements have been welded into one, and there has been no serious schism.

Four characteristics worthy of note are present in her unity:

(1) There is a basic agreement in doctrine. Besides the acceptance of the Bible as the Word of God and the doctrines commonly associated with the evangelical faith, all the movements uniting in her have held deep convictions concerning the doctrine of Holiness as defined in this thesis.[12]

(2) In each case a genuine attempt has been made to consult all the local churches in a denomination seeking union. In the case of each of the three movements under review no church was compelled to participate in the union against its will.

(3) Each uniting denomination has been made to feel a part of the Church of the Nazarene, and so far from merely settling down in a larger denomination has been encouraged to take part in the denominational outreach.

(4) In the context of unity in fundamental doctrines and in the proclamation of full salvation, liberty is given in the mode and time of baptism and the belief in the Second Advent. In church government, Episcopacy has been blended with Congregationalism.

Recent in origin and pursuing an independent but not uncharitable course, the Church of the Nazarene is not without significance for the Church today.

NOTES ON CHAPTER 9

[1]*The Social Teachings of the Christian Churches*, trans. O. Wyon (London, 1931), Vol. II, 994.

[2]E.g. Jehovah's Witnesses.

[3]Ford, *op. cit.*, pp. 65-67.

[4]Troeltsch, however, says, ". . . it is a great mistake to treat all the ideas which underlie the preaching of Jesus as though they were primarily connected with the 'Social' problem. The message of Jesus is obviously purely religious. . . ." *Op. cit.*, Vol. I, 50. See also p. 40.

[5]H. Richard Niebuhr, *The Social Sources of Denominationalism* (New York: H. Holt and Co., 1929), p. 21.

⁶T. R. Warburton, "A Comparative Study of Minority Religious Groups: With Special Reference to Holiness Groups and Related Movements in Britain in the Last 50 Years." (Thesis for Ph.D. in Sociology in the University of London, May, 1966), p. 364.

⁷*Op. cit.*, Vol. I, 334.

⁸Though once a sect is started the duty of unity is usually strongly urged. In the Church of the Nazarene today denominational loyalty figures prominently.

⁹There is a good spirit now between the Parkhead Congregational Church and the Nazarene Parkhead Church.

¹⁰Often important principles are involved in trivial occasions. See "The Story of the Leeds 'Non-Cons'" in *Proceedings of the Wesley Historical Society*, Dec., 1965, p. 85. ". . . it was dislike of the organ that created and detonated the constitutional crisis."

¹¹The title, "The Church of the Nazarene", is not a reference to Nazirite but to Jesus the Nazarene.

¹²Doctrine plays a larger part in the sects and the denominations than in the churches and any unifying endeavours must take account of it. One of the objections to the Ecumenical Movement by some in the Church of the Nazarene and in other evangelical denominations is the belief that the final apostasy will be a world church subservient to Antichrist.

Bibliography

PART I—HOLINESS

Relating particularly to the Church of the Nazarene, the International Holiness Mission and the Calvary Holiness Church, and to the modern "Wesleyan" Holiness Movement in general.

Books

ARTHUR, WILLIAM. *The Tongue of Fire*. London: Hamilton, Adams, & Co., 1856.

ATKINSON, J. BAINES. *The Beauty of Holiness*. London: Epworth Press, 1953.

BANKS, S. *The Golden Highway*. London: Japan Evangelistic Band, n.d.

BARKER, J. H. J. *This Is the Will of God*. London: Epworth Press, 1956.

BEDWELL, H. KENNETH. *Black Gold*. Cape Town: Cape Town Times, n.d. (c. 1936).

BEGBIE, HAROLD. *The Life of William Booth*. London: Macmillan & Co., 1920.

BOARDMAN, MRS. *The Life and Labours of Reverend W. E. Boardman*. London: Bemrose & Sons, 1886.

BOARDMAN, W. E. *The Higher Christian Life*. Edinburgh: Alex. Strahan & Co., 1862.

BOARDMAN, W. E. *In the Power of the Spirit*. London: Daldy, Isbister, & Co., 1879.

BOOTH, MRS. CATHERINE. *Aggressive Christianity*. London: Salvationist Publishing and Supplies, 1880.

BOOTH, MRS. CATHERINE. *Papers on Godliness*. London: Salvation Army I. H. Q., 1890.

BRENGLE, S. L. *The Guest of the Soul*. London: Marshall, Morgan & Scott, 1936.

BRENGLE, S. L. *Heart Talks on Holiness*. London: Salvationist Publishing and Supplies, 1925.

BRENGLE, S. L. *Helps to Holiness*. London: Salvationist Publishing and Supplies, 1927.

BRESEE, P. F. *The Certainties of Faith*. Kansas City: Nazarene Publishing House, 1958.

BRICE, J. I. *The Crowd for Christ*. London: Hodder & Stoughton, 1934.

BRICKLEY, DONALD P. *Man of the Morning. The Life and Work of Phineas F. Bresee*. Kansas City: Nazarene Publishing House, 1960.

BROCKETT, H. E. *The Riches of Holiness*. London: Chas. Davy & Co., 1950.

BROCKETT, H. E. *Scriptural Freedom from Sin*. Turnbridge Wells: C. Baldwin, 1939.

BROWN, C. E. *The Meaning of Sanctification*. Anderson: Warner Press, 1951.

CARRADINE, B. *The Better Way*. Cincinnati: God's Revivalist Office, 1896.

CAUGHEY, JAMES. *Revival Sermons and Addresses*. London: R. D. Dickinson, 1891.

CHADWICK, S. *The Call to Christian Perfection*. London: Epworth Press, 1936.

CHADWICK, S. *The Way to Pentecost*. London: Hodder & Stoughton, 1932.

CHAMBERS, O. *The Philosophy of Sin*. London: Simpkin Marshall, n.d.

CHAMBERS, O. *The Psychology of Redemption*. London: Simpkin Marshall, 3rd ed. n.d.

CHAMBERS, O. *My Utmost for His Highest*. London: Simpkin Marshall, 1930.

CHAPMAN, J. B. *A History of the Church of the Nazarene*. Kansas City: Nazarene Publishing House, 1926.

CHAPMAN, J. B. *Holiness: the Heart of the Christian Experience*. Kansas City: Beacon Hill Press, 1963.

CHAPMAN, J. B. *The Terminology of Holiness*. Kansas City: Beacon Hill Press, n.d.

COOK, THOMAS. *New Testament Holiness*. London: Epworth Press, 1958.

COOKE, MRS. SARAH A. *Wayside Sketches*. Grand Rapids: Shaw Publishing Co., rev. ed., n.d.

CORLETT, L. T. *Holiness the Harmonizing Experience*. Kansas City: Beacon Hill Press, 1955.

CROSSLEY, MISS E. K. *He Heard from God. The Story of Frank Crossley*. London: Salvationist Publishing and Supplies, 1959.

CUMMING, J. E. *Through the Eternal Spirit*. Stirling: Stirling Tract Enterprise, 1937.

CURNICK, E. T. *A Catechism of Christian Perfection*. Chicago: Christian Witness Co., 1885.

David Thomas. Founder of the International Holiness Mission. London: International Holiness Mission, n.d., c. 1933.

Discipline of Pillar of Fire. Zarephath, W. J.: Pillar of Fire, 1926.

DRYSDALE, J. D. *Holiness in the Parables*. London: Oliphants, 1952.

DRYSDALE, J. D. *The Price of Revival*. London: Oliphants, 1938.

DRYSDALE, J. & L. *Emmanuel. "Fourteen Years After."* Birkenhead: J. & L. Drysdale, 1931.

DRYSDALE, J. D. & L. M. *"Emmanuel." 25 Years After*. Birkenhead: J. D. & L. M. Drysdale, 1941.

DUNNING, N. G. *Samuel Chadwick*. London: Hodder & Stoughton, 1933.

286 • *In the Steps of John Wesley*

FAIRBAIRN, C. V. *Purity and Power.* Chicago: Christian Witness Co., 1930.

FINNEY, C. G. *An Autobiography.* London: Salvationist Publishing and Supplies, n.d.

FINNEY, C. G. *Lectures on Systematic Theology.* London: Wm. Tegg & Co., 1851.

FINNEY, C. G. *Sanctification.* Fort Washington: Christian Literature Crusade, 1949.

FORD, J. *What the Holiness People Believe.* J. D. Drysdale Memorial Lecture. Birkenhead: Emmanuel Bible College, 1954.

FOSTER, R. S. *Christian Purity.* New York: Hunt & Eaton, 1869.

FRAME, G. *Blood Brother of the Swazis. The Life Story of David Hynd.* Kansas City: Beacon Hill Press, 1952.

GEIGER, KENNETH (comp.). *Further Insights into Holiness.* Kansas City: Beacon Hill Press, 1963.

GEIGER, KENNETH (comp.). *Insights into Holiness.* Kansas City: Beacon Hill Press, 1962.

GEIGER, KENNETH E. (comp.). *The Word and the Doctrine.* Kansas City: Beacon Hill Press, 1965.

GIRVIN, E. A. *Phineas F. Bresee: A Prince in Israel.* Kansas City: Pentecostal Nazarene Publishing House, 1916.

GODBEY, W. B. *Bible Theology.* Cincinnati: God's Revivalist Office, 1911.

GOVAN, I. R. *Spirit of Revival.* Edinburgh: Faith Mission, 1938.

GOVAN, J. G. *In the Train of His Triumph.* Edinburgh: Faith Mission, 1946.

GRUBB, N. P. *J. D. Drysdale: Prophet of Holiness.* London: Lutterworth Press, 1955.

HALL, C. W. *Samuel Logan Brengle. Portrait of a Prophet.* New York: Salvation Army, 1933.

HARRIS, READER. *The Atonement.* London: Partridge & Co., 1920.

HARRIS, READER. *The Beatitudes.* London: P. L. Publishing Depot, 1912.

HARRIS, READER. *Is Sin a Necessity?* London: Partridge & Co., 1896.

HARRIS, READER. *Power for Service.* London: Christian Literature Crusade, 1953.

HARRIS, J. RENDEL. *Aaron's Breastplate.* London: National Council of Evangelical Free Churches, 1908.

HARRIS, J. RENDEL (ed.). *The Life of Francis William Crossley.* London: James Nisbet & Co., 1900.

HARRIS, J. RENDEL. *Union with God.* London: Hodder & Stoughton, 1898.

HILLS, A. M. *Fundamental Christian Theology.* Pasadena: C. J. Kinne, 1931.

HILLS, A. M. *Holiness and Power.* Cincinnati: Revivalist Office, 1897.

HILLS, A. M. *Scriptural Holiness and Keswick Teaching Compared.* Manchester: Star Hall, n.d., c. 1912.

HOOKER, MARY R. *Adventures of an Agnostic. Life and Letters of Reader Harris.* London: Marshall, Morgan & Scott, 1959.
HUNT, JOHN. *Letters on Entire Sanctification.* London: Wesleyan-Methodist Book-Room, 1849.
JAMES, M. G. *Facing the Issue.* Burnley: Pilgrim Publishing House, 1948.
JAMES, M. G. *I Believe in the Holy Ghost.* Nelson: Coulton & Co., 1964.
JERNIGAN, C. B. *Pioneer Days of the Holiness Movement in the Southwest.* Kansas City: Pentecostal Nazarene Publishing House, 1919.
JESSOP, H. E. *Foundations of Doctrine.* Chicago: Chicago Evangelistic Institute, 1949.
JESSJP, H. E. *The Heritage of Holiness.* Chicago: Chicago Evangelistic Institute, 1950.
JESSOP, H. E. *I Met a Man with a Shining Face.* Florida: Holiness Book Ministry, 1956.
JESSOP, H. E. *We the Holiness People.* Chicago: Chicago Evangelistic Institute, 1948.
JONES, MRS. D. B. and her sons. *David Jones. Ambassador to the Africans.* Kansas City: Beacon Hill Press, 1955.
JONES, E. STANLEY. *Abundant Living.* London: Hodder & Stoughton, 1946.
JONES, E. STANLEY. *Victorious Living.* London: Hodder & Stoughton, 1946.
JONES, E. STANLEY. *The Way to Power and Poise.* New York: Abingdon Press, 1949.
JONES, W. *Entire Sanctification.* London: C. H. Kelly, 1892.
McDONALD, W. *The New Testament Standard of Piety.* Chicago: Christian Witness Co., 1882.
McDONALD, W. *Scriptural Way of Holiness.* London: Partridge & Co., n.d.
McRITCHIE, K. M. *Overcoming Life's Handicaps.* London: Marshall, Morgan & Scott, n.d.
MAHAN, A. *The Baptism of the Holy Ghost.* London: Elliot Stock, n.d., c. 1876.
MAHAN, A. *Christian Perfection.* London: Primitive Methodist Book Room, n.d.
MAVIS, W. C. *The Psychology of Christian Experience.* Grand Rapids: Zondervan Publishing House, 1964.
MORRISON, J. G. *Our Lost Estate.* Kansas City: Nazarene Publishing House, 1929.
MURRAY, A. *Absolute Surrender.* London: Marshall Bros., 4th ed.
MURRAY, A. *The Power of the Blood of Jesus.* London: Marshall, Morgan & Scott, 1936.
MURRAY, A. *The Spirit of Christ.* London: James Nisbet & Co., 1899.
PALMER, MRS. PHOEBE. *Entire Devotion to God.* London: Salvationist Publishing and Supplies, rev. ed.

PATTISON, MARY W. DUNN. *Ablaze for God. The Life Story of Paget Wilkes.* London: Oliphants, 1938.

PEARSON, B. H. *The Vision Lives. A Profile of Mrs. Charles Cowman.* London: Oliphants, 1962.

POWERS, H. C. *Manual. Church of the Nazarene, 1908-1958. Comparisons and Comments.* Kansas City: Nazarene Publishing House, 1958.

PURKISER, W. T. *Conflicting Concepts of Holiness.* Kansas City: Beacon Hill Press, 1953.

RAVENHILL, LEONARD. *Why Revival Tarries.* Minneapolis: Bethany Fellowship, 1962.

RAVENHILL, LEONARD. *Meat for Men.* Minneapolis: Bethany Fellowship, 1962.

REDFORD, M. E. *The Rise of the Church of the Nazarene.* Kansas City: Nazarene Publishing House, 1951.

REES, S. C. *Fire from Heaven.* Cincinnati: God's Revivalist Office, 1899.

REES, S. C. *The Ideal Pentecostal Church.* Cincinnati: Revivalist Office, 1897.

REID, ISAIAH. *Holiness Bible Readings.* Boston: Christian Witness Co., 1895.

RUTH, C. W. *Bible Readings on the Second Blessing.* Chicago: Christian Witness Co., 1905.

SHARPE, GEORGE. *A Short Historical Sketch of the Church of the Nazarene in the British Isles.* n.d., c. 1926.

SHARPE, GEORGE. *This Is My Story.* Glasgow: Messenger Publishing Co., n.d., c. 1948.

SHAW, S. B. (ed.). *Echoes of the General Holiness Assembly, Chicago, 1901.* Chicago: S. B. Shaw, n.d., c. 1901.

SIMPSON, A. B. *Wholly Sanctified.* Harrisburg: Christian Publications, 1925.

SMITH, ALLISTER. *The Ideal of Perfection.* London: Oliphants, 1965.

SMITH, HANNAH PEARSALL. *The Christian's Secret of a Happy Life.* Welwyn: James Nisbet & Co., 1964.

SMITH, TIMOTHY L. *Called unto Holiness. The Story of the Nazarenes.* Kansas City: Nazarene Publishing House, 1962.

SMITH, TIMOTHY L. *Revivalism and Social Reform.* New York: Abingdon Press, 1957.

STALKER, C. H. *Holy Ghost Messages.* Leicester: J. W. Hemmings & Capey, n.d., c. 1919.

STEELE, DANIEL. *The Gospel of the Comforter.* Chicago: Christian Witness Co., 1917.

STEELE, DANIEL. *Half-Hours with St. John.* Chicago: Christian Witness Co., 1908.

STEELE, DANIEL. *Half-Hours with St. Paul.* Chicago: Christian Witness Co., 1909.

STEELE, DANIEL. *Love Enthroned.* New York: Eaton & Mains, 1875.

STEELE, DANIEL. *Mile-Stone Papers*. London: Partridge & Co., 1878.

SWEETEN, H. W. *Must We Sin?* Kansas City: Nazarene Publishing House, 1919.

TAYLOR, RICHARD S. *A Right Conception of Sin*. Kansas City: Beacon Hill Press, 1945.

The Double Cure: or Echoes from National Camp Meetings. Boston: Christian Witness Co., 1887.

The Right Way. A Symposium of Teaching on The Way of Holiness. London: Oliphants, 1964.

To the Uttermost. Southport Methodist Holiness Convention. London: Epworth Press, 1945.

TURNER, G. A. *The Vision Which Transforms*. Kansas City: Beacon Hill Press, 1964.

UPHAM, T. C. *Principles of the Interior or Hidden Life*. London: R. D. Dickinson, 1895.

G. W. *The Work of the Holy Ghost in Modern Times*. Leicester: J. W. Hemmings & Capey, 1919.

WATSON, G. D. *God's First Words*. Cincinnati: God's Bible School, 1919.

WATSON, G. D. *Holiness Manual*. Dallas: Chandler Publications, n.d.

WATSON, G. D. *Our Own God*. Cincinnati: Revivalist Office, 1904.

WATSON, G. D. *Soul Food*. Cincinnati: Revivalist Office, 1896.

WATSON, G. D. *White Robes and Spiritual Feasts*. Cincinnati: God's Revivalist Press, 1883.

WAUGH, T. *The Power of Pentecost*. Rochdale: Thomas Champness, 4th ed., n.d.

WESLEY, JOHN. *A Plain Account of Christian Perfection*. London: Epworth Press, 1960. (His main works are given in the General Bibliography.)

WHITE, ALMA. *Looking Back from Beulah*. London: Pillar of Fire Society, 1902.

WHITE, S. S. *Cardinal Elements in Sanctification*. Kansas City: Beacon Hill Press, 1963.

WHITE, S. S. *Eradication*. Kansas City: Beacon Hill Press, 1954.

WILEY, H. ORTON. *Christian Theology*. Kansas City: Beacon Hill Press, 1959.

WILLIAMS, R. T. *Sanctification. The Experience and the Ethics*. Kansas City: Nazarene Publishing House, 1928.

WILLIAMSON, G. B. *Preaching Scriptural Holiness*. Kansas City: Beacon Hill Press, 1953.

WILLIAMSON, G. B. *Roy T. Williams. Servant of God*. Kansas City: Nazarene Publishing House, 1947.

WILSON, J. P. *Scriptural Proofs of Full Salvation from Sin*. London: Partridge & Co., 1888.

WINCHESTER, C. W. *Wells of Salvation*. Chicago: Christian Witness Co., 1906.

290 • *In the Steps of John Wesley*

WINCHESTER, OLIVE M. (ed. R. E. Price). *Crisis Experiences in the Greek New Testament.* Kansas City: Beacon Hill Press, 1953.

WOODS, J. A. *Perfect Love.* London: Salvationist Publishing and Supplies, n.d.

WOOD, J. A. *Purity and Maturity.* Boston: Christian Witness Co., 1899.

Periodicals

Beulah Items (U.S.A.); from 1892, the *Beulah Christian*.
Emmanuel.
The *Flame.*
Herald of Holiness (U.S.A.).
Holiness Advocate; from 1891, *Pure in Heart.*
The *Holiness Herald;* from 1934, the *Way of Holiness;* from 1953, the *Way.*
The *Holiness Mission Journal;* from 1953, the *Way.*
The *Nazarene* (U.S.A.); from 1900, the *Nazarene Messenger.*
The *Peniel Herald* (U.S.A.).
The *Preacher's Magazine* (U.S.A.); from 1964, the *Nazarene Preacher.*
Tongues of Fire; from 1916, *Spiritual Life.*
The *Way of Holiness* (Published by Star Hall, Manchester, 1909-1928).

Minutes and Official Books and Documents

The Calvary Holiness Church

Articles of Doctrine and Government of the Calvary Holiness Church, enrolled in the Central Office in the Supreme Court of Judicature, January 6th, 1939.

The Calvary Holiness Church. What it is, and what it stands for. Nelson: Coulton & Co., n.d., c. 1942. Official pamphlet.

Executive Council Minute Books of the Calvary Holiness Church, 1934-1955.[1]

Minute Books of the Delegates Conference of the Calvary Holiness Church, 1935-1955.[1]

Minutes of Joint Meeting of Calvary Holiness Church Executive Council and the Church of the Nazarene British Isles Advisory Council, 8th-9th February, 1955.

Minutes of Ministers' Meetings, 1944-1955.[2]

The Old Cross Mission, Ashton-under-Lyne. A short unpublished thesis by the writer.[2]

Rules and Regulations of the Calvary Holiness Church. Manchester, 1943. Addenda to 1947.

The International Holiness Mission

E. A. J. Bolt, *From the Church of England to the International Holiness Mission.* London: International Holiness Mission, 1920. Pamphlet.[2]

Doctrine and Rules of the Holiness Church. Leeds: W. Davy, 1902.[3]

Holiness Church, Hull. Buisness (sic) Meeting Minute Books, 1904-1954.[3]

I.H.M. Overseas Missionary Department. Numerical Statistics.[2]

International Holiness Mission. Constitution. n.d.[2]

International Holiness Mission. Constitution of the South African Branch. n.d.[2]

International Holiness Mission Minute Book Executive Council, 1935-1952.[3]

Memorandum and Articles of Association of the International Holiness Mission. Incorporated 3-11-20.[2]

Minute Book of Holiness Church Conferences, Hull and Leeds, 1900-1913.[3]

Minutes of the I.H.M. Ministerial Conference, 18-3-35 to 30-3-37.[2]

Proposed Deed Poll for the Legal Binding of the Holiness Church of Hull and Leeds. n.d., c. 1906.[3]

Thomas Memorial Church of the Nazarene, London S.W. 11. London: 1957. Pamphlet.

The Church of the Nazarene in Britain

Minute Books:
Gildersome Pentecostal Church, 1914-1934.
Parkhead Congregational Church:
Deacons Court, 1894-1913.
Parkhead Pentecostal Church:
Deacons Meetings, 1906-1918.[4]
Holiness Bible School, 1908-1914.[4]
Sabbath School, 1907-1937.[4]
Pentecostal Church of Scotland, 1909-1915.[4]

Minutes:
British Isles District of Pentecostal Church of the Nazarene, 1916-1919.
British Isles District of Church of the Nazarene, 1920-1966. (Called "Proceedings" from 1924).

The Church of the Nazarene in North America

Manuals:
General Church:
Pentecostal Church of the Nazarene, 1907-1915.[5]
Church of the Nazarene, 1919-1964.[5]

Local Churches:

Church of the Nazarene, Los Angeles, 1898.[6]
> The People's Evangelical Church, organised July 21st, 1887. Revised Manual.[7]

Minutes:

General Assemblies:
> Pentecostal Church of the Nazarene, 1907-1919.[5]
> Church of the Nazarene, 1923-1964.[5]

Local Churches and Associations:
> Church of Christ, organised by Rev. R. L. Harris at Milan, Tennessee, July 9th, 1894.[8]
> Records of the People's Evangelical Church of Providence, R.I., July 21st, 1887.
> Secretary's Records of the South Providence Association for the Promotion of Holiness, commenced May 12th, 1886, and continuing as Records of People's Evangelical Church of Providence (above).[7]

Miscellaneous:
> Report from the Education Commission of the Church of the Nazarene, January, 1964, entitled "A Study of the Educational Structure in the Church of the Nazarene".
> R. L. Harris, *Why We Left the Methodist Church*. Memphis, 1893. Pamphlet.[9]

The Methodist Episcopal Church, U.S.A.

> *Minutes of the Northern New York Conference*, 1889-1901. (Statistical Office, Chicago.)

N.B. The Items referring to the Church of the Nazarene in North America and to the Methodist Episcopal Church, U.S.A., are specified because they are mentioned in the thesis. They are part of the information collected by the writer when he visited North America in 1957 (January to May). Research was done in the libraries of the colleges at Nashville, Tennessee; Bethany, Oklahoma; Pasadena, California; Nampa, Idaho; Red Deer, Alberta; Kankakee, Illinois; Boston, Massachusetts; and in the Nazarene Theological Seminary and in the International Headquarters in Kansas City. A number of persons able to give information concerning the origin and development of the Church of the Nazarene were interviewed and notes were made. Further information was also gathered during tours in 1960 (March to June) and 1964 (June to August).

[1] and [2] In the writer's custody.

[3] and [4] Lent to the writer.

[5] I.H.Q. Archives, Church of the Nazarene.

[6] Library, Pasadena College, Pasadena, California, U.S.A.

[7] In the files of the First Church of the Nazarene, Providence, R.I., U.S.A.

[8] and [9] In the files of M. E. Redford, Trevecca Nazarene College, Nashville, Tenn., U.S.A.

Letters to the Writer

(Quoted in the Thesis)

Writer	Date	
Rev. Stanley Banks	25-3-65	
Mrs. I. R. Edwards	18-7-58	
Miss E. Howarth	6-4-64	
Rev. Maynard G. James	22-4-47,	29-8-51
Dr. H. E. Jessop	21-7-62	
Mrs. D. B. Jones to Rev. R. E. Jones	29-7-59	
Miss M. K. Latta, M.B.E.	6-1-57	
Rev. J. H. Liversidge	31-3-65	
Rev. A. J. Lown	7-9-61	
Rev. J. B. Maclagan	18-9-58,	2-10-58
Rev. R. C. Purvis	18-9-58	
Miss Joan Reid	Jan., 1957	

Interviews and Conversations

(Quoted in the Thesis)

Pastor James Bedwell, London, 27-11-58.
Rev. H. C. Best, London, 25-11-58, 8-7-59.
Rev. Peter Clark, Forfar, 21-10-57.
Miss E. K. Crossley, Crowborough, 26-11-58.
Mr. J. A. Cunningham, Glasgow, 16-10-57.
Mrs. J. Dyson, Carnock, nr. Dunfermline, 15-10-57.
Rev. C. Filer, Royton, date not recorded.
Rev. George Frame, M.A., D.D., Sheffield, 22-9-58.
Dr. Mary Frame, Glasgow, 17-11-56.
Rev. J. E. Griffiths, Lawton, Lancs., 6-10-59, Ashton-u-Lyne, 7-1-60.
Rev. William Henson, Manchester, 11-8-61, 22-9-61.
Mrs. M. R. Hooker, Ridgelands Bible College, Bexley, 20-6-55, 23-11-58, 3 & 4-2-59.
Mrs. Charles Hunter, Glasgow, 17-11-56.
Rev. Maynard G. James, Oldham, 31-10-57, Manchester, 22-9-61.
Dr. H. E. Jessop, Birkenhead, 1-8-57.
Rev. J. B. Maclagan, Manchester, 12 & 13-3-58.
Mr. Sydney M'Caw, Manchester ('phone), 20-12-61.
Mr. & Mrs. H. Pickles, Leeds, 7-10-57.
Mr. & Mrs. John Place, Leeds, 6-10-57.
Rev. R. C. Purvis, Glasgow, 21-10-57.
Rev. Hugh Rae, M.A., Ashton-u-Lyne ('phone), 16-10-58.
Mr. Andrew Robertson, M.A., Uddingston, 17-10-57.
Mr. H. Saville, Leeds, 7-10-57.
Rev. John E. Watson, Morley, 28-1-58.

PART II—GENERAL

Books

ANDERSON, W. K. *Methodism*. Cincinnati: Methodist Publishing House, 1947.

AQUINAS, THOMAS. *Summa Theologica*. London: Burns Oates and Washbourne, 1935.

ARMINIUS, JAMES. *The Works of James Arminius*. Trans. James Nichols. London: Longman, Hurst et al., 1825.

BAKER, E. W. *A Herald of the Evangelical Revival*. London: Epworth Press, 1948.

BARABAS, S. *So Great Salvation*. London: Marshall, Morgan & Scott, 1957.

BARCLAY, R. *An Apology for the True Christian Divinity*. Glasgow: R. Barclay Murdoch, 1886.

BAXTER, R. *The Reformed Pastor*. London: R.T.S., 1829.

BINNEY, A. & STEELE, D. *Binney's Theological Compend Improved*. New York: Methodist Book Concern, 1902.

BIRTWHISTLE, ALLEN. *In His Armour. The Life of John Hunt of Fiji*. London: Cargate Press, 1954.

BLISS, KATHLEEN. *The Service and Status of Women in the Churches*. London: SCM, 1952.

BLOCH-HOELL, NILS. *The Pentecostal Movement*. London: Allen and Unwin, 1964.

BREADY, J. W. *England Before and After Wesley*. London: Hodder & Stoughton, 1938.

BROADBENT, E. H. *The Pilgrim Church*. London: Pickering & Inglis, 1931.

BROWN, W. ADAMS. *Christian Theology in Outline*. Edinburgh: T. & T. Clark, 1924.

CALVIN, JOHN. *Institutes of the Christian Religion*. London: James Clarke & Co., 1953.

CANNON, W. R. *The Theology of John Wesley*. New York: Abingdon Press, 1946.

CELL, G. C. *The Rediscovery of John Wesley*. New York: H. Holt & Co., 1935.

Centenary Souvenir. E.U. Congregational Church (Ardrossan), 1837-1937. (Pamphlet)

CHARDIN, P. TEILHARD DE. *Le Milieu Divin*. London: W. Collins Sons & Co., 1965.

CLARK, E. T. *The Small Sects in America*. New York: Abingdon Press, 1949.

COX, L. G. *John Wesley's Concept of Perfection*. Kansas City: Beacon Hill Press, 1964.

CROSS, WHITNEY R. *The Burned-over District*. New York: Cornell University Press, 1950.

DAVIES, J. G. *The Early Church*. London: Weidenfeld & Nicolson, 1965.

Bibliography • 295

DAVIES, R. E. *Methodism*, Harmondsworth: Penguin, 1963.

DAVIES, R. E. & RUPP, E. G. *A History of the Methodist Church in Great Britain*. London: Epworth Press, 1965. Vol. I.

DIMOND, S. G. *The Psychology of the Methodist Revival*. London: O.U.P., 1926.

DOBRÉE, BONAMY. *John Wesley*. London: Duckworth, 1933.

DRUMMOND, A. L. *German Protestantism Since Luther*. London: Epworth Press, 1951.

ELLIOTT-BINNS, L. D. *Religion in the Victorian Era*. London: Lutterworth Press, 1936.

FABER, F. W. *Growth in Holiness*. London: T. Richardson & Son, 1860.

FIELD, B. *Handbook of Christian Theology*. London: Hodder & Stoughton, 1896.

FIGGIS, J. B. *Keswick from Within*. London: Marshall Bros., 1914.

FITCHETT, W. H. *Wesley and His Century*. London: Smith, Elder & Co., 1906.

FLEW, R. NEWTON. *The Idea of Perfection in Christian Theology*. London: O.U.P., 1934.

FLEW, R. NEWTON & DAVIES, R. E. (ed.). *The Catholicity of Protestantism*. London: Lutterworth, 1953.

FLUGEL, J. C. *Man, Morals and Society*. Harmondsworth: Penguin, 1955.

FORSYTH, P. T. *Christian Perfection*. London: Hodder & Stoughton, 1899.

FOX, GEORGE. *Journal*. Cambridge: C.U.P., 1952.

FREND, W. H. C. *The Donatist Church*. Oxford: Clarendon Press, 1952.

GARVIE, A. E. *The Ritschlian Theology*. Edinburgh: T. & T. Clark, 1902.

GEE, D. *The Pentecostal Movement*. Luton: Assemblies of God Publishing House, 1949.

GOODALL, N. *The Ecumenical Movement*. London: O.U.P., 1964.

GOULBURN, E. M. *The Pursuit of Holiness*. London: Rivingtons, 1869.

GREEN, J. BRAZIER. *John Wesley and William Law*. London: Epworth Press, 1945.

GREENSLADE, S. L. *Schism in the Early Church*. London: SCM, 1953.

GUYON, MADAME. *Autobiography of Madame Guyon*. Trans. Thomas T. Allen. London: Kegan Paul, Trench et al., 1898.

GWATKIN, H. M. *Early Church History to A.D. 313*. London: Macmillan, 1912.

HEARD, G. *Morals Since 1900*. London: Andrew Dakers, 1950.

HIGHET, J. *The Scottish Churches*. London: Skeffington, 1960.

HILDEBRANDT, F. *From Luther to Wesley*. London: Lutterworth Press, 1951.

HOPKINS, EVAN H. *The Law of Liberty in the Spiritual Life*. London: Marshall, Morgan & Scott, 1957.

HORNE, C. S. *A Popular History of the Free Churches*. London: James Clarke & Co., 1903.

HORSCH, J. *Mennonites in Europe*. Scottdale, Pa.: Mennonite Publishing House, 1950.

INGE, W. R. *Christian Mysticism*. London: Methuen & Co., 1933.

INGE, W. R. *Mysticism in Religion*. London: Hutchinson's University Library, n.d.

INGLIS, B. *Private Conscience, Public Morality*. London: A. Deutsch, 1964.

INGLIS, K. S. *Churches and the Working Classes in Victorian England*. London: Routledge & Kegan Paul, 1963.

JAMES, WM. *The Varieties of Religious Experience*. New York: Longmans, Green & Co., 1902.

JONES, RUFUS M. *Spiritual Reformers in the 16th & 17th Centuries*. London: Macmillan & Co., 1928.

KEMPIS, THOMAS A. *Of the Imitation of Christ*. London: James Finch & Co., 1891.

KNOX, R. A. *Enthusiasm*. Oxford: Clarendon Press, 1950.

KOBERLE, A. *The Quest for Holiness*. Trans. J. C. Mattes. Minneapolis: Augsburg Publishing House, 1938.

KUYPER, A. *The Work of the Holy Spirit*. Grand Rapids: W. B. Eerdmans Publishing Co., 1956.

LAW, WM. *Works* (IX Vols.). London: 1893. Vol. III. *A Practical Treatise upon Christian Perfection*. Vol. IV. *A Serious Call to a Devout and Holy Life*.

LIETZMAN, HANS. *The Founding of the Church Universal*. London: Lutterworth Press, 1950.

LINDSTROM, HARALD. *Wesley and Sanctification*. London: Epworth Press, 1956.

LITTELL, F. H. *The Anabaptist View of the Church*. Boston: Starr King Press, 1958.

MAITLAND, S. R. *Facts and Documents Illustrative of the History, Doctrine and Rites of the Ancient Albigenses and Waldenses*. London: 1838.

MARSHALL, W. *The Gospel Mystery of Sanctification*. London: Oliphants, 1956.

MILEY, J. *Systematic Theology*. New York: Methodist Book Concern, 1892.

MOEDE, G. F. *The Office of Bishop in Methodism*. Zurich: Publishing House of the Methodist Church, 1964.

MORRISON, SYBIL. *I Renounce War*. London: Sheppard Press, 1962.

MOWAT, C. L. *Britain Between the Wars, 1918-1940*. London: Methuen & Co., 1955.

NEATBY, W. B. *A History of the Plymouth Brethren*. London: Hodder & Stoughton, 1901.

NEILL, S. *The Unfinished Task*. London: Lutterworth Press, 1957.

NIEBUHR, H. RICHARD. *The Social Sources of Denominationalism*. New York: H. Holt & Co., 1929.

ORCHARD, W. E. *Modern Theories of Sin.* London: James Clarke & Co., 1910.
ORR, J. E. *The Second Evangelical Awakening in Britain.* London: Marshall, Morgan & Scott, 1953.
OTTO, R. *The Idea of the Holy.* London: O.U.P., 1939.
PAGE, I. E. (ed.) *John Brash.* London: Charles Kelly, 1912.
PANKHURST, CHRISTABEL. *Unshackled.* Ed. Lord Pethwick-Lawrence. London: Hutchinson & Co., 1959.
PARRIS, J. R. *John Wesley's Doctrine of the Sacraments.* London: Epworth Press, 1963.
PELLING, H. *Modern Britain, 1885-1955.* Edinburgh: T. Nelson & Sons, 1960.
PERKINS, H. W. *The Doctrine of Christian or Evangelical Perfection.* London: Epworth Press, 1927.
PETERS, J. L. *Christian Perfection and American Methodism.* New York: Abingdon Press, 1956.
PHILIPOU, A. J. (ed.) *The Orthodox Ethos.* Oxford: Holywell Press, 1964.
PIERSON, A. T. *Forward Movements of the Last Half Century.* New York: Funk & Wagnalls, 1905.
PIETTE, M. *John Wesley in the Evolution of Protestantism.* London: Sheed & Ward, 1938.
POLLOCK, J. C. *The Keswick Story.* London: Hodder & Stoughton, 1964.
POPE, W. B. *A Compendium of Christian Theology.* London: Wesleyan-Methodist Book-Room, 1880.
RAHNER, K. *The Dynamic Element in the Church.* London: Burns & Oates, 1964.
RAHNER, K. *Theological Investigations.* Vol. I. London: Darton, Longman & Todd, 1961.
RALSTON, T. N. *Elements of Divinity.* Ed. T. O. Summers. New York: Abingdon Press, 1924.
RATTENBURY, J. E. *Wesley's Legacy to the World.* London: Epworth Press, 1938.
ROBINSON, H. W. *The Christian Doctrine of Man.* Edinburgh: T. & T. Clark, 1952.
ROBINSON, H. W. *The Christian Experience of the Holy Spirit.* London: Nisbet & Co., 1928.
RUPP, GORDON. *The Righteousness of God.* London: Hodder & Stoughton, 1953.
SANGSTER, W. E. *The Path to Perfection.* London: Hodder & Stoughton, 1943.
SANGSTER, W. E. *The Pure in Heart.* London: Epworth Press, 1957.
SCOTT, C. A. ANDERSON. *New Testament Ethics.* Cambridge: C.U.P., 1948.
SIMON, J. S. *The Revival of Religion in England in the Eighteenth Century.* London: Robert Culley. 37th Fernley Lecture.

SIMONS, MENNO. *The Complete Writings of Menno Simons.* Trans. L. Verduin and ed. J. C. Wenger. Scottdale, Pa.: Herald Press, 1956.
SMELLIE, A. *Evan Henry Hopkins.* London: Marshall Bros., 1920.
SOUTHEY, R. *The Life of Wesley.* London: O.U.P., 1925.
SPINKS, G. S., ALLEN & PARKES. *Religion in Britain Since 1900.* London: A. Dakers, 1952.
STARBUCK, E. D. *The Psychology of Religion.* London: Walter Scott, 1901.
STEVENS, A. *The History of Methodism.* London: Wesleyan Conference Office, new ed.
SWEET, W. W. *The Story of Religions in America.* London: Harper Bros., 1930.
SWETE, H. B. *The Holy Spirit in the Ancient Church.* London: Macmillan & Co., 1912.
SWETE, H. B. *The Holy Spirit in the New Testament.* London: Macmillan & Co., 1910.
TAYLOR, JEREMY. *Works* (XII Vols.). London: 1847. Vol. III. *Rule and Exercise of Holy Living and Holy Dying.*
TELFORD, J. *The Life of John Wesley.* London: Hodder & Stoughton, 1886.
TENNANT, F. R. *The Sources of the Doctrine of the Fall and Original Sin.* Cambridge: C.U.P., 1903.
THOMSON, D. *England in the Twentieth Century, 1914-63.* London: Jonathan Cape, 1964.
TODD, J. M. *John Wesley and the Catholic Church.* London: Hodder & Stoughton, 1958.
TOWNSEND, WORKMAN AND EAYRS. *A New History of Methodism.* London: Hodder & Stoughton, 1909.
TROELTSCH, E. *The Social Teachings of the Christian Churches.* Trans. O. Wyon. London: Geo. Allen & Unwin, 1931.
TYERMAN, L. *The Life and Times of Rev. John Wesley, M.A.* London: Hodder & Stoughton, 1890.
UPHAM, T. C. *The Life of Madam Guyon.* London: Allenson & Co., 1961.
VERDUIN, L. *The Reformers and Their Stepchildren.* London: Paternoster Press, 1964.
VIDLER, A. R. *The Church in an Age of Revolution.* Harmondsworth: Penguin, 1961.
WAKEFIELD, G. S. *Methodist Devotion.* London: Epworth Press, 1966.
WAKEFIELD, G. S. *Puritan Devotion.* London: Epworth Press, 1957.
WARFIELD, B. B. *Perfectionism.* New York: O.U.P., 1931.
WATKIN-JONES, H. *The Holy Spirit from Arminius to Wesley.* London: Epworth Press, 1929.
WATKIN-JONES, H. *The Holy Spirit in the Mediaeval Church.* London: Epworth Press, 1922.
WATSON, P. S. *Let God Be God.* London: Epworth Press, 1947.

Bibliography • 299

WATSON, RICHARD. *The Works of Richard Watson.* (Vols. 5 and 12.) London: John Mason, 1858.

WEATHERHEAD, LESLIE. *Psychology, Religion and Healing.* London: Hodder & Stoughton, 1959.

WEBER, MAX. *From Max Weber.* Ed. Gerth and Mills. London: Routledge, 1947.

WEBER, MAX. *The Sociology of Religion.* London: Methuen & Co., 1965.

WESLEY, JOHN. *A Collection of Hymns for the Use of the People Called Methodists.* Comp. John Wesley. London: J. Paramore, 1780.

WESLEY, JOHN. *The Journal of John Wesley.* Standard Edition. Ed. N. Curnock. London: Epworth Press, 1938.

WESLEY, JOHN. *The Letters of John Wesley.* Standard Edition. Ed. J. Telford. London: Epworth Press, 1931.

WESLEY, JOHN. *Notes upon the New Testament.* London: William Bowyer, 1755.

WESLEY, JOHN. *The Works of John Wesley.* (XIV Vols.) London: John Mason, 4th ed., 1840-42.

WESLEY, JOHN. *Christian Library.* London: T. Blanshard, 1819-27.

WILLIAMS, C. W. *John Wesley's Theology Today.* London: Epworth Press, 1960.

WILLIAMS, G. H. *The Radical Reformation.* London: Weidenfeld and Nicolson, 1962.

WILSON, B. R. *Sects and Society.* Heinemann, 1961.

WOODWORTH, R. S. *Psychology.* London: Methuen & Co., 1944.

Encyclopaedias

HASTINGS, JAMES (ed.). *Encyclopaedia of Religion and Ethics.* Edinburgh: T. & T. Clark, 1908-26.

The Mennonite Encyclopedia. Scottdale, Pa.: Mennonite Publishing House, 1956.

Articles

EARLE, RALPH. "The Arminian View of Inspiration." in *Preacher's Magazine,* July, 1959, pp. 20-23.

HUGHES, J. T. "The Story of the Leeds 'Non-Cons'." in *Proceedings of the Wesley Historical Society,* December, 1965, pp. 81-87.

MACDONALD, RAMSEY. "The Labour Movement and Its Implications for Christianity." In *An Outline of Christianity.* Ed. A. S. Peake and R. G. Parsons. London: Waverley Book Co., n.d.

POLLET, J. V. M. "Zwinglianisme." In *Dictionnaire de Théologie Catholique,* 1950, col. 3745 ff.

Unpublished Theses

BROWN, RAYMOND. "Evangelical Ideas of Perfection." Ph.D. Dissertation, University of Cambridge, 1964.

GADDIS, M. E. "Christian Perfectionism in America." Ph.D. Thesis, University of Chicago, 1929.

JORDEN, E. E. "The Ideal of Sanctity in Methodism and Tractarianism." Ph.D. Thesis, University of London, 1958.

WARBURTON, T. R. "A Comparative Study of Minority Religious Groups: With Special Reference to Holiness and Related Movements in Britain in the Last 50 Years." Ph.D. Thesis, University of London, 1966.

www.ingramcontent.com/pod-product-compliance
Lightning Source LLC
Chambersburg PA
CBHW061632040426
42446CB00010B/1377